THE
MEN
WHO
CHOOSE
LIBERTY

SETH IRVING HANDASIDE

CREATING A REPUBLIC: THE AMERICAN WAY
VOLUME ONE 1732 - 1775

READ ABOUT THE MEN WHO WALKED TOWARD DEMOCRACY

The Men Who Choose Liberty

© 2022 Seth Irving Handaside

ISBN 978-1-66786-610-9

eBook ISBN 978-1-66786-611-6

Ukrainians who have put their lives on the line in their pursuit of democratic liberty.

The founding Patriots who saved freedom from being buried in an unmarked grave.

Skip Sommer, Petaluma historian whose encouragement I could never repay.

My wife, Shray, the sweet pea of my life and my light, who put up with my long hours of research.

And hopefully, to show, not tell.

TABLE OF CONTENTS

CHAPTER 1

The Wild Child

The man who stood revered in the county of Hanover, Virginia, took a step back at the Shelton Tavern in 1766 and chuckled when he heard his son's name, Patrick Henry, mentioned from a table nestled by a crackling fire. The face of the sixty-two-year-old John Henry, the county surveyor, colonel of his regiment, and presiding judge of the county court, lit like the dawn. He called out across the room to the group of men chatting by the fire.

"My son ranks as an orator in the class of Cicero, competes in Sunday dances, and birds and their calls grip his imagination."

Taking a lazy swallow of whiskey, he stood straight and tall, his pride visible to all in the tavern.

He recalled the day he was fishing with Patrick and John's younger brother Patrick in the summer of 1748 when Patrick was twelve years old. John understood. He knew that his son now preferred developing his mind rather than existing in the dark void of ignorance.

John Henry did not always say that about his son. He remembered that quite well.

"Pa, education bores me."

"Son, the time of idleness and dreaminess and a disregard for books must now cease."

The tug of a fish at his hook caught Patrick's attention. He smiled openly, his dark-blue eyes sparkling like a clear stream.

"But I prefer fishin' rods and rifles to books."

"Children," his younger brother, the rector of St. Paul's Parish in Hanover, declared, "One must reach," as he focused on Patrick, "a time when they stop being disorderly in dress and slouching. Reject living as a vagrant without ambition. Stop roaming in the woods, loitering on river banks, and preferring the lives of trappers and frontiersmen to those who toil in the civilized life."

Bored, Patrick tugged at his hair and stared into the distance.

"To this point in your life," said his father, "you have given no hint nor token, by word or act, of the possession of any intellectual gift that could raise you above mediocrity, or even up to it."

Patrick, the younger, focused on the brothers.

"Readin', writin', and 'rithmetic – borin'!"

"We know," said his uncle, "you prefer the bubbling spirit of your mother's family, the Winstons. But unlike them, you lack conversational skills or have any gift for music or eloquent speech."

"Mom says the young should pursue the fondness of country life, the pleasure of living, their love of fishing and hunting, and the mystery and charm of the outdoors."

John Henry glanced at his brother, who shot him an awkward grin while shaking his head.

"I like," said Patrick, "sittin' on a rock, listenin' to the wind, and smellin' my place here."

They stood like the stillness of a falling leaf.

The tension in their shoulders eased as both men took heed and knew they were pursuing the proper course.

"This is why we must take personal charge of this matter," said his father.

In frustration, he gestured to Patrick. "No son of mine is going to be a wild child!!"

Patrick, the elder, nodded in agreement.

"Patrick, you will acquire some knowledge of Latin and Greek," added his uncle, a Scottish classicist, "and greater knowledge of mathematics."

Patrick grimaced, his face resembling a dried prune.

"Mathematics!"

Irritated with impatience, his father frowned and peered straight at his face.

"The latter being the only branch of book-learning you have shown some skill in."

"You must," concluded his uncle, "develop industry, order, sharp calculation, and persistence."

Patrick drew his eyes away, fast, on purpose, as he always did. Thinking, he preferred the advice of his Welsh mother, "Do what makes your heart light."

1749 Patrick Henry Takes Up Learning

The following year Patrick was pulled away from his mother's pocket by his determined father.

Under the trees, the green grass, with the wild, mountains in full view, Patrick stood upright along with twenty other pupils reciting Greek in melodious voices.

Patrick, a syllable behind, mimicked the words.

That evening he told his mother, "I know father and uncle said my translation passed, but they also said some passages needed correction. They must think I am hopeless."

"Men will be men, my son, do not let it get you down."

Perplexed, he pined for the wooded hills and lavender-tinged mountains. He tried to put his suffering aside, but his mind remained open to the dogwood, and he relished the honeysuckle that waxed in full bloom.

The next day, with his brain numb after three hours of Greek and Latin, his uncle queried, "Name the maxims I asked you to live by."

Quickly, he abided, "Be true and just in all my dealings. To bear no malice nor hatred in my heart. To keep my hands from picking and stealing. Not to covet other men's goods. To learn and labour truly to get my living, and to do my duty in that state of life unto which it shall please God to call me."

His father listening by his brother's side, said, "Brother Patrick, I would like young Patrick to have some time off this summer. Fishing, hunting, swimming, singing, wrestling would be a good reward, and doing some chores."

"When enjoying nature's great harmony," said brother Patrick, "he can harvest the wild grapes and plums and the honeycomb in the tree hollows."

"And use his flintlock for fresh meat and his rod for fish."

By midsummer, to his anguish and with a half shrug, Patrick moved on to Virgil, an ancient Roman poet, and Livy, Roman historian of the pre – and early Common Era, through repeated drilling in the language.

Years later, according to Thomas Jefferson, the seed of his intellect sprouted, and the man who "gave the first impulse to the ball of the revolution," mounted his learnin'.

Under a Loblolly Pine, nearly a hundred feet high, his brown eyes squinting from the filtered light, Patrick lay watching his line in the water, a rifle by his side.

The river caught the bright blue of the sky, glistening and sparkling as it flowed silently.

Focused on the space beyond the riverbank, he sighted the horns of a buck above a patch of butterfly weed.

Clutching his weapon, he aimed, but before his finger pressed the trigger, a breeze blew open the book's pages by his side. He looked down, his attention caught.

He read, "Words, to its possessor, glow like a golden crown, in which solace and entertainment unite with intrinsic worth."

His finger relaxed, and he found himself lying on his back upon the soft earth, rooted in reading *The Life and Opinions of Tristram Shandy*.

The water bowl of his mind filled to the top – he liked it, remembering words.

He rose and gave the forest a long look. "See you later."

By the beginning of fall, the church gripped Patrick's attention. He stood in the back of the building with his hands on his hips, listening to Reverend Samuel Davies, who moved to Hanover County, Virginia, in 1748.

As a non-Anglican, he attracted attention throughout the colonies and drew satirical criticism from the Church of England's elite.

"Wise and good rulers have justly accounted for an extensive blessing to their subjects."

The twelve-year-old reached for his mother's hand as they enjoyed Davies's voice echoing off the church walls.

"Justice is an amiable attribute in itself, and it appears so to all rational beings but criminals."

The Reverend, he learned, filled the hours of his day writing poetry and composing hymns.

"The LORD reigns; let the earth rejoice; let the multitude of islands be glad!"

Patrick, intent on learning how Davies used his voice from a whisper to grand heights, studied the preacher. This skill of how Davies controulled his listeners' emotions became more important than hunting and fishing, and Patrick craved to master the technique.

"Brethren, our nature, our circumstances, and the important prospects before us," preached Davies, "are such that it is high time for us to look about us for some sure foundation upon which to build our happiness."

"Now is the time for us to find the refuge," said Patrick as he imitated the Reverend on his way home with his mother, who thought the recitation by Patrick sounded faithful to the Reverend's words.

"It will be too late." He thrust out his arms, smiling up at his mother, proud he could recite as well as the Reverend. "When all created supports drift away," he said, repeating Davies's words, "and this solid globe itself dissolves beneath our feet into a sea of fire."

His mother knew Patrick not only tapped on the door of knowledge but pushed it open.

"Repeat my favourite," she asked.

"Time is an ever-running stream perpetually gliding on and hurrying all the sons of man into the boundless ocean of eternity."

"You sound just like the Reverend. I know not the difference."

He put his hand in her pocket, holding tight, knowing that he would grow past the need of this safe place soon. So filled, he found his own heart's joy.

1750 Hanover, Virginia

A year later, his father asked, "Have you read the *Virginia Gazette*?"

"Yes, mother, asked me to recite the Reverend's letter to her."

"Do you have a favourite passage?"

"Wealth—will prove a vain shadow — honour will prove an empty breath – pleasure – will prove a delusive dream — your righteousness — will prove a spider's web!"

To his astonishment, Patrick liked similes and analogies. He found himself sliding his fingers over words, taking a paragraph or two, and committing it to memory.

After another long day, John Henry plopped down for a moment, organizing his ideas on going forward, the times being tough. His heart hurt, and so did his savings. He bit into a hard apple. Patrick sitting by him, smelled a cascade of flavour: sweet, nutty, fruity, and a bitter sensation.

"Son, my financial situation smells like manure," he said in 1750, "I think it best to put you behind the counter of a local merchant."

"I know, father, the support of a large family calls for sacrifice."

A dull ache settled into John Henry's soul, and his eyes drifted away from his son.

"After a year, I will set you up in trade."

1751 Patrick Takes Up Business

A grimace gripped Patrick's face. He tried to smile but knew he would like the retailing and bookkeeping drudgery – as little as a colt does a cart.

After the first few months of being in business for himself, Patrick addressed the door to his store in a quiet tone as he opened up, "I make mistake after mistake. If I cannot do it right, why the hell bother to be a storekeeper? I will never get all of this done, so why start in business. Being a storekeeper stinks, nothing good about it at all."

1751 Patrick Learns the Violin

Later that day, a customer who needed a sack of rice traded an old violin with a bow to Patrick. He placed the instrument on some sacks of flour and stared at it. Intrigued, he picked it up. Always wanting to learn to play, he ran his fingers over its strings and rested them under his chin. The bow fit in his hand, naturally.

Too often than not, he forgot to order inventory on time and knew he never did things right, except for that old fiddle that made him chuckle despite himself.

"Can I pay you half Patrick? The harvest is not good."

"Your credit is good," his heart replied

"Still learning the violin?"

"Playin' it well, if I dare say so. Been readin' too on liberty and republicanism."

"Well," said the farmer, "you have a fine porch to breathe the insight of that which dwells in them books."

On a walk with John Shelton and his daughter Sarah, the rain came down hard on their heads as Patrick plopped down under a 100-foot tall scaly-bark hickory tree after venting his frustration.

"Well, I believe my failure in merchandise covers the situation," he said to John Shelton.

"Mistakes happen," answered Shelton.

"Why me?" asked the now eighteen-year-old Patrick as he extracted some pale and compressed hickory nuts from their thin shells.

He handed one to father and daughter.

"Have you thought of taking up farming for your livelihood?" asked his father-in-law to be.

"The invitation to work the earth is difficult to resist."

"600 acres."

"It seems daunting, Sir."

"Oh, Father, thank you for the wedding gift," voiced Sarah Sallie Shelton, who savoured the sweet kernel.

Patrick pushed over his failure at merchandise.

"Your family and ours, Patrick, cherish the fact that love entered your life."

"I hope I am up to the task."

"That is why God gave us hands."

Patrick married Sarah Shelton in 1754, and the two went on to have six children together.

For three years, he laboured with the slaves on the land to obtain scanty support for his family with his hands, but the barren earth and spring drought defeated any agricultural skill he possessed.

"Son," his father-in-law said, "the times stink and money, scarce."

The words rang a bell, worse in memory, thought Patrick.

Woefully, he blurted out, "I feel like a failure. Therefore, I am a failure."

Shelton put his arms on his shoulders, "You must forget about the fire that levelled your house last month. Come with the children and move into my tavern."

"How will I support my family?"

"A storehouse near the main road," said Shelton, "and near the courthouse owned by William Parks, who I know. I will inquire."

He engaged in merchandise, again, and settled into the new job.

"Need two pounds of molasses," asserted the baker.

"Have you ripped the cotton cloth?" questioned the seamstress.

"No, maybe by Friday," responded Patrick as he weighed the molasses.

"The sugar arrived?"

"No, a French ship hijacked the shipment from St. Croix."

A customer rose on her toes and in a voice, he thought, like a violin played with a poorly rosined bow, said, "What do they expect us to do? Use our whiskey as a sweetener?"

Though he spent most of his time trying to pay the bills, Patrick developed a sharp sense of the human comedy surrounding him.

When home, he told Sarah, "Whenever a company of my customers met in the store and were themselves sufficiently gay and animated to talk and act as nature prompted, without concealment, without reserve, I listen as if under the influence of some potent charm."

"Do you take no part in their discussions?"

"No, I study their mannerisms. For example, the baker links his hands behind his head when he asks a question. A woman today rose on her toes before speaking."

"What do you do if, on the contrary, they remain dull and silent?

"I, without betraying my drift, task myself to set them in motion and excite them to remarks, collision, and exclamation."

"My dearest husband, nothing suits you better than to start a debate and listen, I imagine with great amusement."

"I compare the debaters and ascertain how they would act in a particular situation."

"I am sure you take delight in relinquishing your silence and regale the patrons with tales."

"The blacksmith told me I had achieved a high mark of character in my struggle to command language."

She smiled, "That is not news to me, husband." Her eyes open wide in admiration.

The compliment left his face red.

"Are you still drawn to geography and reading the historical works of Greece and Rome?"

"Yes, and excuse me for saying, my dearest one, I fell in love with Titus Livy."

He paused, grinned, and blew her a kiss.

Her face fixed with a warm gaze; she said, "I remember father mentioning him; he wrote a history of Rome and the Roman people."

"Quite a book. I experience surprise and admiration from the words. Livy's vivid descriptions and eloquent harangues have become part of me. Even when I close the store to indulge in hunting and fishing, he enters my conscience."

The dormant power of his genius awakened, she realized. Their eyes locked in a mutual understanding.

"I know, Patrick, that you breathe uncomfortably in an unpromising world, but continue to play your violin and flute, read more books, and let your curious inspection of human nature continue."

PH Takes on a Republican Spirit

"I find myself on the path to a republican spirit."

She realized he made her think. "Find a way to use it for your family."

He nudged beside her.

She wanted to stroke his hair, put her arm around him, but it was the afternoon.

They lingered.

He promised Sally to keep his mind targeted on business and not let failure happen, but inside he assumed it would not work out, so why even try? His cash sales, not being sufficient to support his wife and children, required him to give up storekeeping at the age of twenty-four. As he walked away from the store, he turned and gave a last glance, knowing that his latest adventure was another giant misstep.

Thrice failed in earning a living and in debt, he closed his eye, trapped by his dark thoughts, but decided to delve deeper into books to find the road to a livelihood. When not readin', he worked for his father-in-law at the tavern: serving guests, tending bar, and entertaining the customers with his fiddle playing.

As he and his family approached his close friend Colonel Dandridge's house, he unchecked his sunken cheekbones for the Christmas holidays. He opened his eyes, looking across space and time without speaking. Bewilderment and fear flew off. For the first time in a week, he smiled.

Memories danced through his mind, piling up against the hope of his future. Watching his children run into the arms of his hostess, an idea rumbled through his mind.

CHAPTER 2

Papa's Boy

Tossing his head and sending a flurry of red hair flying, the two-year-old Thomas Jefferson, managed in the hands of a slave, turned with warmth and love to his father.

"Put him up on the horse and be careful!"

"Yez, Sir, Master Jefferson."

The father of the future president shifted the saddle and said, "You take heed; destiny awaits my boy. He will make a mark on the world one day."

Peter Jefferson noticed a look of confusion welling from the face of his slave Sawney.

The only destiny waiting for Sawney was to work from sunrise to sunset and maybe a day of rest – as the good pastor spoke of last Sunday.

Peter Jefferson, who married well, social status outweighing money, loved his wife and never rested on the benefits of the marriage. He strived to have a higher societal standard through his hard work, gaining a real respect by his family.

He knew how to run his plantations. From iron hoes – broad for weeding and narrow for hilling – to an English plough that prepared heavier soils, he turned tobacco into gold.

"A small dose of decency would not affect your margin," said the pastor to Virginia's gentlemen planter.

Peter observed the lean, frail man, and by the words and guidance of compassion, resolved to try, "try, unlike others." he said to himself, "and not look upon his slaves as bales of hay."

"Kindness, just as he showed to my brilliant steed; I could show that to Sawney," he mused. Determined to encourage his son's moral and intellectual growth, the man, who also excelled at hunting and riding, fixed his eyes on his child, whispering, "Remember son, God's word tells us they need someone to guide them through the strange land they left. Their skin makes them lower than white people."

Thomas leaned forward in the saddle with a long face.

"Creation is nature's signature," said Peter.

Thomas made no answer.

"Son, it will not harm to be tender."

Black as a moonless night, the large hands of Sawney placed the child of Welsh descent onto a pillow, atop the saddle gently.

Peter gave his son a loving nod, a great deal more than Sawney ever observed from his master.

The tyke lit with life, releasing a swift and stunning smile.

Peter Jefferson's tall, graceful stallion pinned its ears as it sidestepped something gliding on the ground, kicking out and grazing the virile man's leg. Startled, Thomas's father moved back from the steed; his rectangular face noticed a viper swirling away. His sturdy jaw narrowed, his brown, small eyes flashed heatwaves at the snake as the pain from the horses' hoof shot through his leg.

The boy rubbed his pointed chin and rolled his eyes, imitating his father's gesture. Catching Thomas's eye, Peter winked, then patted his son on the cheek. Sawney, whose head of hair was the colour and texture of old spaghetti, turned to Peter Jefferson.

"'Tis your lucky day master. Them cottonmouths, deadly."

"That is right, Sawney; that sure is right."

In 1745, Peter Jefferson looked with some trepidation to what lay ahead.

"Time, I guess, to fulfil my friend and your cousin's wishes, the late William," Peter said to his wife as they boarded a carriage. He did not like leaving his beloved Shadwell; uprooting the family brushed against his better judgment.

His wife, Jane, nodded, pursed her lips, and let her eyelids drop, "I look forward to living in eastern Goochland County and caring for Thomas Mann Randolph." Peter winced. He thought, some people would say he was taking advantage of the situation, but as Jane said, "None of their business!"

Sawney, keeping an eye on young Tom, strode alongside the rig on the 50-mile journey. The boy humming, birds singing, and the south wind whispering through the countryside. The bottomlands, covered with tall grass, rippled like a lake of green.

As Peter's modest dwelling receded from sight, his face turned red, and he clenched his work-scarred hands into a fist; his eyes sent short, intense glances from point to point at Shadwell. He shunned any second thoughts of not honouring the terms of Randolph's will that called for his "dear and loving friend Mr. Peter Jefferson" to move to Tuckahoe until Randolph's orphaned son came of age. He knew his duties as justice of the peace, a judge of chancery court, and a lieutenant colonel of the militia in Albemarle County must wait.

As they approached their destination that evening, Jane closed her eyes, testing that the two-story, four-room abode, built on the rising ground, still retained its splendour.

A minute passed without a word. Jane's eyes never left the house. Peter's hands twitched, and his thoughts darted as he whistled the tune, "The Drummer's Call."

"Peter, I feel refreshed. The commanding view of the James River on that side," she pointed easterly, "and the Tuckahoe on the other remain breathtaking."

Her arm wrapped as far around his waist as it could, and she pressed against him. A combination of love and awe heated his face as he gazed at William Randolph's estate while Jane seemed to skip with joy to the front door. Peter knew any thoughts that his wife would want to return to their simple weather-boarded house without a view vanished like youth's blush.

Thomas settled into his new surroundings at Tuckahoe faster than he could have imagined. He spent his early years in school, learning English grammar and spelling from a tutor with his three sisters and three cousins.

"Here," his father said, "discipline of your noble mind must begin."

When not reading George Anson's *Voyage Round the World*, Thomas walked the 3,256-acre Tuckahoe tract with his cousin, Thomas Mann Randolph, always seeing slaves toiling in the scorching sun.

Thomas Mann Randolph yelled at a group of slaves taking a break in the shade, "Get to work or else!"

Momentarily, they glared at him. He turned to his cousin Thomas, "Did you know in the New Testament, Paul returned a runaway slave, Philemon, to his master?"

Thomas shook his head sideways.

"The Greeks had slaves; the Romans had slaves. It is the natural state of humanity."

And this was before Thomas Mann and his cousin; Thomas read Aristotle's *Politics*, a gift to the boys from Peter Jefferson.

"For that, some rule and others be ruled is a thing not only necessary but expedient: from the hour of their birth, some are marked out for subjection, others for rule . . . ."

Observing the slaves at Tuckahoe with Randolph before returning to Shadwell in 1752, he said to the nine-year-old, "According to Aristotle, cousin, the slaves need to have masters tell them what to do because they cannot think properly."

Thomas raised his eyebrows and thought for several seconds, "I guess they are lucky because they would not have known how to live their lives without masters."

"To reason with slavery," said Randolph, "as it has existed for ages, is to argue with brutes."

"If the present generation allows slavery," said Jefferson, "it does not lessen the right of the succeeding generation to be free."

"Have you noticed," said Randolph, "that love seems with them to be more an eager desire than a tender, delicate mixture of sentiment and sensation."

"In memory, they are equal to the whites."

"In reason much inferior," said Randolph. "One can scarcely be found capable of tracing and comprehending Euclid's investigations."

He gave a manly snort.

"In imagination, they are dull, tasteless, and anomalous," said Randolph.

"I know," said Thomas, "that among the Romans, about the Augustan age especially, the condition of their slaves was much more deplorable than that of the blacks on the continent of America."

"Misery is often the parent of the most affecting touches in poetry," said Randolph. "Among the blacks is misery enough, God knows, but no poetry."

He blurted out, "Where do we get the right to whip and mutilate slaves?

Thomas Mann Randolph replied, "In the Bible, Abraham owned slaves."

Thomas listened to sentences, which were not enjoyable. Words both familiar and strange, hateful, and heartbreaking. "I will say," said Thomas, "I have observed that the slaves are more ardent after their females than whites."

The pot calling the kettle black in Jefferson's future acts.

"They secrete less by the kidneys," said Randolph, "and more by the skin's glands, which gives them powerful and disagreeable odour."

Thomas blinked, wondering if he was in a dream. His cousin concluded, "They are property and such."

Young Jefferson came to know that you are either in or out when it came to slavery, and try as he might and write as he did, he picnicked at the table of bondage.

In his years living at Tuckahoe, Peter Jefferson gained renown as a cartographer after meeting the Albemarle County surveyor, Joshua Fry. Along with Doctor Thomas Walker, the two men formed the Loyal Land Company, petitioning for an area of land consisting of 800,000 acres. Dr. Walker explored Kentucky in 1750, 19 years before the arrival of Daniel Boone.

Fry and Jefferson participated in an expedition from September 10, 1746, to February 24, 1747, through the strange land to draw the "Fairfax Line." This journey marked Lord Fairfax's property across Virginia and West Virginia, crossing the Blue Ridge, the Valley of Virginia, the Allegheny's, and the High Lands of West Virginia.

A lot of lands.

In 1749, the two men mapped the line between Virginia and North Carolina across the Blue Ridge. Peter's fame as a surveyor spread in all directions. Thomas Lewis, kin to Meriwether Lewis, documented the trek in a journal. In 1750, Lewis Burwell, the acting governor of Virginia, recognized the two men's accomplishments and commissioned them to produce a map of the colony that was completed and printed the following year. They created the first map of Virginia.

Young Thomas ran into the parlour and stood beside his father; his hands balled into fists at his sides. His focused eyes stared straight at Peter, "Tell me about your trip!"

"Where should I start?" said Peter, who settled back in his chair.

"Anywhere!"

Chortling, Peter leaned forward to tell his son a tale. "Often having to defend ourselves against the attacks of wild beasts during the day, our eyes scanned in every direction, and at night we slept in trees for our safety."

Thomas tried to picture his father, a man of enormous strength with remarkable powers of endurance, untiring energy, and indomitable courage sleeping in a tree.

"By the end of December, our supply of provisions began to run low, and my comrades, overcome by hunger and exhaustion, fell, fainting beside me."

"What did you eat?"

Peter's eyes, red as a bobcat's, smouldered with amusement. "Raw animal flesh or whatever found to sustain life."

"Yuk," said Thomas as his face squinted. Thomas knew amidst all these hardships and difficulties, his father's courage did not once flag.

"I pressed the men on, and we persevered until completing the task."

He jumped into his father's arms. "You are my hero."

Peter squeezed his son, "All in a day's work, son."

When not out in the wilderness, Peter lusted for Jane, and between 1746 and 1755, he left her pregnant ten times, missing her successful births, and the death of Peter Field in 1748, a month after delivery, and a stillborn son in 1750.

When returning to his temporary home at Goochland, he shared his tears with Jane and took even a stronger attachment to Thomas. He kept it to himself, but he supposed, *God let me down.*

"Did I not render to a man according to his work?" he declared to Jane, who dug into her soul and strengthened her faith in the Almighty. Jane prayed to God, "I know in your heart, and all your soul and your vital force, there must be a reason you took my two sons."

In 1752, they returned to Shadwell, named after the parish of his wife's birthplace in London. Jane's face was full of joy; when she approached home, envisioning the added dining room complete with expensive new furnishings: oval tables, matching side chairs and armchairs, various matching sets of dining wares for different foods or courses for a meal, and sparkling silver tea and coffee accoutrements. As she sauntered into the new main entrance that separated the interior living spaces from the outdoors, she purred.

Thomas studied the new clothing: pumps and sacks and gowns of lutestring India chintz, various items to aid in personal hygiene, dressing tables, wondering why. He observed his father's eyes shining again with delight to be master of his home. He thought ahead and developed the property during his absence by improving the dwelling house into four spacious ground floor rooms and garret chambers above, adding outbuildings, and constructing a water mill on the Rivanna River. And Jane's diligence encouraged him to continue to ascend the ladder of luxury.

With a fast spirit, she advised him to make Shadwell the centre of civic culture in Albemarle. At first, caution and fear played on his mind as he listened to his wife's advice, but the recognition he received from Dr. Thomas Walker, a close family friend, erased any doubts he harboured. Feeling relieved that everything proceeded so well, he made a hard decision for a man – to listen to his wife and follow her lead. While sitting at her sewing table, Jane's jaw tightened as a hand; then, a body appeared disturbing her tranquillity.

"I want Papa. I . . ."

She shot him a jealous eye. The near ten-year-old Thomas lurched back. A smile pushed from his face. Jane thrust from her chair and left her son in midsentence, thinking of how she resented his unadorned love for his father.

She blurted out, "When are you going to stop nibbling on your fingernails?!"

Thomas, slightly slumped, like a depressed older man, appeared to carry a high weight. After walking about the room, she stopped by the door and threw up her hands.

"Sall" needs me," she said. "Stay out of trouble!"

She sauntered down the hall, calling out "Sall."

Thomas sat on the floor, his eyebrows scrunched together, and his head tipped to the side.

"She hates me," he murmured.

He glanced at the empty chair, then swivelled about and went to look for his hero.

"Father, why do I always see you with a book?"

"As my education reeked of neglect, I desired to improve my knowledge."

"Teach me. I want to be like you."

"Son, the sign of a healthy mind means not just what you know but how you act when you do not know what to do."

The youngster thought himself blessed to have such a man in his life.

"It is how you bridge that gap between the known and unknown that separates man from the lower primates," said Peter, amazed by his words.

Thomas heard each word. His eyes looked straight at his father.

The self-educated father who mapped Virginia and accurately depicted the Allegheny Mountains, showing the route of "The Great Road" from the Yadkin River through Virginia to Philadelphia to be a distance of 455 miles, said, "Knowledge remains as the true predictor of success."

In late 1755, the sun peeked brightly from behind the mountains, ready to start a new day with a light that burst through the open window, playing on Jane's face. She filled her lungs with the scented air, then exhaled as the wind whispered through the trees.

Peter stood up, stretched, and stepped from the bed to the window in the corner of their room. He looked out at his landed estate (now over 7,200 acres), hearing birds singing gently.

He approached his wife, slid his hands around her waist, and lifted her so effortlessly. "Jane, my successful ventures in buying land and building this estate will give our son the adequate resources to be a real gentleman."

Under her breath, Jane wondered how a timid, shy, reserved boy with lips tightly sealed, slumped in a lounging manner, on one hip commonly, and with one of his shoulders elevated much above the other, could meet her husband's expectations. And make a mark in Virginia.

"I want, my dear Jane," as he hugged her, "for my son to have all the advantages denied me."

Maybe, she mused to herself, *overcoming adversity separates the wheat from the chaff.*

"I expect him," she said, "to be a model aristocrat like the members of my family."

But that was like trying to get blood from a stone.

Reacting to his wife's silence, Peter cradled his thoughts and said, "I know he seems moody, quiet, and withdrawn, but something unique to him exists. I know and sense it."

"Really," she said. "I get angry when I think your son speaks behind my back."

At a loss of words, Peter's shoulders rose, his head level.

"I feel something special about the boy."

Jane remembered his kicks and twists during her uncomfortable pregnancy. It still annoyed her. Try as she might, and Peter often reminded her, "It was the nature of giving birth that caused you such discomfort, not our boy."

She listened to his words but knew her other children came out quickly and caused her little or no pain. Thomas made her pay the price of giving birth. She never forgot the anguish and took it personally. Sometimes, when in Thomas's presence, she sighed deeply and cried inside for her failure to forgive. Is that not what her pastor and her readings directed her to do? In black-and-white terms, she believed her son a bad boy. She remained perplexed even when comfortably occupied.

The 43 books in Peter Jefferson's library rested in their places. They seemed to nod at the boy, holding an adventure for him. While biting his lip and tapping his finger against his chin, Thomas scanned the various titles hoping to find something to bury his loneliness. He considered Paul de Rapin, Thoyras's *History of England*, and John Ogilby's *America*, but settled with Virginia's map. He relaxed at his father's desk, running his finger along his journey through the wilderness. A distant high-pitched shriek sent shivers down his spine.

"Sall, get him down here, now!"

Sweat stung his eyes, and he jumped up; wiping his face on his shirt, remembering his first intimacy came from the slave, Sall, who breastfed him, sang him to sleep, appeared by his side when he cried in the night, and took his hand and walked with him along the banks of the Rivanna River at Shadwell.

Never a happy mother, she stood by the door upon his return from any activity. Jane patted her daughter's shoulder before rising. "Help me to teach him to dance." Quickly, she turned and stared at Thomas as he entered the room. His eyes seemed lifeless. He shifted his slouch and thought, "Why me?"

"Come here and stand straight," she demanded, "and put your hand around your sister's waist."

He stumbled towards them. His fists clenched so tight they ached. His mother's glare at him lodged in his throat – it never relented as the years moved forward, and his mind recalled her unpleased look.

"I labour much to raise you to the same standards of propriety that your father and I have known. I expect you to be a very gentle, well-dressed young man. Remember, Virginians look more at a person's outside than his inside."

Limply, his hands hung by his side as he wondered why she always lectured him.

"Must I remind you again that Aristotle ranked dancing with poetry and said a proper good dancer personified manners, passions, and actions?"

His head turned to his older sister, hoping for an ally, but she turned to Mary, their youngest sister. From his readings, he knew her statement's correctness and repelled at the given information, not the content.

"Do not look away while I am talking to you, young man. For these and other reasons, I expect you to be spotless, neat, and appear attractive at all times."

He tried to look at her, but his eyes fell to the floor.

"Do not expect any grace and civility from me if you defy my wishes."

About to speak, she cut him off.

"You bring shame to the Randolph name."

"I am a Jefferson," he uttered, "and care not that you come from an accomplished London and Virginia merchant."

"My ancestry dates back to the early mists of Scottish and English history. Do not speak lightly of this!"

At best, her family was of modest means, he thought incorrectly, and not aristocratic in any sense of the word. She hovered over Thomas like an apparition as he glared at her.

"I never want anything to do with silly noble manners."

"Well, lest you forget, your father comes from the Gentry, Peter Jefferson Gent!"

Thomas took two long breaths, and his head reeled at the information.

"Too many complications exist in life for you to understand," she said.

He gazed at her. "For you!" he shouted.

His heart rumbled like an angry beast.

Speaking at the top of her voice, "I am not your father who grants you too much freedom of thought and speech."

His eyes beamed with delight for telling her what he thought.

"Go to your room and stay there until you apologize to me for your selfish behaviour; you ungrateful, spoiled brat."

He thought she sounded like a sow in heat, excitable, and more vocal.

He still wanted to love his mother but stood with a glare that humbled the devil. With a dirty look that contorted her face, Jane rushed towards him and dragged him by his red hair to his room. Her voice pierced his ears, "You have no idea how much trouble you cause me!"

He cowered in a corner, clutching his arms to his chest, shaking convulsively. Jane's face was as red as a beet. "The world does not revolve around you. You will soon find out how hard it is."

Feverishly, she stomped around his room, slamming books shut and throwing others to the floor, and then scanned the four walls looking for something special of his. Breath avoided his lungs. Every movement by her sent waves of pain through him. Before she departed his sanctuary, she gathered his writing instruments. He hoped she would take the Bible by his bedside, but she left it undisturbed. Hate sprinted through Thomas's veins. He tried to open his mouth, sighted his mother's eyes, and remained silent.

"Ponder your four walls and try to be humble like Jesus."

As the door slammed shut, his cursing began, and he swore until he could not swallow, well aware that "cursed are those who curse you."

While walking down the hall, her look could have blackened toast. She murmured, "The spoiled wretch will never change, damn his heart!"

Next morning, he heard a key unlocking the door and then a knock. Bouncing into the room wearing Peter's pyjamas, all smiles, Jane lit up the vicinity with a festive glow on her face as if nothing had happened the day before. Curled up like a cat in front of the hearth, Thomas wished for his father's return.

"Oh, Thomas, are you feeling better today? You must be famished."

For the first time, he smiled genuinely and wondered, a strange way to say, "Sorry."

"I brought you some food." She paused and turned. "Dinah!"

The house slave winked at him as she entered the room carrying an oblong silver tray. Smelling crisp hash browns and scrambled duck eggs, and garlic in the fried spinach, he grabbed the glass of goat milk and took a big gulp.

"Thomas, I wish you would make eye contact with me as you do with your father. I enjoy seeing your hazel eyes. They complement your freckled face."

He knew her next sentence. "Do you always have to dress in slippers and corduroy breeches to annoy me?"

"Thank you for the food, mother."

His mouth smiled, but his eyes did not. The dancing lesson scarred his relationship with his mother, who he could never quite forgive. Wanting to ask her why she did not criticize him when they assembled in his father's presence, he held his tongue. In his hidden diary, he documented that Jane was agreeable, intelligent, lively, cheerful, humorous, and fond of writing letters when not around him, and, he admitted, she wrote readily.

He understood all too well that his father adored her – many nights when home from surveying, he heard the sounds of intimacy, his father's pleasure standing up and howling. This fact never slipped Thomas's mind when his father arbitrated family tensions.

After returning from another survey, Peter Jefferson burst into Thomas's room. He observed books stacked on his desk, flowers wilted in

THE MEN WHO CHOOSE LIBERTY

a vase, clothes strewn about, and mismatched shoes lying in corners. The contrast between the decoration Jane put into the front rooms and Thomas's room startled him.

"Son."

"Father, I want to tell you how much I miss you."

Peter looked delighted.

"Did you and your mother get along?"

"I do not understand her. Why am I different from her? She says one thing and the next . . ."

His father wrapped his arms around him, comforting him as his voice cut him off.

1752 Thomas Jefferson Goes to School

"Being that you will be nine years old in a few days, I want you to attend a Latin school run by a Mr. Douglas, a clergyman from Scotland."

"When will I begin?"

"Two weeks hence."

"Come down in half an hour so we can eat together."

After his father left, Thomas opened the door of his room. He wanted to skip down the hall but returned to his desk, arranging his notebooks by subject. Before departing, he went through the fruitless task of grooming.

"Son, I have been pleased with your progress in educational pursuits."

Thomas listened in all the right places but knew what was coming next.

"I need to know you and your mother will get along when I am gone surveying."

Thomas's mind galloped north then headed east, trying to fathom not spending a minute under Jane's glare.

That night Peter gave him a firm handshake and said, "For both of us, listen to your mother."

In the remaining weeks, Jane and Thomas avoided each other as cats and dogs do, and his mother's upper lip curled when her son strayed too close.

Isolated and smart enough to steer clear of his mother, he read, sketched, and walked the fields of Shadwell while the days for the appointed hour of attending school dragged on.

Initially, a permanent flash of light reflected in his eyes as he listened to his teacher speak Gallic with a Scottish accent. His master's broad, wrinkled face appeared hard to him, and his small eyes that yielded no emotion reminded Thomas of his mother.

On a Sunday morning, Peter Jefferson, just returned from the distant forest, asked Thomas, "What do you think of Mr. Douglas?"

"He knows French, but only a little Latin and little instruction in Greek."

"Regardless, you will learn the basics of classical education from the rudiments of these languages."

"I wish to dream of the men of antiquity and ignore Christian saints and modern historical figures."

Jane glanced over at Thomas and grinned. *Must put on a good show for Peter*, she thought, her face withholding a sour look. She winked at her husband.

"Little boy," she wanted to say, "in life, strive for the attainable. Big goals pass like a breeze in the air and leave you with a sour taste."

She noticed; Thomas imagined the stain on his shirt. With an ache in his heart, he squinted into her eyes. He might as well be deaf, for all the good his mother's words were going to do for him. Before Jane could speak, Peter answered, "Yes, dream, as long as you do not ignore my library of Shakespeare, Swift, and Addison."

"I will make them my playtime and never sit down in idleness."

Jane stood up abruptly. "Excuse me; I have some letters to write."

She withdrew with Peter wondering why her frown.

"Son, let us men take a walk. I want to explain the business of capital investments made at Shadwell."

They slid out of the house and streamed past an assortment of laborers.

"Father, why do you have slaves?"

The question startled Peter Jefferson. He tried to open the door of his mind, but words eluded him. He thought to tell his son slavery existed throughout history and was the natural state of life. The Greeks owned slaves, the Romans retained slaves, but he shifted the subject.

"Do you understand what makes Shadwell successful, son?"

A bolt of anxiety rushed through Thomas's mind. He eyed the cleared land, observing dwellings, stores, barns, vegetable and flower gardens, tobacco and grain cultivation, a grist mill, and livestock.

"The horses, cattle, pigs, and sheep," he said, "provide transportation, food, hide, and fibre."

His father showed him his hands. Thomas thought they looked like the leather on some of the house books.

"Son, my properties in Albemarle County double the next in value, and I am the second-largest slaveholder in the county, owning more than fifty slaves."

Thomas stepped back, absorbing the information.

"And," Peter said, his eyes scanning his property, "We are debt-free."

Thomas looked up and smiled some.

"We controul our life."

Having no idea what his father was talking about, Thomas changed the subject.

"Will you buy more slaves?"

Peter Jefferson stepped back and beheld his son

"Good question. What do *you* think?"

Without taking his eyes off his father, Thomas shrugged, oblivious to the brutal tradition of slavery that allowed families to be comfortable and overflow with conceit.

Peter informed his son, "Their work allows me to attain my dreams. For even as hard as I do without them, we would be beneath my thoughts."

"I understand, father; they make it so we can be happy."

"I want my industry and hard work to enable you to grow up to be anything but an ordinary man."

"I will rise early, before dawn, and fill every hour with useful pursuits, father."

"You will see how much gets done. What will you do today?"

"My doings shall include horseback riding with my friend and neighbour, Jake Walker, exploring the woods of Shadwell."

He stopped and thought, then said, "Two hours on the violin, three hours making sketches of buildings, an hour of penmanship, followed by Greek and Latin translation. And I want to begin Shakespeare's *Measure for Measure*."

Peter Jefferson greeted this information with a broad grin; Thomas took note of his crooked teeth as Peter tried to forget Jane's accusations towards his son.

"I studied the book by da Vinci you purchased for me."

His father remembered the disgust that swept over Jane's face when he let slip of this present. The light danced on Thomas's face as he asked, "Do you think man will be able to fly?"

"Curiosity inspires invention, son."

Both smiled and, observed for a moment, forgot the woes of life. Thomas broke the silence. "I am proud that you, father, have become a member of the House of Burgesses."

"Just for one term, son. Something I always wanted to accomplish."

As his father stepped forward, Thomas observed a radiance on his face.

"Son, Reverend Maury wants me to consider an expedition to the West up to the Missouri River, to discover whether it has any communication with the Pacific Ocean."

"Can I go with you?"

Peter cast a look over Thomas's shoulder, wondering what he should say, but before he answered, Thomas, changed the subject.

"Father, I am reading *Tom Jones*."

"I just learned that Fielding died on October 8, 1754," said his father.

"Do you know from what?

"No, said Peter, "but death at forty-seven." He shook his head.

Three or four plump rabbits stopped nibbling on wild grass and stared at them. Thomas wondering what it was like to be a bastard like Tom Jones. Would he ever meet one, and how would he react if he did? He would meet one, and he turned as purple as a plum when he did.

Peter, listening to the wind and how it felt compared to surveying the Ohio River watershed.

"Life is about accepting the challenges along the way," he said, "choosing to keep moving forward, and savouring the journey."

He enjoyed that the Ohio River was fast in some places and slower in others and planned on returning the following fall, wishing to draw a stretch of the scenery. However, death shut down Peter Jefferson's lids at Shadwell in 1757; his close friend, Dr. Walker, the family physician and one of his will's executors, was by his side. How was Thomas to bear the change? Thirteen years under Peter Jefferson's guidance, the mildness of his temper seldom allowed him to impose any restraints, and now the shadow of his mother's authority was in his face, hovering like insects at a swamp. Sorrow came, a hard regret for Thomas in the shape of a disagreeable consciousness.

His brain went numb, and then a headache thundered: he held his hands on his fourteen-year-old head as he believed no relative or friend lived to advise or guide him. Day after day, feeling hopeless and depressed, he twisted and turned in the mirror of loneliness. Jane provided the family with a level of care, skill, and prudence that may have chafed her oldest son's sense of entitlement yet kept the family in the black.

CHAPTER 3

Long Ago and Far Away: Alexander Hamilton's Roots

A s the Atlantic quietly and softly drew boats filled with enslaved people, their numbers increasing rapidly, the wind's heartbeat in the Caribbean Sea skipped a beat for the men and women considered chattel.

In 1740, at age 11, Rachael Faucett watched her parent's marriage disintegrate in Nevis's lush and hilly southern foothills, a 36-square-mile island under the British government. The intelligent, alluring, and determined Rachael relocated to St. Kitts, a 68-square-mile island under British rule, along with her mother. In 1743, Rachael's father, John, had made out his will, declaring Rachael the sole beneficiary.

Remembering the too many times she was startled out of her sleep by the hateful screams of her parents, Rachael's face turned as pale as the linen her mother wove.

"Keep your grubby hands off me!"

"Watch your tongue, woman!"

"Do not come on to me with your lust."

"Do not debate about my right and your duty."

Puckering her lips, Rachael snickered, recalling her father's constant lust for her mother. She gazed upward to soft cauliflower clouds. Turning to hope and to her future, she threw up her arms, tossed back her head, and thought of building castles in the air. "Catch the moment," she uttered, "and enjoy the journey. But her thoughts wandered to her past. Confusion raced through her memories as they streaked through her mind. For the first time in her life, doubts existed in her sense of identity. Trying to ignore the echoes in her heart, she grunted, wondering, about her youth?

No birds sang from the branches, she said to herself.

Rachael recalled before hesitating, measuring her thoughts about her mother, Mary, and her older husband, and her father, John, a physician. They just did not get along, and Mary was stung by their rage when she, as a child, lived on Nevis.

Remembering the too many times she was startled out of her sleep by the hateful screams of her parents, Rachael's face turned as pale as the linen her mother wove.

"Keep your grubby hands off me!"

"Watch your tongue, woman!"

"Do not come on to me with your lust."

"Do not debate about my right and your duty."

Rachael puckered her lips and snickered, recalling her father's constant lust for her mother. She blushed, redder than that night's sunset, as she thought of her parent's relationship.

"Stay away from me. I have suffered satisfying your disgusting urges!"

"Do not blame me for your inhibitions."

"I want distance from you and off this godforsaken, blighted island."

"The law considers you my lawful wife."

"Well, I have no hunger in answer to Shakespeare."

The physician believed what resided within her lovely head was lost like a leaf in the wind, but Rachael knew how her mother liked to quote the Bard's "lawful as eating" from *The Winter's Tale*: Act V Scene III.

"I want out of this union," said Rachael's mother, Mary, "and demand the property I brought to the marriage and enough money to begin anew."

"You seek to abandon all our years together?"

"Without much content, Sir."

"I labour for you and the child fourteen hours a day."

"So much to my good comfort," she sneered, "as it exists."

"Your love for me is gone?"

"An understatement, Sir."

"Never good?"

Rachael laughed and recalled he would then give her an innocent, pitiful, feel sorry glance.

"I am ready to bargain so I can have no more of the smell of your flesh."

"You have lost all sense of your well-being. Why do we have this discussion repeatedly?"

"Save your questions for your patients."

"No curative?"

"Yes, a detachment potion that relieves me from your suffocation."

In a mirror hanging over a dresser, she studied her face and thought, *women having the same rights*, she told herself, *as animals at the slaughterhouse*. She saw the women of her family racing against the wind in a yacht so white it hurt her eyes, realizing that her mother refused when required to be quiet, reserved, or reticent. Her situation made her independent and assertive, she realized. As a woman of beauty, charm, and ambition, she rejected the command of a man's control, *a rare trait for a woman, indeed*, Rachael thought.

Her mother, denied a better life, worked as a seamstress to support Rachael. She stopped and saw her oval face with red cheeks and her black bands of hair in the mirror.

"Home life, a dog's life, when two dissonant tempers meet up," she told herself. "Yesterday trumps tomorrow no matter how hard you try to change the hand dealt you."

A frown marred Rachael's brow as she realized her mother's marital situation bordered on the absurd. The sun below the horizon, twilight cast sunbeams in every direction before the big ball of fire morphed from dark orange to a dull yellow. The dusk of the day then materialized. The horizon momentarily blushed pink before gliding black—the sunset, ready to start another night. Rachael dreamed of running on the beach of opportunity, but her future actions would bring her to the ocean's edge.

Hope, soft and quiet, covered her mind. She circled her situation, but the reality of her mother's life, she realized, made it hard for her to live in the present and her previous history filled her mind with thunderclouds. Her goal, she told herself again, was "to make the future a formidable distance from the past."

She stood like a statute as nature's globe highlighted her yellow hair, her mind silent, showing signs of wear as the wind whispered above the sea, sadness drifting over the ocean's surface. Pulling optimism into her body, her shoulders rose as she sighted her past and sang with her head raised.

> 'Twas in the merry month of May,
> When bees from flow'r to flow'r did hum
> Soldiers through the town march'd gay,
> The village flew to the sound of the drums.

An ocean chill hovered under the night breeze as a series of clouds blocked the stars. She shivered, then chattered, smelling decaying seaweed.

Hours later, in clothing wetter than a fish in the sea from spending the night at the water's edge, she frowned but not because of her condition. She could not shun the picture of herself as a youth lying at night in her bed curled up in a ball, her hands clasped on her knees and tears raining down her face.

In 1745 Dr. Faucett, passed, leaving his property to Rachael. Mother and sixteen-year-old daughter settled on St. Croix, an 82-square-mile island under Dutch rule in North America. They resided at No. 9 Company's Quarter, one-and-a-half miles southwest of the capital, Christiansted, at the sugar plantation of Rachael's thirty-two-year-old half-sister, Anne, and her husband, James Lytton.

"What a handsome dwelling built of stone with a piazza! Big and spacious!" exclaimed Mary.

"I like that it stands on the summit of a little hill," added Rachael.

"Wait till you smell the jasmine," said Anne, "that lines each side of the walk to the house."

Anne pointed at waving branches that surrounded the home.

"Spreading tamarind, flowering cider covered with flowers, sister, and orange trees, limes, cocoa nuts, palmettos, myrtles, and citrons that provide shade."

"The flowers of all hues leave an impression of peace that I feel deep down," said Rachael.

Seeing a quick, sad smile from Rachael, Anne said, "Your lives have been a bucket overflowing with tragedy."

"Witnessing all five of your siblings' death, three in one month," added Mary, "a tragedy I could do without."

"Having to abandon a life of comfort," said Rachael and take flight with you when your marriage came to an end is not what I wanted!"

Extremely bored, slightly vexed, and jealous of Anne, due to her stepdaughter's affluence, Mary sat wondering if her life could be any more mundane, any more staid.

As if by magic, Johan Michael Lavien appeared, impressing Rachael's mother when introduced by Anne. A former merchant from Nevis, an acquaintance of the Lyttons, and an aspiring planter on St. Croix, he now landed in the life of the Faucetts.

Mary was impressed with neither his looks nor his gift of gab. After some chit-chat about the weather, he smiled. Mary ignored the words spewing from the mouth of Lavien. His black trousers, blue vest with silver embellishments over a white shirt with ruffles of exquisite lace, his wide-brimmed hat turned up on three sides, and the silver shoe buckles reflecting the light roused her admiration. In her mind, his low-heeled leather shoes negated the bravado of the braggart.

"My recently purchased cotton plantation, No.12b Company's Quarter, is not far from the Lytton home."

As the hand of the clock wound on, he ignored the fact that he paid far more attention to the great house where he would reside than the wind and cattle mill, the boiling house, the curing home (the place for fermenting the liquor or wash, from which rum is distilled), the storehouse for grain, and the stock house. All the accessory buildings required improvement. And the slave huts were built of stone; the roofs were not well-hatched or as comfortable as they should be.

Mary reached out and draped Anne's hand and said in a calm voice. "The best-dressed man I have ever seen. He wears clothes more exquisite than the petals of a rose. He would be the perfect husband for Rachael."

The sixteen-year-old's world was about to fall like the leaves of autumn.

"Her mother is not thinking," said Anne to James, "that one unhappy union should not be rushed straight into another."

The fortune hunter failed to inform Mary that he spent his time peddling household goods of late.

The innocent Rachael Faucett represented a new prey. Her snug inheritance would have allowed her to feel comfortable but was an "I do" from departing.

Rachael was resting on her heels by her mother's side, anguish on her frightened pallid face.

"He is older than you!"

Mary blushed. "Thirty-two is not that old."

"He looks like forty and acts even older."

"The marriage will be good for the family."

"Financial and social prospects mean nothing to me."

"When you gain in years, you will understand and thank me."

Lavien availed himself to shoot James Lytton a wide grin two tables away.

"Slaves that run the boilers," Lytton said to Lavien, "constitute the most valuable men on a plantation."

Lavien, sitting at the table with his left leg crossed over the right, lit a cigar.

"Want of attention to this ruined many an aspiring plantation owner."

But the only mentation in Lavien's mind was Rachael's tautened thighs, developed by her long walks.

"Special care must occur in constructing boiling houses," informed Lytton.

The face of Lavien was as blank as an empty bottle.

"The heat," continued Lytton, "required to produce four or five kettles that contain not less than a hogshead (63 gallons) apiece requires a robust and clear fire to boil the sugar to its proper consistency. They should be built very high and lofty, covered with shelving boards that admit the air freely as well as give vent to the steam."

In his mind, Lavien dreamed of the ripe Rachael, un-robing.

"You will know it is correct when they boil to their height, and those in the room can endure the heat."

With arousal boiling beyond the consistency of sugar, Lavien tasted the sweet virgin. "Mind you," continued Lytton, "you never have enough manure, and every successful planter must obtain this great article. You should hoard it with the utmost care, and large dunghills composed of the ashes from the boiling kettle, the bruised canes, the cane's spilled leave, the cleaning of houses and dung of the stables should be turned up and kept everywhere until ready for use. Never should infant cane be placed in its pit without a sufficient quantity."

Lavien, a Dane, or a Jew, probably neither but of North German extraction stuck to Rachel like glue. Forced to marry, the sixteen-year-old forfeited the bloom of her youth. The boorish, little man of repulsive fibre did thrust his cane in Rachael's pit. They produced a son, Peter, in 1746.

The night hummed with intrigue and the moon full of delight as Lavien watched Rachael's reflection in a mirror. The creep savoured the thought of ravishing her but said, "The boiler house burnt to the ground, killing two enslaved people."

"What about my money?"

"Lot 12b needs to go for sale."

"And my money?"

"I have entered into a contract to purchase, at a bargain, I might add, half of an adjacent tract at No.19."

Lavien's posture bent like a broken finger as Rachael realized her life was as insignificant as a whisper in a boisterous crowd. It dawned on her how little she cared for him.

"Enough of you, husband. For too many years, you have irritated my patience."

"Get undressed."

He attempted to grip her, but she landed on the bed, his fingernail scratching her face. Her hand grazed his lips, and she smelled liquor on her fingertips. She rolled on her side, her heart missing several beats.

A thought assaulted her mind. "Damn that man!" She decided to leave. "Lavien never showed me any respect and used physical force to get his way and made me out as a fool."

"Worse, I let him again," she realized.

She needed to think, not sleep, and sleep evaded her that night.

The moon rifled its reflection in the window, making her blink. The curtains, drawn back so she could enjoy the breeze and the night birds rippled, shifted, and moved until the smoky-grey of dawn merged with the mist. Lavien passed out beside her, exposed, vulnerable, drunk on cheap port. She thought of smothering him with his red wine-stained pillow, but instead, she rose with the sunrise and departed from four years of pain and torture on a bright morning.

Furtively, she glanced behind for fear of Lavien. Halfway down the path, she thought she heard footsteps behind her – smelled the stench of the cheap port, and desperation crept ever closer. She quickened her pace, jumping at the slightest sound, even pebbles creaking under her feet, never realizing her imagination playing with her.

Sometime after leaving Lavien, she met Johan Jacob Cronenberg, a Danish land surveyor who arrived in St. Croix in the winter of 1747 and was mapping the island. She lived with him till the fall of 1749. Learning of a Dutch law that allowed a husband to charge his wife with committing "such mistakes, which were indecent and very suspect for married people," Lavien had her put in jail. The chauvinistic law, a shadow of justice for the fair sex, imprisoned the wedded wife for having resided with Cronenberg for a long time in fornication until the court reached a decision. Cronenberg was also charged with fornication by Lavien and jailed.

Entering one of two adjoining rooms on the south side of the fort, Rachael grimaced genuinely. She stared at the wood partition with a connecting door that separated the cells. Her delicate beauty stood up in intense light. Her cell's small, barred windows faced west and offered an unimpeded view of the wharf area and King Street's eastern end. The western sun's breath warmed her body, and she wrapped her thoughts around her freedom from Lavien, the brick floor cooled her anger. Truly, alone for the first time in her life, she promised not to give up hope and vowed to listen to her own wishes.

Rachael counted her days at the fort, almost a month she realized, but cared not. She cherished her freedom from Lavien. She watched as cannonballs pierced the hulls of pirate ships that tried to cross the coral reef and boats traversing Gallows' Bay from the windows of her confinement. Not dreaming of sailing to a new life, she resolved to start anew and looked upon her confinement as the first chapter. The eight-by-ten-foot cell shrank in her mind, and the food – boiled yellow cornmeal mush, salted herring and codfish – represented a step up from her mother's cooking.

Several pounds lighter, she continued to languish at the fort.

"I am impressed with your resilience," said the fort's captain.

"What choice do I have?"

"You could return to his bed."

"I am only twenty-one, and I will be damned to waste more years with that ogre."

Her warm, vibrant, chocolate eyes were still full of hope for the days to come. His eyes fixed on her, admiring her vibrant, unpainted round, rosy face, and attractive smile that lit up even on the gloomiest of days. He wanted to run his fingers through her curly chestnut hair that complimented her eyes and small, round nose and kiss her defined mouth.

"You remind me of a blossom in May that refuses to wilt."

On an early Tuesday morning, after eight months of confinement, he entered her cell.

"You can go," he said.

"What!" exclaimed Rachael.

A whip of panicked excitement cracked through her as he led her from subjugation.

"Your husband, tired of choking on the weeds of hate, took to attending church."

"I can see him praying for my reformation and cherishing the thought of having me back in his bed."

"He dropped the suit, believing you as a wedded wife would forsake your unholy way of life and live correctly with him."

The man in charge of the fort was thinking her life bruised and her soul branded as they walked to the guarded entrance to the fort.

He looked at her. "He wants you to return home."

"His hope is as futile as giving food to a corpse," she shot back, thinking a vulture's derriere would be more pleasant at her side.

"What will you do?"

"Get as far away as I can from the balding, pock-marked lifeless swine, probably to an English island."

"I want to take my son."

"Your rights of legal separation," he stopped to think, "are slim at best under the Dutch law. According to the island's jurisprudence, guardianship goes to the father."

"Then, I will go alone without remorse."

On an afternoon of a fall day in 1750, Rachael lit another cigarette, her fifth, as she and her mother waited for a boat to remove them from St. Croix.

Her spirits could not have been higher as she boarded the boat to cross the two-mile channel for St. Christopher, more commonly known as St. Kitts.

"Look, we must anchor where no harbours nor bays exist," Rachael said. She pointed to some carts, near that open road.

Mary was favouring the birds that flapped their wings as they soared through the sky.

"You look invigorated, Rachael."

"I am ready to flap my wings, mother."

Mary looked at her daughter, smiling at her innocence. "How free are the birds," she asked, "from the sky's chains?"

Rachael, too giddy to hear her words, raced upon the shore. She stood at the foot of the island's volcanic cone. Looking up from the base that ascended from the sea and rose from all sides to the mountaintop, she observed sugar cane for about a third of the way up and then a vast green canopy of myrtles, tamarinds, oranges, limes, cherries, and papaya.

Within days, Rachel mingled amongst the 1,900 white inhabitants and 417 free Negroes and mulattoes of the island, who lived quite well and appeared extraordinarily polite and hospitable. he 23,462 indentured servants that inhabited Saint Christopher stood as far from her consciousness as a distant galaxy in the solar system.

"Mother, I enjoy the abundance of freshwater, forests, salt, and fertile soil," said Rachael.

"The natives refer to our new home as Liamuiga or fertile land."

"I am glad you have time to smell the buds and taste the fruit."

"I cherish the colourful profusion of vines and flowers. The fresh, flourishing vegetation ranks above any in the world, a military gentleman told me."

"The cost to live here makes it impossible to stay," informed Mary.

"But cotton is a plentiful shrub, and coffee appears on the creek's banks that flow into the sea."

"That is true. The cotton helps me be a needlewoman, and coffee gives me energy, but we cannot survive on cotton and coffee alone."

"What shall we do?"

"Move to Nevis!"

"Too small and I have bad memories!"

"Look at it as the land of beautiful waters and the cost of living substantially less."

"But mother, that will be a step down economically and socially – I thought this meant something to you."

Mary shut the door to her daughter's new life. "We have no choice!"

A life without choices, Rachael knew, was not a vibrant one – like being on of the walking dead. Rachael listened to Nevis's lush tropical silence being replaced by the humming sound that cultivated sugar cane. The challenge, she told herself, was to act as though she enjoyed her new surroundings. Just try to play the role of an obedient daughter, a child hauling a smile.

"Mother, I need more than this. I must visit St. Kitts."

"The child in you no longer lives. Do as you think best."

Best, an elusive meaning. A hair from the worst.

Mary spent some time on St. Eustatius in July of 1755 and returned to St. Kitts in May of 1756, where she died.

* * * * *

St. Kitts, a long green island fringed with palms and rising to a volcanic mountain in whose crater molten lava moved sluggishly was north of Nevis. It sported a cosmopolitan setting, though less exotic than Nevis.

Her first day there, overflowing with freedom, she found it entirely enchanting. Its seaport warehouses, two ports, shipping depots, small stores, many churches, and a fort with a magnificent view filled her with energy. She attended Lutheran, Dutch Reformed, Anglican, Roman Catholic, and Presbyterian services. Hope here, there, and everywhere.

While exploring the port in Basseterre, St. Kitts, in 1751, the sun's rays flickered through the sky, and she glanced at a man, observing his tanned forearms. She wanted them around her waist. Her world drifted away, absent of all colour but him.

James Hamilton, a watchman wearing a crinkled wide-brimmed cotton hat, a weathered short sleeve brown waistcoat to midthigh with a faded forest green vest, and scuffed leather shoes fastened with worn brass buckles, thought himself dandy. He noticed her stare, removed his hat, and walked towards her.

She shivered as his head nearly collided with a hanging sign. The reddish-blond-haired workman with sparkling violet-blue eyes approached ever closer. Better than icing on the cake, she believed. She mumbled, "I want a taste."

As opposite from my husband as north from south, she said to herself but in truth as faulted.

"Hello."

Her heart dropped this day of 1751.

"Call me, James." His voice touched her, tasted her.

She teased herself with her fantasies, but before he could go on, she fainted. Sputtering upon awakening, the rippled arms that lifted her from the ground stopped in midair. Her breath froze in her lungs as she looked into his eyes, her heart bouncing with desire, but an inner voice warning her to go slowly. She experienced a hand, fragrant as her soap, massaging her forehead.

Her face, still delicate, perhaps more so considering her life since Lavien. The slope of her cheekbones gave her dignity. With pale skin, her youth was robbed, but only she knew. Her hair, pinned up to the top of her head, was a selling point, though her face seemed vulnerable. James noticed a hint of frailness in her beauty but never doubted it.

Impressed with his banter about his royal title, land holdings, and aristocratic status, she dove into a relationship with the charming, penniless fourth son of Scottish nobility. A tenderness coursed through Rachael, leaving her flaming with life. Her eyes beamed through the hours of the looking glass.

"What do I have to lose?" she thought, forgetting about eggs in a nest.

She sent out sparks like a wildfire, alive with life. Her eyes could beam through the night. So warm with love, she refused, at first, to hold his hands for fear of burning them. They produced two children, James Junior sometime in 1752 or 1753 and Alexander in 1754 or 1755.

Due to constant debt, the ever-failed James Hamilton withdrew from St. Kitts to Sint. Eustatius and became a sailor on a merchant vessel, leaving Rachael to nourish for herself and raise James Junior and Alexander. Taking heed of her situation, she moved back to St. Eustatius and found employment in a store while James sailed upon the sea.

CHAPTER 4

Mules Are Always Boasting

aron Burr, the younger, entered life in 1756 upon the tenets of religion on both sides of his family. His grandfather, Jonathan Edwards, noted pastor of the Congregational Church in Northampton, Massachusetts, author of the *Edwardian Theology*, a fundamentalist John Calvin, possessed an original mind in pre-Revolutionary America. He gained notoriety in 1735 for his sermons against moral decay and spiritual apostasy. His revival pioneered the Great Awakening a few years later. Edwards loved to quote the Bible, "A city that is set upon a hill cannot be hidden."

But his dogmatic self-righteousness caused his popularity to wane, and after angering his congregation, Edwards was relieved of his pulpit at Northampton. He relocated to the forest-bound frontier village of Stockbridge, Massachusetts, where he worked trying to marry the man-centred theories of Locke and Newton to the God-centred doctrines of John

Calvin. He grappled with the age-old question of the nature of human free-dom, but try as he might to declare the marriage to the world, he failed.

'Tis a shame he didn't pursue his earlier scientific studies at fifteen or sixteen. He discovered water to be a compressible fluid, a fact that was not given to the world by scientists until 1763, and one if Edwards had pursued it further might have led him to Benjamin Franklin's theory of electricity before Franklin discovered it.

Aaron Burr's father, Aaron Burr senior, opened his eyes to the sermons of Edwards. He saw the "footstool of sovereign grace" and God's Son in the Gospel, as an all-sufficient Saviour. As numerous beliefs existed and preached their God, for religion needs a home and money to pay the expenses, the Reverend Burr went to work as an apprentice at a small church in Hanover, New Jersey.

The flock of the First Church at Newark abandoned ship for the newly established Episcopalian church, and the "urban, lenient, and charm-ing Burr" was called forth from Hanover. After a year of probation, he was ordained as the minister at Newark. Aside from his pastoral duties, which he handled with aplomb, he helped found in 1746 the fourth college in America, the College of New Jersey, at Elizabethtown. Upon the first presi-dent's death, its Presbyterian pastor, Jonathan Dickinson, he took charge of the college and its eight students. The college resided in Newark for three years, and Burr received no salary. The enrolment increased "to between 40 and 50" by 1751, but the successful thirty-five-year-old man lamented that he had everything but a wife.

The Reverend Burr, hearing of an Edwards daughter, visited and soon married the eighteen-year-old Esther, "amicable in her person, of great affa-bility and agreeableness in conversation, and a very excellent economist." In December of 1756, the Burrs moved to Princeton, New Jersey, into a house adjoining the newly constructed Nassau Hall of the College of New Jersey.

Esther dined in silence and drank her hot water, always looking at her eight-month-old son, Aaron Burr, Jr., who she believed to be on "the borders of eternity." With a concerned, cautious look, she informed the doctor. "For three days, he has breathed with difficulty."

The doctor gave her a quick, level-headed look, "The child will not live till morn."

"Oh, God!"

She dropped to her knees and prayed, "I struggle to overcome the sin of possessiveness and accept your will for my child. I know I must submit! For the Lord giveth and the Lord taketh, and I will bless your name. I know Lord, you have the first right, and the child is not mine; he was lent, and I must freely return him and say, Lord, do as seemeth good in thy sight."

At dawn, a streak of light awoke Esther. She experienced a finger running down the back of her neck and turned, but no one was there. Hearing her son crying, she thought herself dreaming, but the cries continued. Realizing they emanated from Aaron, her heartbeat wildly. She jerked her head up.

"Oh, God, I thank you for his recovery. I knoweth you have set him apart for some special purpose, and I will undertake to prepare him for an outstanding future."

Looking up, she asked, "What obligations, Lord, am I laid under, to bring up my child in a peculiar manner for you?"

She heard the Lord say, "Children are inherently tainted by sin and, thus, must be instructed and disciplined."

Looking at her son, she sighed before picking him up. She squeezed him in her arms, saying as she looked up, "There will be a time for every activity, a time to judge every deed."

As the days passed, God's child confounded Esther. She thought of him as a little dirty, noisy boy and wrote, "Very different from Sally, almost in everything. He begins to talk a little, is very sly and mischievous, and exhibits more sprightliness than Sally, and most say he is more handsome, but not so good-tempered. He is very resolute and requires a good nanny to bring him to terms."

Baby Aaron often perceived a chill when in the presence of the "good governess." The urge to lift his head, roll over, sit up, look over his shoulder, and crawl away governed his actions toward his independence.

A few weeks after Aaron Burr Senior's death in late September of 1757 at age forty-one, Esther wrote her father, "My little son suffers from the slow fever, and brought again to the brink of the grave. But I hope in mercy; God shall bring him up again. But how good is God! He hath not only kept me from complaining but comforted me by enabling me to offer up the child by faith. I saw the fullness there was in Christ for little infants and His willingness to accept of such as offered to Him."

By the end of the day, Aaron's gaze returned to her and held. She liked what bordered on the reflection of hope. Suddenly, her heart pounded, and she ran her fingers through his black hair. With a sigh of relief, she cradled him in her arms. She walked to the window with him.

Looking out, she noted her childhood self with skinny arms, a crumpled skirt, and messed hair as a rainstorm began. She turned a little and stared at her son, thinking life was worth waiting for. Kissing his forehead, she then carried him into the bedroom. The evening was quiet and spent in prayer.

Sleeping in her arms, he dreamed that they were falling and falling.

"The dirty little boy" soon lost his mother to smallpox.

Convening at a simple square pine table, he breathed, soft and shallow, amid the burning candles as he wondered if God sought to prepare him, to soften the tragedy that soon unfolded. But considering it highly unlikely that God determines who lives and who dies, he decided it best for him not to believe in the hand of a controulling God.

Silence pierced the room before a dull moan of outrage arose from two men; moonlight penetrated an open window, and a slow, careless breeze rustled the maple trees' red-orange.

"Not fair," the men said simultaneously.

"All those deaths in eighteen months, what was God thinking?" said Edward Shippen to his brother.

With no joy in his eyes, William folded his arms and responded, "Do not expect me to judge God. But let it not be forgotten that exceptional blood flows in the veins of the boy."

"His father and I," said William, "helped found the College of New Jersey."

"I communicated with the famous divine of the northern colonies several times," Edward Shippen replied, "before his premature death."

"Jonathan Edwards, the boy's maternal grandfather, asked me to care for the boy if anything happened to him."

"Well, dear brother," said Edward, "You better keep your word with the man some said went to the mountaintop and spoke with God."

"What a tragedy to have the boy's parents and the Edwards' grandparents die before he reached the age of two."

"Too often than not, reality arrives like an unwelcome guest," said Edward.

"What should we do?" asked William, who thought mules always boast that their ancestors galloped as horses, the truth holding court in the boy's case.

Catching Edward's eye, William winked, then gave his brother a pat on the back. "We will do our duty."

Over a thunder of grief, Edwards shed a tear for this departed friend, Aaron Burr Senior.

* * * * *

Aaron Burr and his sister, Sally, found themselves at the William Shippen residence in Philadelphia.

His sister's right arm wrapped around his waist as she put her left hand on his face.

He welcomed the comfort of her attention. He let her warm his body. "Never leave me."

With a cheerful look and manner, she said, "Of course."

Amidst a house of hallways and many doors, Aaron discovered half-smiles, worried frowns, backs of heads shaking to and fro, and whispers.

"Oh! The poor, unfortunate children."

"What lies down the road?"

What could he say to them? He thought. He smiled a little while looking up.

When the smells and sights of the City of Brotherly Love started to feel natural, and the hugs and tender caress of Mrs. Shippen provided comfort, his uncle, Timothy Edwards, arrived at the residence.

Little Aaron gawked at him, his curiosity on tiptoe. The man wearing a wool suit with pants that stopped at the knee, stockings, leather shoes, a shirt with a vest over the top, and buttoned to the neck explained. "I am your uncle. I have gained custody of you and Sally." The faces of the Shippens grew smaller as the horses pulling the carriage galloped towards their new life. Aaron's tears greased the carriage's wheels, Sally, and Aaron on the road again.

His uncle settled next to Aaron and gave him an odd, searching look.

Aaron sent him an unappreciative glance.

He turned to Sally and whispered in her ear, "Uncle's mood scares me. He does not like me. It must have been something I did. Otherwise, he would smile back at me."

On the way to Stockbridge, Massachusetts, Uncle Timothy explained in a serious, quiet manner. "As the grandson of the dignified Edwards, the great American luminary of divinity, and President Burr's son, whose burning light shone in the churches, you have a destiny. Your heritage."

The sun slanted on Aaron's face in the open carriage. Twisting his fingers around each other, he nodded. Uncle Timothy bit his lip and tapped his finger against his jaw. Aaron shrugged at the weight of mystery on his shoulders and grimaced. "My destiny?"

Aaron's only memory was a stop in Manhattan and a night or two at Walter Livingston's residence, other than Sally holding him tightly, during the long, bumpy ride.

"Little brother," her soft, silky voice resonated, "everything will be all right. I will always be here for you."

Aaron tried to believe her, but death lurked everywhere. As he grew in years, he realized, in the end, only kindness matters.

By the time he reached the age of four, Aaron knew the Bible and was compelled to memorize portions of it. At the age of twenty-one, the hard-working and dependable Timothy Edwards married Rhoda Ogden, the belle of a prominent family from Elizabethtown. They became mothers and fathers to seven orphans, several under fifteen. Aaron bonded with Rhoda's younger brothers, Matthias and Aaron Ogden, in his new home at Stockbridge.

Aaron Burr and the Ogden brothers accompanied Uncle Timothy on several visits to an Indian village. His grandfather, Jonathan Edwards, who has served as a missionary to the Stockbridge Indians, informed them,

"Accept the Massachusetts General Court's word that your land will never be sold."

A cheering thought to the Indians and the sight of the great man cemented this statement. At the village, Aaron befriended Hendrick Aupaumut, the chief Sachem's son, and helped his Indian friend learn to speak English. The tribe would support the rebels during the coming Revolutionary War. After the war, the patriots of Massachusetts broke their word and imposed a relocation to New York. In the end, the tribe ended up in Wisconsin.

"You look disappointed, husband," said Rhoda.

Timothy looked back and forth, a blank stare plastered on his face. "Expectations and demands require my aspirations of a career in law to be set aside."

Her bright blue eyes observed his face turn the colour of a red rose; his fists clenched tightly.

"The realities of life tend to quash one's plans."

"Yes, the cold facts dictate mouths need food and bodies clothing. I must take up a mercantile career to succour our new family."

She bore the intelligence well. "You make me proud to be your wife."

Timothy looked down.

"Promise me, husband. Do not abandon your dreams of the law."

He lifted his head, admiring her long, brown, wavy hair tied in a ponytail. "I promise."

"I know that your well-developed powers of concentration will provide for our family."

"And, we must adhere to the voice of the Lord."

A hush settled instantly. Timothy raised a brow and shifted forward. He suffered no doubts, sounding so dogmatic.

From her oval face, the small, slim woman said, "Move to Elizabethtown."

Before a split second elapsed, he pulled the trigger on her suggestion. He cupped her face with his hands, thinking her beautiful, especially when she smiled.

"You always display a good mood."

"As a wife should."

His eyes fastened upon her.

She observed light in his eyes. His love for her swelled as they stood and swirled together beside the oil lamps of Elizabethtown that hung as an ornament to British America. At its door, the Revolution creaked, and the town evolved into a community of zealous Whigs who desired to limit royal power, increase parliamentary influence, and defend civil liberties.

"Boys," said merchant Timothy to the two Aarons and Matty, "change hangs in the air – be ready."

The three boys looked at each other, then looked back and forth, with a blank expression on their faces. They preferred the location of Elizabethtown and that it abutted the water on Newark Bay. They explored Staten Island, able to row to Newark's town and then another short jaunt by water. When not on the water, they walked and explored the numerous activities abutting the intersection of Kings Highway and the Old Post Road, two significant paths of commerce, a coach stop between New York and Philadelphia.

The three boys loved the moment and roamed the rolling hills, hiked into steep valleys, dashed into swift-moving streams, fished and hunted in the swamps, sailed their skiff, and swam in the waters. They spotted many sails and commercial ships visiting the wharves saddled by Manhattan Island docks.

A bearded sailor, tall and skinny as a broomstick, invited the boys to board. "I'm da ferst mate, ye boys wanna lok ebout. Me lookin fer a caben boy. Wanna com and explor da sea? We erf te Cheena."

The attraction in Aaron's eyes caught Matty's attention.

"Thank you, Sir, for the offer."

He threw his massive arm over his friend's shoulder and demanded, "Come, Aaron."

Aaron tried to resist but was no match for Matty.

"Aaron," Matty snapped, "what makes you want to see over the horizon and not what lies before you."

"I am intrigued by all the activity of life and the energy of the world around me. I want to experience life."

Matty thought the path to their destiny hides from view when one fails to see what lies within.

"Aaron does not mean to ignore his studies," said Rhoda.

"Life must be serious in the Edwards household. God commands it," snapped Timothy.

"He does not mean to cross your stern eye, husband."

"Stubborn as a mule and always crossing the line."

"Something seems to erupt in him."

"What offense did the tutor cause him when he ran away for three days, thwarting all efforts to find him?"

Rhoda remembered he slept in a nearby orchard living on fruit and dreamed of the future: willing to be wooed, hoping for more.

"And the time Mrs. Pompousarse visited."

"Oh, yes, the prim and moral woman."

"Our guests have the right to stroll in the garden on a warm summer evening and enjoy the declining sun."

Rhonda remembered her costly dress of white silks and how she glowed like an angel.

"What was he thinking atop that cherry tree?"

"I do not think he was thinking but just eating the sweetest and juiciest, his palette salivating, I imagine."

"How could he stain the purity of her cloth?"

"I can still hear her shrieking," said Rhoda with a slight giggle. "'Wait till I tell your uncle; a whipping awaits you.'"

"I see no humour in this!"

"But dear husband, you did not see her facial features reseeding inwards to a most grotesque state and her crooked tea-stained teeth looking like a rocky cliff."

"Never once did he stop pelting her with the berries," exclaimed Uncle Timothy, "as she accelerated to the front door. He persisted in reddening the back of her attire, knowing a whopping would march his way."

Rhoda neglected to tell her husband that Aaron told her, "I do not live for people's amusement, but they for my enjoyment. If a thumping awaits me, I might as well enjoy the moment."

She believed she brought out the best in Aaron and Sally by being positive and cheerful. Did not Aaron trust her as much as Sally and find her honest and say what he thinks? She thought, *we bonded to each other, and he never seemed bored in my presence. I could tell if he was up to mischief or lying even if he kept a straight face! He never knew how, but I could read it in his eyes.*

"Husband, remember life taught him at an early age that existence can end at any second. Yes, things come to those who wait, but you will see tomorrow without a guarantee."

Timothy neglected what he heard.

"Like Henry Fielding's Tommy Jones," Rhoda continued, "Aaron is an inoffensive lad amidst all his roguery. He loves you, my sweet Timothy."

"Son," she remembered her husband saying to Aaron, "Order exists so that society can crawl forward."

Aaron pleaded not, as he paddled him badly.

Rhoda knew he did not want to crawl but to sprint. She thought one generation never sees who you are, and the other fails to understand what you are forced to become.

Timothy announced while leaning back against a table, a half-smile on his face, and his attention centred on his wife, "Education lodges in the Burr-Edwards family. I have hired Tapping Reeve, a College of New Jersey graduate, to tutor Aaron and Sally."

Aaron decided it would be more strategic to listen than protest.

Bursting through the door and out of breath, Timothy screamed, "God help me!"

His body, shaking like a young tree in the wind.

"Gone again?" asked Rhoda.

"Yes," said Timothy, his face looking as deep as the grooves and lines on a century-old tree's bark. "Ran away again, this time, to New York with a desire to go to sea."

He wants to start fresh, thought Rhoda, free from the bonds of the shadows that chill his soul.

INTERLUDE I

POMPOUS AND FERTILE IN IMAGINATION

Spawned in 1757 on the backwater of the Patuxent River of Benedict, Maryland, James Wilkinson's critics said he was, "more a shark than a saltwater creature."

Joseph Wilkinson, James's father, represented the lesser landed gentry, a class of men with humble beginnings who achieved limited economic success.

"Know yourself, your strengths, weaknesses, and ambitions," the father told his son.

James gave a wry grin, knowing he did not have to hide his expression.

The boy enjoyed spending time with his father and followed him about the plantation, seeing how it functioned.

"Son, trust your instincts. You live or die by them."

The words ran through the boy's veins, and he never deviated from them.

"Let pride be your standard and never lapse into regret."

The boy nodded slowly.

Seeing a warm, understated smile, his father let out a subtle, soft breath of approval.

Fair enough, thought James. He never expressed any doubt about his father's advice. He lived his life without a morsel of regret.

Betty, his mother, gave him a sound constitution and a sense of justice and the Christian faith. She spent her days sticking with her beliefs. As the hills and piles of her life became less manageable, her faith in God increased.

His father died when James was six. His last words, "My son, if you ever put up with an insult, I will disinherit you."

The child believed it and acted on it throughout his life. Friends and foes would learn that was how things stood. By the middle of the next year, James still pined for the companionship of his father. His image of the deceased man left in him a ripple of sentiment to his dying day.

He awoke late on a Saturday under a dull winter light to the smell of baking bread. For several minutes he lay silent, enjoying the voices of his two older sisters, brother, mother, and grandmother. He heard the fire crackle as his brother Joseph added another log. The comforting heat called him, but he remained in bed, hoping for some distance and some time.

Joseph entered the room. James's eyes widened but showing no amusement.

"Join us for some food," and he turned to return to the warmth of the fire.

"You are the only one in the world who makes me feel good about myself; stay!" said James.

Joseph's chin lifted just an inch, and a broad smile stretched across his face. He coaxed his brother from the room. The family ate, in between heaving sighs. James could not remember being so sad over a meal.

"You sure?" asked James in a tone somewhat aloof, but friendly "Do you want to have that last slice?"

Slowly smiling, Joseph pushed it towards him. Thirty minutes streaked by before James settled his sorrow, and the corners of his mouth turned up.

"Come on, Nanna, you do not want to leave me alone, do you? Just stay, and I will tell you a story, and you can bake a cake."

The fact that he asked made her happy and for a moment stood in complete accord.

"I want you to know that your father's plantation must be sold to meet his debts."

"Where will I live, grandma?"

"Your dad's friends and creditors have allowed your mother to keep the land that she inherited."

"I do not feel as bad, knowing that."

"Remember, James; you possess a distinctness from the unruly and rebellious nature of most men. Consider yourself like our baronial neighbours in the nearby counties across the Potomac, the Carrolls of Prince George and Ann Arundel, and the Washingtons of Mount Vernon."

"Mother wants me to become a plantation owner with Joseph."

"Your lineage as a gentleman runs deep. Wilkinson men must be above horse racing, cockfighting, and cards. Necessity requires that hierarchy organizes society, and your place resides at the top."

The second son and youngest of four children gasped, and his lips twitched as he leaned back in his chair.

"Do you not want more than a life of telling men where to hoe and shovel?"

Surprised by the question he cocked his head aback, "I guess."

"You have a liveliness and charm that will be wasted indulging in farming. I want more for my grandson."

"But mother wants me to stay close to the land."

"You must find your uniqueness. You have a quick intelligence and need a proper education."

"Who will provide me with this?"

"I have found a private tutor, David Hunter, a graduate of the University of Glasgow."

James grinned as he realized he would be getting a better education than the sons of the Maryland planters.

"Classical education grounded in English literature, grammar, rhetoric, and Latin is what the doctor ordered," explained his grandmother.

On the practical side, he mastered mathematics and mainly surveying. The most beautiful English decorated his conversation. He considered himself more talented than others, never able to acknowledge his self-limitations.

"Once again," he said to his youngest sister, "I stepped in and saved Joseph. I should have objected more strenuously when mother appointed him to wipe down the horses, but I let her silence me, despite my better judgment."

"Oh, James, you exaggerate."

"After all I have done for you; this is how you treat me."

"I will tell mother."

He interrupted her. "No, when I said that, I did not mean that. I meant it like this." A tear rolled down his cheek, and he wiped it with this forefinger.

"Boys," said their mother, "You must be inoculated against smallpox."

Thirteen-year-old James and his brother covered this territory before, but as soon as their horses passed the bounds of former rides, his brother asked, "You sure this is the correct direction?"

James pointed westward, "Baltimore, two hundred miles distant."

"I miss Mom," said Joseph.

"I promise, no arguments for a week if you will not discuss her."

"OK."

"I must admit, Joseph, that sensations affect the bosom that I have never before experienced."

"Inoculation is an occult art; why must we go?"

"Do you want spots on your face, neck, and arms that become pustules and then turn to sores with ugly purple scabs or worse, death?"

His older brother grimaced, "Is not there someone other than Doctor Stevenson, who is closer?"

"He is the lone advocate."

"'I am afraid."

"Try not to worry. The doctor is acquiring a great celebrity in the southern states by his success in preventing smallpox."

"Is it a frightful reality?"

"As devastating as the London plague of 1665."

James told his brother, "I did not want to put trepidation in your bosom when ten miles from Baltimore, but the journey seemed more distant and perilous than a voyage to China."

He refused to tell his brother that the town pulled him. When entering Market Street, which extended from Gay Street to a short distance west of Calvert Street, James turned to Joseph.

"The active scenes of business, the commixture, passage, and re-passage, of men, women and children, wagons, drays, carts, dogs and horses, and the numerous tawdry signs swinging over the street, excite a degree of admiration and astonishment that abates my solicitude for what we left."

"Which way to the doctor's mansion?"

"Stevenson's folly is across that common ahead."

"Why do you say that?"

"Because it is unfinished."

"How wide is the common?"

"Near half a mile," James imparted, as they crossed the water. "See, our high leather books keep our feet dry."

"You were right. I am sorry I questioned your wisdom."

The inoculation class consisted of John Custis and James Wormley of Virginia, James and Perry Frizby of Maryland, with half a dozen other young gentlemen from the southern provinces.

"Young gentlemen, by Jasus, you will be peppered if you fail to adhere to my regimen."

"His frequent alarms do not scare me," James exclaimed to Joseph."

"I want nothing to do with an eruptive fever."

"A slight one is acceptable, said James.

"I have three pustules. How about you?"

"One." He put his forefinger to the right side of his chin. "I am going to stay with my friends every day unless you bring back hay for the horses by the time I get home"

At first, the natural gaiety of his disposition silenced his partiality for our birthplace scenes, Joseph wrote to his mother. *As far as James is concerned, life is a pretty good deal. He spends his days doing what he enjoys and receives enough attention from all the parties involved.*

Amusements, with his new companions, occupy all his time. The attractions of Baltimore, the bonds of local attachment, the walnut and the cedar and the cherry trees, under whose shade he sports – the lawn on which he frolicked, and the limpid fountain from which he drank, no longer delight him, and the sweetest ligaments of human affections remain broken. Your tender embraces, and his birthplace beckons us.

Through green hills and valleys, they travelled, hardly aware of the scenery until reaching home. James dismounted from his horse and drank in the vista. He cherished the scent and taste of the land. Having been in this spot a hundred times, it still soothed him. The need to talk overcame him. He walked towards his brother. "Leaving the bustle and excitement of Baltimore to the isolation of plantation life is not hard."

"I must admit this surprises me."

"I need to pursue my studies."

The next day James rose at sunrise and spent the morning and afternoon studying. The excitement he experienced when he opened a book was something that he never could explain to his family or friends. No one grasped the satisfaction he gained from knowledge.

Most of his acquaintances thought books were a dread. To them, the words, the paragraphs, the feel of the pages evoked a sickness. To James, they meant hope and a better life. Reading convinced him there existed an endless amount to know about human nature, and he devoted his free time to learning, watching, and listening.

With a pleasing countenance and an intelligent and keen eye, considered handsome or very near it, he mastered his address and knew himself in great luck.

After a passage of three years, at the age of sixteen, the stimulation of urban life beckoned. He jumped at the opportunity, courtesy of his grandmother, to study at a medical school in Philadelphia.

He travelled mostly by water, down the Chesapeake and up the Delaware rivers from Calvert County, Maryland. Before entering his lodgings, he came upon British barracks where troops paraded.

He wrote home, "A more impressive spectacle never seen – It appeared like enchantment, and my bosom throbbed with delight. Some things seem right immediately. This is one of them."

From that day forward, in 1773, he welcomed the strongest inclination for military life.

In his bare webbed feet, this child of a respectable couple looked ordinary. He stood five foot seven-and-a-half inches. His brow was wide and high, his lips, bow-shaped and hard, like the mouth of a man who knew what he wanted to say and say he would.

Before liquor and lard made him the mirror image of a croaking bullfrog, he maintained a symmetrical and graceful model that attracted attention. With a personable face and maintaining the most gracious of manners, he could have been a "ladies man," but most women did not interest him. They were not an appetizer nor an entrée to power.

Later in his life, he often joked to his sons, "How different history would have been if I came across a circus of acrobats, rope-dancers, jugglers, and clowns interspersing their acts between equestrian displays. As my horsemanship was second to none, I could have joined up and made a name for himself."

He preferred the circus of life, and by the sleight of his hand, he dealt deception to the leaders of his time.

"Well, hello there, Mr. Wilkinson," an officer said while grinning. Their eyes met.

"Have not seen you since yesterday."

"Hey," James answered, giving the officer a small nod. "Tell me about Philadelphia."

"With a population of over thirty-thousand, it is the largest city in the thirteen colonies; only London exceeds it as a centre of business in the British Empire."

"Philadelphia boasts paved streets," trumpeted another officer, "and a university, a hospital, theatres, firefighters, and library."

Wilkinson stood admiring the officers of the British regiment, the Royal Irish, who garrisoned the City.

"You look like a young man who knows what he wants."

"You inspire in me that love of all things military."

"May it be the guiding star of your life."

"I hope for the flame of future escapades," sported James.

"Be careful your cup not runneth over and stain the parchment of history."

He frowned at the thought. His mouth became soft, hesitant. Life can be simple, he hoped, drawing his dream closer.

CHAPTER 5

Life After Peter Jefferson

"Upon my word," Jane Jefferson wrote her brother,
William, a merchant in Bristol, England, "My head hurt, my
body hurt, everything hurt for a fortnight."

Perhaps it was not fair to expect her to mourn for a more extended period, but life's facts required her to plan for her future. The thirty-seven-year-old Jane in 1757 absorbed her loss and assumed responsibility for her eight children, sixty-six slaves, and more than 3,000 acres. Her routine changed little. She wrote letters to her family and friends, kept meticulous notes.

"Am I a terrible mother?" she said as she offered Reverend James Maury a glass of wine.

Maury's eyes scanned the parlour, admiring the fancy silverware and plates, the beautiful crockery, the well-made furniture, and the exquisitely attired Mrs. Jefferson.

"I want to place my slow-paced, timorous, and unready son at your school."

She stopped her mouth firm.

"He needs help to make him a better man."

I will consider it a challenge, Mrs. Jefferson. My home is not far from Shadwell. Your son will be able to spend some weekends with you."

Maury noticed a slight contort appear on Jane's face.

"Where exactly is it?" she asked.

"Near Charlottesville."

She knew the fifteen miles, too close, but it was better than having him in the house.

Abruptly, she stood, and for one awkward moment, thought of changing her mind.

Running her fingers through her hair, she asked, "What will he study?"

"History, science, and the classics."

Studying his face, she said, "His father would be pleased."

Maury raised a finger at her and, in a confident voice, said, "You will not regret your decision."

Young Jefferson, hurting from head to toe from his father's loss, propelled forward under "the correct classical scholar."

He developed a love of Greek and Latin and relished the separation from his mother.

'The two Ancients are critical," Maury informed his students, "for men who might take place in society."

The Reverend ingrained in Jefferson the desire to further ascend the ladder of Virginia society. "Not for your mother," the mentor said, "but a confirmation of your father's faith in you."

Jefferson sat still and listened to Maury, but his thoughts of achieving a place in society were thumping like approaching horses.

"Education," Maury said, "allows those who wish to make a reputation, a reputation."

"I will dedicate my life to those words," said Thomas.

Maury noticed a look in his pupil's eyes that made him feel proud. He nodded, and without taking his eyes off his student, said, "You are ready, you are ready because you invite knowledge."

Taking a breath, Maury thought Thomas looked pleased.

Three months later, while he crouched beside Maury, his mentor said as he jabbed his finger on a map, "Allow illimitable freedom of the human mind to guide you."

After a self-satisfied glance towards Maury, Thomas tipped his head down at the map.

"The Missouri River is not a myth. Your father and I talked about an expedition up the river."

Jefferson remembered his father's voice and how he still had trouble living without him.

"I know your father would be proud of you," said Maury.

Jefferson's eyes returned to the map of the North American continent.

"See," Maury's finger wiggled, "there must be a large river in that direction, mountains are there, and beyond them must be a stream to correspond with the vast river on this side of the chain. A great highway to the West will someday open in that direction."

A beam infiltrated Thomas's mind. He grabbed the glorious possibilities of the great West, then little-known. He thought of following the river and keeping a journal of the country passed through, the distances travelled, and what worth of navigation those rivers and lakes afforded.

He filed it away and said, "Someday."

The next day a peculiar thing happened to Thomas. Friendship dropped on him at Maury's school. He met Dabney Carr, a boy of the same age. They talked literature on the weekdays and, on occasion, visited Shadwell.

In the morning, drinking coffee so potent, they all but stood up and growled.

Dabney blurted out, "I'll race you to the oak on that mountain you dream of living atop."

They rode through the woods called Monticello, the Italian word for "little mountain."

He knew Thomas would beat him, but he wanted to boost his friend's confidence.

Jefferson sprawled out amidst acorns. Dressed in shabby clothes that obscured his bowed shoulders, a book on architecture and the novel, *Tom Jones*, lay by his side. He ceased writing in his notebook as his friend dismounted. Happiness conquered his blue disposition. He smiled at Dabney.

"I see you are as usual making notes," said his friend. "Have you gathered and recorded any useful knowledge you would like to share with me?"

"Just designing where my future gardens will be."

"Of course, they will be efficient, productive, and convenient to the house," winked Dabney as he ambled forward.

"As life should be, but tell me what took you so long?"

"Stopped to help a damsel in distress."

Jefferson focused on Dabney. "Is there a sister?"

"Two, as a matter of fact. Are you up to the task?"

Thomas wished it. He forgot his insecurity and rose.

"Let us be off."

A tight-lipped grin appeared on Dabney's face as he averted his eyes and tilted his head away from his friend, his face shining. "Just joking."

Thomas dropped his notebook on a cluster of nine shallow-fingered lobed leaves. He pondered the meaning of friendship as his companion relaxed across from him. Frowning, he shook his head sideways, thinking of Tom Jones and wondering if he would ever be appealing enough to have an author write about his exploits.

Light filtered through the ancient red oak's twisted arms, leaving a golden hue on the trunk. It caught Thomas's attention. His eyes danced with the beauty of the image. He recalled when he and Dabney first stopped to rest under its branches two months earlier.

Patterns of sunlight shun on their faces.

Today, he sighted light and shadow on Dabney's face. "I am so lucky to have you as a friend."

Two young squirrels raced around the ancient oak's twisted arms as Thomas envied how carefree they were.

Turning to Dabney, he said, "Are you going to invite me to your thoughts, or would you prefer I just keep silent?"

"If I die before you, would you bury me here?"

"Not a subject I think about since the death of my father."

"Do you regret, Mr. Jefferson, that you never tracked alongside your father upon the frontier wilderness he charted?"

Thomas looked at the squirrels as they continued to race up and down.

He thought they live for the moment; it was no use going over his father's death again.

"I did not mean to rekindle your sadness," said Dabney, "but there is something about the tranquillity of this setting."

Thomas exhaled slowly cleared his throat, "Yes, there is something special here."

An exhilaration pumped through his heart. Not good at expressing his emotion, he tried to fight off a tear and realized his friend possessed more of the milk of human kindness, indulgence, softness, pleasantry of conversation, and conduct than anyone he knew.

A thought closed in from behind. Thomas glanced to his right and came face-to-face with Dabney. Words appeared with a sincerity. "Well, let us make a contract: whoever survives the longest promises to bury the other under our genus Quercus."

The corners of Dabney's mouth turned up, "Sounds good to me."

After a lull, Thomas jumped to his feet and stretched his legs. He looked down at Dabney and asked,

"What are your expectations for your future?"

Dabney met his eyes, "Easy question," he said. "A lawyer. And you?"

Standing restlessly, he thought for a few seconds. "Mr. Maury sparked my curiosity about the unknown land beyond the Mississippi River."

Dabney blurted out, "Thomas Jefferson, the Marco Polo of British America."

"Who knows? But I would like to think so," said the unripened laddie.

The boys sat listening to each other talk about life, marriage, the thrill of school, and Tom's mother as dusk arrived. It went right for Jefferson at school: the Greek, the Latin, the radiant attention of Maury. He stood in the front and enjoyed it.

After two years, the Reverend advised his protégé, "I spoke with your mother's cousin, Peter Randolph, and he agrees with me; it is time for you to go to college."

"Are you sure?"

"You have learned all you can get from me."

A thrill danced through his body. He gathered his thoughts and focused on the future, "I will not disappoint you," thinking any talk of exploration would be in Williamsburg's habited town.

Upon leaving for college, his mother glared at him through the open door. The sight of her sickened him. Nausea hit like morning sickness. Slowly, he strode towards his horse as a skull-cracking headache developed.

A scowl wider than the sky draped his face.

"I will watch your progress," she said, "and it will be good if you could make new friends and stop speaking in a soft voice as if you are whispering."

He did not look back. It was time, he thought, for a final departure from this wicked person. She hid her pleasure, and with her daughters, watched the six-foot-one, awkward, raw-boned, shy adolescent of seventeen mount his horse. A warm breeze ruffled his uncombed hair. His right hand gripped the reins as his feet slid into the stirrups.

Jane turned to her girls and jerked her head back, and imparted to her son, "The universe does not revolve around you. You will soon find out how complicated life is."

His heart burst with delight as he shifted on his horse. Straight, muscular, and broad-shouldered, he sat in the saddle, his clothes too small for him. Observing an air of stiffness in his body as he rode, she wondered for a moment what his fate would be, and in truth, she cared not. She skipped back to her front door, relieved that her eldest boy's whims would entwine her no more.

Free of her faded and torn love, Thomas's freckles danced as he galloped off one shoulder elevated above the other, in the winter of 1759 to Williamsburg, located halfway between the York and James Rivers, to attend the College of William and Mary.

Pursing his lips, he blew softly towards the whispering wind. His thoughts skidded from the past, expecting to dent the future. He could not wait to let his hair grow, wear whatever clothes he wanted, achieve the status of a natural aristocrat like his father, not an artificial one like a Randolph.

And he thanked God, not to have to read her favourite passage from the Bible, "As long as I am in the world, I am the light of the world."

Jane watched as Buella moved his belongings into a corner of his room, the slave thinking Jane embarrassed him more times than not and failed to give him the hugs and kisses children need. Understanding life is hard to explain; Jane promised herself to try and make amends. She remembered looking into his eyes for the first time as she closed the door to his room, but the experience from his birth brought back the memory of pain. Filing the past in a dark crevice in her mind, Jane Jefferson continued to squelch the need to tell her son she loved him, her words forever a silhouette of silence.

CHAPTER 6

Of Scottish Nobility

Sunlight shot through the fog, landing on the water surrounding the island of St. Eustatius in the spring of 1758. Sitting, the four-year-old Alexander smiled up into the filtered rays and enjoyed the tinged greenish-brown water. He wondered what colours an artist needed to paint the scene. Trying painting in the past, he hated getting it on his fingers; it made holding a book uncomfortable.

His life gently, rhythmically swung as he cast a sceptical eye at the unrelenting sea, wondering about the future, *his* future. *Alone*, he thought.

Suddenly, a school of gulls circled an outgoing vessel. Alexander's eyes locked in on the gulls, admiring their patience. Just as suddenly, the predators descended to the sea, fielding their prey.

His past then dropped into the wide corridor of his mind, bringing forth memories.

"What is wrong, my sweet?" asked his mother.

"Nothing." He looked down, his eyes red and wet.

"Where is your brother?"

He shrugged his shoulders. His chin came up, but he remained silent.

"You have been so depressed that you are not able to see the feet in front of your face."

"Mean things have been said to me that upset me. They rattle around my mind."

"Alexander, they are nothing but scared mice disguised as roaring lions. The world is full of too many people like this."

His head rotated back and forth.

She turned so they were face-to-face.

"Do not feel unloved, unwanted, alone, and scared, my precious one."

Her eyes inspected the vibrant blue of his.

"Need I remind you of your father's Scottish ancestry, which separates you from being a West Indian outcast."

"Father talks more to James when he returns from the ship he sails on, so he must like him more than me."

"Oh, Alexander."

"He does not love me. I will always be lonely."

"Oh, honey, not as long as I breathe." She brushed his hair back from his face.

He wrapped his arms around her, and her warmth melted his turbulent thoughts. Sparks flew from his eyes.

Rachel pulled back and winked at him as she smiled.

"Mère, you make me feel comfortable and safe." Now lit with life, he told her, "You inspire me to be a better person."

She enjoyed the glint that was back in his look. Still fixed on his eyes, she let her hand glide down his cheeks. His joy spread, swelled, beat faster. Wanting to run up and down the street, he arched, trapped in his web of delight. Soft, firm, warm, smooth rays of hope burgeoned.

He side-stepped the new growth in the herb garden outside the door as he ran into the morning rush. His hair flowed about his face, wild yet glorious as he pranced through the Nevis streets of Charleston. His head was high, smelling the sweet fragrance of ginger root, cinnamon, and nutmeg. Freed from his dark thoughts, he stood out like a dream within sleep.

Sitting on a bench on Main Street outside St. Paul's Anglican Church, he wondered why he let the kids he did not care about depress him. He kept his eyes level with the church and believed it ugly yet formal.

Before entering, he held the door open for an older woman, letting her go first. The interior gripped him, stroked his senses. An organist playing music by John Blow filled the room. He brushed his hair back from his face and experienced a lightness in his heart. Letting loose a chuckle, he viewed his future, warm and bright, as something to achieve.

Looking upon a bas-relief on the altar's back wall of Jesus with his arms raised, he glanced again, wondering if men would ever follow his prescripts. After leaving the church, his chest puffed out, he sat outside for a while, thinking, why do I always see life as obscure? Escorting waves that resembled a wall of water; towards the admiralty court, he believed himself the supreme commander of a fleet about to enter a battle.

Ten minutes later, satisfied and free of regrets, he entered the admiralty court and scrutinized swaggering pirates, in manacles, at trial before being sentenced to hang. He surmised many of the buccaneers, tools of the warring European powers that played upon a nation's sovereignty. Annoyed with the court, he turned to the door and exited.

His thoughts were scattered as he approached an auction. As the auctioneer barked, a bitter taste resided in his mouth as he scrutinized slaves who stood waiting, then sorted to match each other in size and strength. His gaze swept over the men, women, and children. Their pain shot through him with a terrible intensity.

He counted, and every ten had a driver who walked behind them, holding a short whip and a long one. They were naked, male and female, down to the girdle. The whip's uniform application rattled his mind as these mortals were ushered towards dusty roads, singing beyond shame and pain and above the present moment.

"The inferno of white gold," he said, "always surrounding them as they are regularly ranged. Each with a little basket, which they carry up the hill filled with manure, shall return to the mill with a load of canes. They go up at a trot and return at a gallop."

An ocean breeze whipped his face. The gulls cawed and squawked overhead. The smell of anger clung to the ocean mist on his face. He muttered to the wind, "Equality seems invisible like the air."

He ran his fingers through his hair and finished his memory on the treatment of the slaves, "Stallions not gelded, but in every way castrated by misconduct on the part of avaricious men who wield the hammer of the law."

After watching some light-hearted banter of a school of seals, he remembered his mother talking to his dad.

"He learned French early on."

"I understand he has intellect."

"What cruises through his blood and makes him different defies explanation, James."

Alex's father stood back, wondering where the conversation was going.

"His gift," she said, "is not possessed by everyone."

Embarrassed, James tossed his head back. "Really."

He paused. The conversation made his head pound.

"Like those before and those that come after, he will have to make the best of it."

Two years later, his Huguenot mother shrugged, avoided confrontation, and arranged to tutor him at a Sephardic Jewess school in a separate building near the synagogue in St. Eustatius.

"Hello, Mr. Hamilton," said Mrs. Silva.

After examining the schoolroom and engaging in innocuous conversation, Alex settled into a chair. As he studied the lines on her face, his teacher let out a light laugh. Her eyes were warm and intense. *Voice, too,* he thought.

"I know what you sense, Alexander, the life of an outcast."

At first, he did not believe her.

"I escaped persecution in Brazil from the Inquisition and came from Barbados to Nevis in 1743 with my fleeing family."

He shrugged. Puzzlement and interest flickered over his face. "Good government," she told him, "allows the oppressed to lift themselves from the depths of religious intolerance into freedom."

He sat straight, studying the implication of her statement. He spread his hands on the desk. "I can see why my mother brought me to you."

He was inundated in sweat, his face pale as parchment, as he climbed the side of the mountain, Mount Misery, his "Mount Sinai," to practice an assignment for school. Finding slopes steeper than others and trails more devious than complex, he moved slowly and swiftly until he stopped to catch his breath. Glancing over a cliff's edge, he perceived the Ark of the Covenant on the waters beyond. He scowled before waving his hand to the Lord above. The wind that blew in his face stilled as he recited the Ten Commandments –the Decalogue – in Hebrew for his teacher, till he could say it backward.

A lush, leafy country lane flanked by a sturdy stone wall connected the cemetery to the synagogue and school. Without any pangs, Alexander rushed along the path. His mind, free of any doubt that he would not excel when his turn came to recite the Decalogue. After returning home, he climbed into bed, excited for the morning. He slept some but for hours stared at the ceiling.

Called to enumerate the homework, the six-year-old Alexander sprang towards the front of the room. Confidence circled about him. The small boy stood on a makeshift table by his teacher's side, unable to see over the podium. His heart pounded, and sweat draped his face as he balanced on the wobbly table. *Will I fall?* he thought as he perched above his chuckling and smirking classmates. He conquered his balance on the rocky structure as his teacher's eyes hissed at her unruly class.

"Oh, wretched idiots!" his teacher said, clenching her fists, "Why do you mock a fellow student. Your dirty, lifeless, wooden words and stone actions reek of sin towards humanity! What do you think? Nothing! What do you see? Nothing! Will you go to heaven? No! You hold to the beliefs of our Lord Jesus, but did he go about tormenting the innocent?"

Her thoughts paused for breath, her blood boiling as she stood up and said, "Quiet!"

Alex let out a nervous laugh, and then his keen, firm voice breezed through the room.

His spirits soared like an eagle in the sky as he began speaking.

Just as he reached the end, his eyes crisscrossed his classmates. He grinned. He sensed his teacher's joy.

"Metsuyyanut" (most excellent) were the words from the heart-shaped face of his instructor, clad in a black hemp dress. She helped him down, inadvertently brushing her hand through his reddish-blond hair.

He turned to the class and said with a chuckle, "Next."

Not one of the stilled pupils rose to take up the cross and follow him.

As Alex walked home in 1760, his attention drifted on Johan Michael Lavien, who he just learned denied Rachael everything she deserved – who wanted to make her more miserable than she could have ever dreamed – to steal everything she possessed.

The breeze bit his nose and mouth. Hate, he thought, ran its course, achieved its goals, and allowed Lavien a comfort that occupied his body and mind.

He used his slaves to bribe the man who would grant him a divorce and label Alex a bastard. The Dutch records revealed that Lavien kept his slaves (sixteen or seventeen) working in the fields of Governor-General Christian Lebrecht Baron von Pröck. They cleared wooded tracts to cultivate more sugar in 1757, the white "gold" of its time.

Lavien, a plantation overseer, filed for divorce in St. Croix's matrimonial court presided over by von Pröck in 1759. (About this time, Rachael and James signed an affidavit as husband and wife for the christening of a friend's child.)

Learning that he charged his mother with "shameless, rude, and ungodly mode of life," and that she "completely neglected her marital duty, and left her husband and child alone by committing such mistakes that among married people are indecent and very suspect and indulged in whoring with everyone," shocked Alexander.

The accusations rained – poured – buckets, on and on and on. They stood close and wrapped their arms around Alexander's love for his mother, whose smile made him smile.

His mind hung from this information, but then he later discovered that two of the three witnesses, people of little or no means, were never questioned in the proceedings. Rachael's summons to appear in court was delivered to her two previous addresses on St. Croix, the Fort, and the captain's old residence. He took the news calmly enough, realizing his mother was the victim of her ex-husband's loathing. Judged guilty of Danish law by von Pröck, she forfeited any current or future claim on the guileful Lavien and was forbidden to remarry.

Alexander discovered a woman and boy (presumably Peter Lavien, age 12) listed as part of Lavien's "white family" in 1758 and 1759. Since their marriage was still binding at that point, the woman's presence should have the same negative legal implications as applied to his mother, but it did not. He concluded that the law allows the corrupted and rotten to prevail, and those with connections and money can use it to smother the less fortunate.

After the recording of the divorce, Johan treated Governor-General Baron von Pröck, the colony's highest judicial authority, to drink and dinner.

"I told you," said von Pröck, "justice can be swift when in capable hands." von Pröck noticed satisfaction in Lavien's smile. The latter's slaves worked on another of the governor's wooded tracts in 1760.

Before leaving St. Croix in June of 1773, Alexander delivered a letter to the local newspaper denouncing the scoundrel.

> *When lies lead to injustice, the time arrives to clear the air. You, Johan Lavien, a cunning, poor-humoured, staid boor, with manners worse than a vulture, are not what a gentleman ought to constitute nor what you claim. Your actions towards an innocent woman deserve notice. You trapped her in your low net by false impressions and made her squirm.*

Putting the words to parchment vindicated his mother to Alexander as he continued his verbal attack.

Your heart, Sir, colder than a wolf's nose.

May your world become as lifeless as a grave and as miserable as the fifth act of a Shakespeare tragedy.

He stopped writing and realized that Lavien bloodline deserved exclusion from the future of humanity.

I stand ready to meet you on the field of honour if you feel I have besmirched your character!

He wept as he recalled his mother's warm hands, massaging his pulsating sadness.

The strut returned to his walk, and questions about the move in May, 1765, which had always confused him, were resolving. The extreme discord that began between his parents after their relocation from the British island of St. Christopher now made sense.

In 1759, the divorce decree by Lavien and its terms settled upon James Hamilton. He exploded.

"Rachael knew for some time," Alexander learned from his niece, Ann Lytton, "But she refused to come and defend herself, knowing it would not go over smoothly with James."

Not surprised that his mother chose silence to confrontation, Alexander lamented that she lived a lie. He remembered her pale face, absent of cabbage rogue, contrasted with her dark eyebrows and forced smile.

"Yes! I knew of the divorce and tried to spare you and the children the pain," said Rachael.

"You lied to me every minute of our life together!" said James.

"You must understand. You must!"

"Why did you do this to me!"

Everyone in earshot overheard the accusations follow one another. Just when they thought they concluded, they started again.

"I hate you!" said James. Ripples of pain started to shoot through James's arms, chest, and head. "You turned my children into bastards! "Pounding his chest, he yelled out, "You made me a common fornicator at best! You stole my self-respect."

"What self-respect?" she yelled back.

Rachael, realizing her marital situation as unstable as her husband's emotional and financial situation, refused to listen as James went on, glad he mate might be out of her life.

The brothers' heads hung low for days, but Alex sprang back with determination.

"Our futures lie beyond, not behind, like a donkey's ass," he told James Junior, whose eyes were half closed.

"I do not possess your resiliency, brother; my pain eats at me from the inside."

"From one bastard to the other, the hell what people say or think, James."

"I feel no humour. I taste the cold, despite the summer sun and warm wind. It will pass," Alex said.

"Being a bastard sucks," James stopped, lost again in his fears.

"The line between very upsetting and amusing, a razor's edge," Alex remarked.

"Well, you cross it!"

"We can rise beyond the circumstances."

"The scars are too deep for me."

James' mind dove deeper into despair.

"The past," said James Junior, who stopped and looked away, "darkens my aspirations and leaves me alone."

Alex absorbed the news, swallowed the words, and kicked his way back to the surface. He promised himself; he would look after James Junior. Love for his brother required nothing less.

As the moon peeked above, Alexander walked around the island, realizing the weight of shame crushed James: the constant reminder, the strain, the embarrassment.

A twang of guilt surfaced, even though he remembered supporting his mother when his father left, but still, that did not make up for that time he displayed anger at her before she died.

Alexander realized the millions of ideas that flooded his mind came from her encouraging him to read the many books she possessed. And the more he read, the fuller his mind and facts and fantasies became the calories of his life. *Damn the past!* he thought, as a cloud obscured the light of the moon. But the over and done would condemn him.

Alexander caught a glimpse of the past when he remembered walking with his mother, and James Junior asked, "Why did you renounce father's name?"

"How do you know this?"

Alex says the poll-tax states your name as Fatzieth and living with two white children."

"I do what I must do. It does not mean I love either of you less."

Continuing down a path in Nevis on the first day of August 1764, the sun glowing, and with rain falling in thin strands, she announced, "I have a surprise."

Feeling exhilarated by the thought of a surprise, Alex skipped along, following the pace of his brother and mother to a back street from King

Street, #34 The Company's Lane, where he observed a man in front of a two-story building.

Her head held high; Rachael announced, "Mr. Thomas Dipnall."

"Hello, boys. Follow me in."

They strode through the entrance. A resounding echo filled the room. Dust flowed freely in the stale air as the open door brought light to the stone floor and the spider webs that hid in the walls' cracks. Alex jumped up and down on the tile to test its strength.

"Firm," he announced.

"Good," replied Dipnall, "because you will need a sound basis for your store."

"Our store?" exclaimed James Junior.

"Yes, said his mother. "Do you think you can fix the walls?"

"No problem, mother."

Alexander grasped the situation immediately.

"We will live above, brother."

The boys raced to the upper level. Alexander liked that he walked barefoot on the wooden floor.

"Look, it juts over the street," said James.

"We will make it our library," responded Rachael.

She wrapped her arms around her sons, "I have added Plutarch and Pope to my collection of history and mythology, philosophy, romance languages, mathematics, and science, bringing the total to thirty-four."

"The perfect spot to read Plutarch," Alex said. He looked at his mother and admired the gallant, persistent, self-reliant woman for having chosen to flaunt certain social and cultural conventions and have the strength of character to live with the consequence.

Rachael's head rotated to her youngest boy, "Your ability with numbers and understanding of the mechanics of business will enable us to run a store. James, your skill with tools will allow us to make it work."

The veil of hope rose like smoke from a volcano. A mosaic of panache whiffed out, masking the storm of adversity surrounding them.

"Now, boys, come with me; we must know where to procure the plantation necessities of pork, beef, salt fish, rice, flour, and apples for our store."

In a white or red skirt, her striking face sheltered by a black silk hat from the sun's breath, they returned. James Junior was carrying most of the materials, as Alex, the ten-year-old referred to by two future presidents of the United States as a "bastard," said to James, "I expect to see a hammer and saw dangling from your belt, and an adze hooked into it."

"We will know you have been working," said Rachael, "when sawdust sticks in your hair."

"Put some shelves here," suggested Alex, "build a counter on that wall, hang a basket over there for the fruit and....."

Rachael glanced at her youngest son with a slight air of disapproval but realized he was unlike all the men in her life who were not looking out for the family's best interest. Her dismay quickly turned to a smile, and she thought how lucky she was to have him in her life.

Alex peeked at her and wondered what brought a smile to her gaunt face. He noticed the anxiety that life imprinted on her countenance. He took her hand and rattled off a poem.

May we take advantage of your sensibility to steal your affections with or without your consent our love floats in a sunbeam witnessed by the hand of the divinity erased.

She grabbed the boys into her arms, their innocence flowing through her.

"Remember, my dear ones," she paused and kissed each forehead, "happiness, like summer, needs the rain to nourish the coming harvest, and sadness makes us value the joys of life."

Beyond the horizon the sun set brightly, announcing the end of the day—the ocean silent, showing signs of sadness. The wind was whispering above, the waves nodding rhythmically, as Alex cradled his past. His thoughts flew over the slick surface of his past, and his shoulders rose as his head hung low.

I must go,
Nobody weeps,
For my future calls,
Far across the sea.

He laughed and attempted to close his eyes to the soft, green hills of Christiansted, St. Croix. In his heart, he hoped to let go of something that he assumed he should keep. The following week Alexander told Mère and James Junior but not before stifling a chuckle when he observed his brother's sawdust beard that clung to his sweat-drenched face.

"I visited the newly established import-export firm of David Beekman and Nicholas Cruger at Nos. 7-8 King Street to acquire more goods. Its buildings there resembled a capital "L." The storefront (the base of the "L") faced King Street. Two rows of warehouses with a narrow passageway between (the leg of the "L") extended along King Cross Street."

James' backaches and blood and aching muscles welcomed a break from his work.

"The owner/merchant, Nicholas Cruger, with a pencil in hand, his dark hair standing erect in his head, thought me lost as I entered to ask for help."

Rachael's pulse beat fast, an exciting feeling of anticipation.

"Sir, my mère, brother, and I support the family by running a small store selling plantation supplies."

"And what supplies would that be?" replied the amused man.

"Our stock of goods include pork, beef, salted fish, rice, flour, and apples."

"How do you procure them?"

"From our landlord, Thomas Dipnall, wholesale, I may add."

"Have you thought about adding to your inventory?"

"I smiled, and the twenty-one-year-old Cruger put his arm around my shoulder, and we walked, talked, and negotiated."

Alexander drew back, wanting to get the situation right and proudly announce, "I brought home a bag of apples nearly as big as a boat."

Rachael let out a hardy laugh that echoed in the empty wood room.

"The New York merchant took to me as a smile does to love and told me, 'I overheard mutterings about Rachael Lavien and her 'unfortunate children.'"

Emotions swirled in Rachael's eyes.

"After conversing with me, he learned the lines between a story are more important than the cover of a book."

Eighteen months later, Cruger offered Alexander, "as an intelligent boy," a job as a clerk. From that time, he got paid to mingle in the centre of the current economic heart of trade.

The world of Christiansted, a busy international port with connections to British North America, Europe, West Africa, and the Caribbean, was better than the best chronicle he ever read.

As their clerk, he recorded in the ledgers of his employers under the heading necessities and luxuries: building materials, plantation equipment and supplies, livestock, furniture, crystal, porcelain, silver, linens, other household goods, clothing, food, and drink. Under the heading local exports: sugar, molasses, rum, cotton, tropical dye, and hardwoods such as logwood, lignum vitae, and furniture grade mahogany. His work under Mr. Cruger's roof provided him with an understanding of commercial activity mechanics and dealings with ships' captains, customs officials, merchants, and planters. His duties in warehousing and retail were the most valuable part of his education.

I must admit," he told Mère, "and I am sure you would agree that the one part of my job I hate the most are the slave auctions that occur either in the compound at the wharf or in the yards of private importers."

He drew back from her, his eyes turning cold as ice.

"Last week, I watched 300 first-class slaves, just imported from the Windward Coast of Africa, sold from Cruger's square. What kind of morality makes a man's hue a crime, and with a dull and heavyweight authority, forces life from the heart?"

An integral part of the Danish traffic of humans, the town received tens of thousands of poor souls brought from Guinea to St. Croix. The hand of injustice ships them across the Atlantic along a route called the "Middle Passage." Unfortunately, it passes through Christiansted, and as Alexander was wont to say. "Abusus non tollit usum." (Rights abused are still rights.)

"The sight of slavery pollutes every pore in my body. I try to close my eyes to it, but it still ripples through me with a terrible intensity. Someday with God on my side, I hope to rid the world of slave-owning's terrible nausea."

CHAPTER 7

Jefferson Meets Henry
for the First Time

"Patrick," said Colonel Dandridge, "Merry Christmas."

H enry grinned. His eyes opened wide. Alertness resided there. A warm gaze fixed on his friend.

"I meant to tell you."

Patrick's eyes opened wide.

"I look up to a man with a high forehead and straight nose, somewhat of a Roman stamp. It brings me back to antiquity."

"Later, my friend," said Patrick, "I will tell you a story or two from ancient times."

"I admire your festive face considering your financial setbacks."

"To wallow in despair will not put bread on the table."

Dandridge motioned to a gawky young man.

"Thomas, meet a close friend."

Jefferson's cold stare fixed on the dark-complexioned, spare, raw-boned man who was his height. Later in his life, he took a step back and noted the event to William Wirt.

"Mr. Henry began his career with very little property. I first became acquainted with him during the Christmas holidays at Colonel Dandridge's home in Hanover in the winter of 1759–60. As I have understood, he acted as a barkeeper in a tavern at Hanover C.H. for some time. He married very young; settled, I believe, at a place called the Roundabout in Louisa, got credit for some little festivity store, but very soon failed. During the season, I met him in society every day, and we became well acquainted, although I was much his junior. His manners exhibited a coarseness in them. His passions were music, dancing, and pleasantry. He excelled in the last, and it attached everyone to him."

That Christmas night, Patrick informed Thomas, "I have decided to start the coming year with a clean slate."

Jefferson gave a weak smile, thinking, really.

"I have turned my views to the law."

Jefferson nearly choked. No way a coarse, rustic, failure can become a lawyer, he thought.

"I considered it while working at my father-in-law's tavern and decided when I arrived here."

"Based on what?" queried Jefferson, who examined him with a predator's resolute concentration.

Henry blinked a few times before speaking. "The opportunity provided by its proximity to the Court House and my conversations with the lawyers."

Jefferson excused himself with his brain numb from talking to Henry for an hour, and his mind clouded from one too many glasses of wine; thinking that a desperate man who failed in all his experiments, that, as a last effort, be determined, of his accord, to make a trial of the law – absurd.

"I wish you well," said Thomas, who did not laugh but wanted to.

In the early spring of 1760, Jefferson, a student at the College of William and Mary, while studying his Greek and Latin and happier than a bee on a cherry tree, heard a knock on his door. Disturbed, he approached the door.

"Come in."

Henry, with eyes like coal, peered by the side of the opening door. His long, dishevelled hair hid his face.

"Col. Dandridge wanted me to give you this book on *Ethics* by Aristotle."

Jefferson gestured to a chair as he took the book. "What brings you to Williamsburg, Mr. Henry?"

The older man observed piles of books in every corner of the room.

"I have come up to the capital to seek admission to the bar."

Perplexed, he contemplated how this man of inadequate knowledge of any sort, who read nothing and owned no books, could be ready to provide legal representation.

Trying to hide his astonishment, he replied somewhat rhetorically, "Since our last time together, you found time to master the law?"

Why yes, man's natural parts can always be improved by larnin'."

The student smirked. "How did you prepare in such a brief interlude?

"Read and reread *Coke upon Littleton* and the Virginia laws."

"For how long?"

"'Bout a month."

Patrick thought he observed a condescending look on Jefferson's face. Jefferson struggled to remain pleasant but did so, preoccupied with the belief that Patrick smelled of desperation.

Henry stared into his eyes. "I look forward to our next meeting."

At work the following week, Jefferson lumbered to a table by the window at George Wythe's office, picked up the Virginia laws, and brought them to his desk. Just as he leaned forward, he recoiled to his side of the desk when he heard George Wythe say that Peyton and John Randolph, lawyers who could qualify a person seeking admission to the bar, endorsed Mr. Henry.

"Though thinking him very ignorant of the law," said Wythe without looking at Jefferson, "they perceived him as a young man of genius and did not doubt he would soon qualify himself."

Wythe stared at his speechless apprentice, who folded his arms. "They signed his license to practice law with much reluctance."

If not from his mentor, the news would have made him doubt. Jefferson mumbled, "Henry passing Virginia statute requirements is absurd as drinking wine for a broken leg."

Wythe chuckled and, in a tone detached, and informed his student, "At first, Nicholas refused but on repeated importunities and promises of future reading, also signed, as did I."

Jefferson lurched back, dumbfounded.

"You look like a student trying to catch the meaning of words in a language he does not understand."

Jefferson attempted not to blush and sat as speechless as a corpse, thinking no accuracy of an idea resides in Henry's head.

Before riding back to Hanover in 1760, the twenty-four-year-old Patrick, dressed in old worn clothes, dined with Jefferson to the cedar and woodsmoke scent of the Raleigh Tavern.

"Consumed I am with elation," said Henry, "but I am also tempered with a serious reflection upon my deficiencies as a future lawyer."

Jefferson listened, wondering how the man who failed in merchandise and farming before turning his views to the law could practice without proper training.

Ignorance rattles through his mind, reflected Jefferson. Weighing his words, he withdrew his thought.

"I know you will do well," he said. "I wish you success."

"I am determined," informed Patrick, "to correct my shortcomings for the sake of everything and everyone dear to me in life."

Upon returning home, Henry pursued with industry and focus the study of his new profession.

The next morning guilt dropped out of a tree and darted into Thomas's heart.

It dawned on him that he only wrote Dabney a brief note since his arrival in Williamsburg.

Dearest Friend,

On the way to college, I stopped at Colonel Dandridge's in Hanover and passed the Christmas holidays there. During the season's festivity, I met Patrick Henry, a married man and a near neighbour. We became well acquainted, altho Henry was much my senior. Though suffering from another business failure, the older man put on a good front; played his fiddle and flute to the delight of the guests. He told me I listened to the music, but I bit my nails with a wooden face and observed. I consider him as being all tongue without either head or heart. I discovered I am energized when alone, but my energy becomes drained when being around people for too long.

Henry asked if I ever get lonely?

Not unless I am with people, I answered.

I tried to explain I need time alone to recharge, but my host and their friends did not understand. As you well know, I like to think about and explore thoughts.

I gleaned information on Williamsburg from the household, and after a fortnight, I continued my journey to the capital of Virginia, population 2,000.

The well-gardened town with one great street stretching along the ridge for nearly a mile, met my expectations. At the extreme west end of Duke of Gloucester Street, lined with shade trees and enlivened with traffic, stood the college.

Gloucester Street, I calculated as ninety feet wide.

The shops & Inns on the Duke of Gloucester Street with painted signboards for the people who could not read surprised me. The long, white wooden building, known as the Raleigh Tavern, was just as described to me. It stands on lot 54 on the Northside of the Duke of Gloucester Street between Botetourt Street and the Capitol. Two stories in height and lit by eight dormer windows on every side, the lead bust of a smiling Sir Walter stands in a portico over the door on Duke of Gloucester Street.

I recall Henry seemed to inspect me at our first meeting. Stepping back, I remembered a quote by him, "Do not follow the truth at the heels too closely, lest it strikes out your teeth.

Jefferson poured himself a glass of wine and stood up to stretch before resuming his letter.

The central area in the tavern, the Apollo, means a banqueting room. It was large and well lit, with a deep fireplace on each side, beside a door adjoined by carved wainscoting beneath the windows and above the mantelpiece. On first entering, the general flow and the activity going on gave me doubts. But my first sight of two buxom barmaids, each giving me a wink, one with the left and the other with the right eye, freed me. My nativity went with the setting sun and a glass or three of wine. I thought of you, who urged me on several occasions to take delight in my new surroundings. I certainly did as my eyes focused on one or the other barmaid.

The following day the Governor's carriage with postilions and outriders dusted me. Drawn from the Palace to the Capitol by six milk-white horses in gorgeous trappings, my face scowled but not for long.

Theatres, taverns, and the House of Burgesses have replaced the rural setting of the estate at Shadwell. I refer to Williamsburg as "Devilsburg."

Glaring at the bottle of wine, Jefferson poured himself another glass. He crossed his long legs.

More acquaintance with Greek and Latin as well as learning something of the mathematics makes me feel I'm ready to master the ages.

A circle of men, all my senior by at least a generation converged upon me. They changed my life forever: Dr. Wm. Small of Scotland, then professor of Mathematics, a man profound in most of the useful branches of science, with a happy talent of communication correct and gentlemanly manners, & an enlarged & liberal mind befriended your shy friend. He made me his daily companion when not engaged in the school, and from his conversation, I learned my first views of the expansion of science & the system of things in that surround us.

He checked his watch and felt that time was of no concern.

Fortunately for me, the Philosophical chair became vacant soon after my arrival at college, and he was appointed to fill it per interim: the first whoever gave in that college regular lectures in Ethics, Rhetoric & Belles Lettres. He told me that he thought me made of stone when I could concentrate on Homer and ignore the scent of spring, but I am not telling you anything you don't already know. He promises to procure for me, from his most inti-mate friend G. Wythe, a reception as a student of law, under his direc-tion. He introduced me to the acquaintance and familiar table of Governor Fauquier, the ablest man who ever filled that office. With him, and at his table, Dr. Small & Mr. Wythe, his amici omnium horarum, & myself, formed a partie quarree, & to the habitual conversations on these occasions, I owe much instruction.

A noise outside captured his attention; he raised his eyebrows and contin-ued writing.

I judge everyone by the standards of Small, Wythe, and Fauquier, the men who have instilled in me a curiosity that encourages my many-sided person-ality. Mr. Wythe, in particular, is a faithful and beloved Mentor, but best of all, instilled in me a love for wine. Little changes when it comes to my studies. A new friend, John Page of Rosewell, says, "I can tear myself away from my dearest friends, to fly to my studies, but you knew that already.

An upsetting conversation with him occurred that I want to impart to you.

"Thomas," he said, "you are becoming smug in your path of wisdom."

"Really!" I replied, "Have I acquired an obnoxious trait."

"Unfortunately, my friend, the lantern you use to pass through the concealed and somber paths of knowledge is not the one and only one."

"I believe," I told him, "my cherished beliefs that you allude to are as accurate as my father's surveying and the circumnavigation of those who disagreed with me are imprecise."

His face tightened, and his thoughts flashed anger, but he just said, "Oh," *and left it at that."* Jefferson's face clenched as he considered the conver-sation. He glanced away, reliving the conversation. *I disdain smugness, but I have more enjoyment reading Shakespeare, Johnson, Milton, Dryden, and Montesquieu in French than playing cards or betting on the horses.*

In closing, I feel I have landed in Nirvana and realize neither wealth nor princely power outshines a noble friend, and you, dearest friend, the noblest.

Adieu.

The following weeks, Greek and Latin and more Latin and Greek, History, Philosophy, and Ethics, continued to grab the student's attention until he encountered a young woman, whose eyes peeked out from under her eyelashes.

Staring at her, he stopped completely, standing, nervous, outside the Apollo Room, the evening of October 6, 1763, a Thursday. Inside, ladies and gentlemen danced minuets, jigs, and reels to two violins and a French horn.

Venturing in, Thomas glanced across the dance floor, hearing the rustle of the ladies' silks swaying from side to side. He tried not to think of her. Not able to not steal a glimpse, his head lifted as he observed three admirers surrounding Rebecca Lewis Burwell of Gloucester County, the sixteen-year-old-sister of a classmate.

He tried to fend off jealousy. She looks happy, he guessed. She said she would dance with me, but he bet she would forget. His attention fixed on her soft-lidded green-blue eyes, her narrow-lined brow, a nose not wide and pleasing in appearance, and her thick, moist lips ready for kissing. With the flick of her wrist, she dismissed her admirers and stepped in his direction.

He recognized he needed to relax and wanted to ask her for a dance but feared to make a fool of himself, and the rank and file would laugh at him. "What if I trip," he murmured, "and fall with my partner to the floor." Her dress, a pale, sky-blue cotton, tight around her petite waist, floated above the surface.

He noticed her skin, radiating with innocence and life against it. Her hair, up in a tight bun held by a black ribbon, reminded him of a ripe, large peach. Thomas wanted to smell its richness, but she frightened him. He turned away for a second or two to recollect his emotions; his face turned blood red in embarrassment. Hearing clanking chains and shackles, he feared for a moment of becoming a slave to her – his life, as barren as a grave.

Asking in a detached and clinical tone, he said, "Rebecca, may I have this dance?"

"Of course, Thomas. I was hoping you would ask."

Remember, he said to himself, *use as much moving language, as you know.*

"Thomas, place your hand a little lower and take smaller steps."

Sweat poured down his face. The cold presence of his mother shivered through his body.

"I want . . . wooooould you."

"Thomas, you are stepping on my foot!"

"Oh, I am sorry."

His mind a fog.

"Thomas, are you alright? Sweat is pouring from your face."

"I have something to . . . Woooooould you consider? No . . . I mean will you . . . Let me startttt."

'Thomas, relax! What is going on?"

"I cannot imagine spending my . . . No, what matters most to . . . I do not want to rush."

"What are you trying to say?"

"So . . . You know . . . What do you suppose?"

He could not utter the words, "Will you become my wife?"

Her blank stare filled the room.

Hearing the words, "You are not the man I thought you were," the sought-after sixteen-year-old turned away from him.

CHAPTER 8

Patrick Henry v.
The Parsons' Cause

D ust blew and rain threatened as George Wythe and young Thomas strolled towards the courthouse. As they came to the stocks near the public jail, they observed several men in the pillory with their earlobes nailed to it.

"The word *pillory*," Wythe said, "dates in English since 1274."

Thomas stiffened and stared at the wooden posts and the holes in them that secured the two offenders' head and hands. The construction of the pillory fascinated him. Did the person who made the first pillory have a mother like his?

"What crimes did they commit?" asked Jefferson.

"The younger man for blasphemy, the older one had relations with a man, and the gentleman on the right coveted his neighbour's wife."

The smell of the mixture of dead rats, excrement, rotten mud, vegetables, and fruit decaying around the grassy area surrounding the pillory sent waves of nausea through Wythe's stomach. He turned and rushed off to the court house.

Jefferson followed, wondering about the wisdom of having a law that allowed public humiliation by the citizens' hands to deter sins against society. Later in his life, Thomas Jefferson learned the verb "to pillor" and used it to expose to public ridicule, scorn, and abuse men outside his political circle.

For months, he sat in the law office of Wythe organizing his thoughts on how to proceed but nary a day went by that Patrick Henry's name did not croak in his head like a frog.

"Colonel Dandridge informed me, in general conversation," said Wythe, "that Henry likes to read and reread a few of the best books. With his excellent memory, coupled with his fondness for the study of human nature, he can grasp the compelling features of any subject."

"I hear," said Jefferson, "he divides his time between lawyering and helping his father-in-law run the Shelton Tavern."

With a searing throb in his heart, Thomas blurted out, "He mixes with clergymen, pedagogue, or legislator, small planters and small traders, sportsmen, loafers, slaves and the drivers of slaves, the good-humoured, illiterate, thriftless consumers of tobacco and whiskey on his tavern porch or the shady side of his country store."

Wythe noticed the colour red revolved around Jefferson's eyes; then they hardened into red-rimmed slits.

"He does," said Wythe, "have the ability to make men laugh, make them serious, and kindle a fire to their enthusiasms."

"His penmanship, punctuation, spelling, and syntax, Colonel Dandridge informed me," said Jefferson, "rivals the letters of the great actors in history."

Wythe turned away, hoping his student's anger, warring with envy, would abate.

"He possesses," Thomas continued, "a superficial knowledge of Latin, barely translates Greek, owns no books, and to his discredit serves as a host-bartender whenever Shelton takes leave." An ignorant, lazy man, Thomas thought, not a gentleman.

The future Sage of Monticello neglected the fact that Henry recorded fees in 1185 suits, besides many other fees for preparing legal papers out of court, and stood fully occupied with the appropriate business of his profession. (Jefferson registered in his fee-books only 504 cases in a similar period.)

Henry's eldest grandson, a student, years later at Hampden-Sidney College, wrote, "His grandfather's examinations of his progress in Greek and Latin were so rigorous that he dreaded them "much more than he did his recitations to his professors."

Contrary to what Thomas believed, enjoying the rustling leaves of the forest and dancing at the Tavern hindered not the "indolent, slovenly Henry" from gaining in knowledge. Like creeping ivy on a wall, he hid the truth from himself. Jefferson chose to see Patrick as a shallow man and not as a copious, poetical, majestic human being. Because of Jefferson's inability to shut down his own insecurity when it came to Henry, he lost the beauty of the Henry's growth. How different the world became because Henry said the strongest things in the finest language, though, according to Thomas, "without logic, arrangement, and in a desultory manner."

"Mr. Wythe, have you heard," asked Jefferson, "of Henry's position on the question of British debts, in the case of Jones & Walker."

"Yes."

"How could the shirtless and shoeless man have searched the pages of the law in a case wholly foreign to his character?" asked Jefferson.

"Thomas, Judge William Nelson last night at dinner with me, his bottle of claret, splendid, I may add, said, 'Henry pled in the Court of Admiralty as counsel for a Spanish captain whose vessel and cargo was libelled.' He knew not how Mr. Henry acquired such a knowledge of written complaints in maritime law, to which he supposed he had never before turned his attention."

Jefferson believed it as absurd as taking a legal brief to the apothecary. He abruptly headed for the door, yanked it open, then slammed it as he left. Wythe swallowed hard and proceeded to work. For Henry, the stakes were high. He taught himself to observe a situation with a powerful, intuitive, swift glance of his eye. For what ordinary men might spend hours toiling, he took in immediately. His memory held everything he wanted and needed.

According to his friends, "All Patrick's resources were at instant command; his faculty of debate, his imagination, humour, tact, diction, elocution were superb and exquisite. He stood as a man of human and friendly ways, whom all men loved, and whom all men wanted to help."

From the beginning of Virginia's history, most persons in the colony above the age of sixteen years supported the Church of England by revenues derived from taxation levied upon tobacco, the staple of the colony. In 1748, a law passed stipulating a pay of 16,000 pounds of tobacco, the colony's staple per year to the clergy. Poor harvests made many subjects sigh and lower their faces as tobacco prices rose from two to six pennies per pound, tripling clerical salaries. A law for the relief of the people passed the House of Burgess in 1755, which stipulated that all tobacco debts be discharged in money at a rate of two pence per pound for ten months.

Hence, the law called the Two Penny Act.

In 1758, tobacco again in short supply, the price advanced, and the Burgesses re-enacted the Two Penny Act for a year. Instead of what the clergy felt due to them, 16,000 pounds of tobacco, they were compelled to take the province's paper money at a great discount. A debate arose, and the clergy led the charge against the legislature of the colony. They wanted to jam their hands into the pockets of the citizens and stomp away, enriched.

When King George II overturned the Two Penny Act, the religious faction sued local farmers and officials to recover their lost salary. Rev. James Maury, the rector of Fredericksville Parish, Louisa, and Jefferson's former tutor, brought suit in the County Court of Hanover on April 1, 1762, for £144 against Thomas Johnson and Tarlton Brown, collectors of the levies in the Parish of Fredericksville, Louisa County. Maury, a man of high standing, continued his school in Walker Parish and taught five boys who became signers of the Declaration of Independence. Three of them would go on to the Presidency of the United States.

The lawsuit, referred to as *The Parsons' Cause*, came to trial. As Patrick aimed for the Shelton Tavern from the Court House, a man with arched eyebrows approached him. He recognized the face, but the man's name drew a blank.

"Mr. Henry, did you know the court of Hanover County delivered a decision in the case of Reverend Maury disallowing the Act of 1758, adjudging the act contrary to the law?"

"Yes, my uncle informed me the ministers were deprived of two-thirds of their salary for the year 1758."

"We want you to represent the people on the writ of inquiry to determine the damages thus sustained by the parson before a special jury."

"You have counsel, John Lewis."

Patrick glanced over, scowled when he thought of replacing Lewis. The one thing you do not do, he knew, is make an enemy of a friend.

"Lewis believes it is a very simple question of arithmetic for the court."

"He does?" said Patrick. That is why he expressed his desire to withdraw from the case."

Henry rolled his eyes before asking, "Is there a Court date?"

"The first day of December for a special jury to examine whether the Plaintiff sustained any damages and what."

Patrick was curious why they would want him to act as counsel for the defendants.

"We need hope's sunbeams to pierce the curtain of the king's veto as a breach of their legislative authority."

He cleared his throat, stood back a foot, "Give me a little time and space to think this over."

He went fishing to help him mull over the request. Upon returning to his office, he knew from a legal standpoint, he should decline the offer. Approaching his desk, he tidied some papers, but upon second thought, destiny barked. He sat down and decided to sit in the vacant chair for the people. He did not fare well the last night of November. As a matter of fact, he slept tighter than his bowstring. For one thing, fellow lawyers kept telling him the law states the proper course, and Rev. Maury should be made whole. Arguing against the church made him uneasy, as he would be attacking his uncle whom he prayed would not be in attendance. And then there sat his father, the presiding judge.

Hearing a great commotion outside the Shelton Tavern on the morning of December 1, 1763, he observed, according to his friend George Morgan, "Great numbers, riding on horseback or in coaches, gigs, or carts, moving towards the Court-house. Perukes on the heads of the gentlemen in coaches and Hogarthian clothes on all."

In the distance were the oaks shedding copper and yellow leaves, crimson speaking from the sumac, bright red berries on the spiky leaves of holly, the dark greens of the cedar and pine, and the jaundiced sedge, thick upon vacant fields.

On the road that led past his abandoned store were throngs of people descending a hill, fording a creek, and then ascending the gentle rise to the village of scattered houses. Some joined the crowd at the tavern or the greater crowd on the Courthouse Green. In the courtyard stood the prominent people of the two parishes of Hanover, and some from parishes far off. There were planters dressed in velvet with powdered hair, long queues, and white top-boots, elbow-to-elbow, under the arched opening of the bench less, roomy Courthouse made of English brick. In the courtroom or on the paved porch were rough-and-ready gentry in homespun standing who could fix a gaff as skilfully as they could crack a whip or plough a furrow. Goosebumps tricked down Henry's arms and legs.

"Wait a minute," he said to himself.

"Ready?" queried his father-in-law, John Shelton.

Patrick found himself between a smile and a frown.

Glancing around the noisy, wooden tavern, he noticed there were half dozen men he knew by name and several others he knew by sight. His shoulders shrugged as he stared at his old wool coat. He recalled how the clergy's case sailed before the wind of the Law. With good reason, the plaintiffs thought their triumph would be complete. Part of him did not want to leave the cozy, safe, and familiar tavern. The demurrer's decision excited a violent unrest among the people and equal jubilation on the part of the clergy. They expected to enjoy the final triumph of their hard-fought battle. "Yes, indeedy, the defendants hired me to plead before the jury on their behalf, and they are goin' to get some pleadin'."

"Son," said his father-in-law, "this is the time in the rush and frenzy of life that every man dreams for." As he put on his coat, he looked up and said,

"Charge the foe and examine for the special jury what damages the plaintiff, Maury, sustained."

A cloud of consternation settled in his eyes, yet; Patrick looked fierce and unnerving. A lull passed before he exited through the door. He walked with Colonel Samuel Meredith, who counselled him to relax as they stood amidst the throng. Another carriage appeared on the heels of twenty parsons; it pulled into the courtyard carrying his uncle, the Reverend Patrick Henry.

Nervously, he approached it and implored, "Please do not come into court today."

"Why?"

"Because as the defence is engaged in opposition to the clergy, your appearance might strike me with such awe as to prevent me from doing justice to my clients."

"Rather than that effect should be produced, I will not only absent myself from the Court House and return home."

Patrick hugged his uncle, then tried to make his way through the crowd but managed to find himself surrounded as he approached the courthouse. He looked up, his eyes agitated but direct, hoping he knew all the answers. The court was packed full of loud spectators, elbowing one another as they jockeyed for space, quarrelling loudly and reeking of spirits. Those not standing in the courtroom crowded in the doorway. He tried to push aside the fears twisting inside him.

On a long bench sat Colonel John Henry, flanked by the other justices and twenty clergymen who felt confident the judicial drama would fatten their purses and prestige under their wigs. Patrick avoided eye contact with his father.

The sheriff went forth to summon jurors and returned with twelve men.

Ridiculous! Thought Rev. Maury as to their impartiality.

Patrick's body tightened. He tried to relax in his seat.

"Men of the Jury," announced the Kings' Council, the beefy Mr. Lyons. "I will state the facts very briefly and explain the decision upon the demurrer, an assertion by the defendant that although the facts alleged by the plaintiff in the complaint may be true, they do not entitle the plaintiff to prevail in the lawsuit. The demurrer puts the act of 1758 entirely out of the way and left the law of 1748 as the standard."

The pulse of the courtroom accelerated, hearts racing most knowing they did not have the money to pay the clergy.

Henry sat nibbling on a fingernail as the corpulent Lyons turned to the jury. A piercing silence settled in the courtroom.

"You are sworn to a single point – the amount of salary due the plaintiff."

Lyons turned to Henry with a smug expression.

"I call Mr. Gist."

Gist was a tall, thin man with perfect skin.

"Sir. What is your profession?"

"A tobacco dealer."

"Inform the court of the market price of tobacco in 1759."

"It averaged 50 shillings per 100 pounds."

"Thank you, sir. You may go."

Patrick, erect in his seat, remembered encountering on a walk with Mrs. Henry several butterflies embossed with brown and black markings on their wings and bodies, amidst a bunch of yellow and the black striped butterflies. She informed him the brown and black ones mimic the poisonous pipevine swallowtail to ward off predators. Marvelling at nature's uniqueness, he hoped he possessed something special to ward off the people's predators.

Lyons said in a loud voice, "I call Mr. McDowall."

McDowall had small hands and a beauty mark on his chin.

"Sir. What is your profession?"

"Tobacco dealer."

"Please inform the court of the market price of tobacco in 1759?"

"It was about 50 shillings per 100 pounds."

"Thank you, sir. You may go."

The spectators in the room were disappointed and observed Henry; as he sat silently. Lyons approached the jury, tried to make eye contact, but many jurors avoided his glance.

"Members of the Jury, at 16,000 pounds of tobacco a year as salary, I compute that Reverend Maury is due 450 British pounds in cash, rather than the approximately 150 pounds he received under the Two Penny Act."

"The simple arithmetic of Mr. Lewis," Patrick said to his co-counsel.

"I submit," continued Mr. Lyons, "as evidence that Rev. Maury's is due the sum of £300. Members of the jury, he is entitled to this amount according to the law. I repeat according to the law."

A hush engulfed the courtroom. Lyons bowed to the jury and plodded towards his seat. He stopped halfway and turned to the jury, "I rest my case." As he sat in his chair, he felt it creak under his weight.

Patrick shot up. He felt some truth in Mr. Lyons' words but refused to grant him any elbow room.

The packed courtroom stared at Patrick, wondering what he would say. No one in the crowded room recalled ever hearing him speak publicly. Curiosity glowed and the collective intake of breath was heard noticeably. The clergy, elbow to elbow, forty eyes focused and unblinking. His father hunched over, his fingers tapping on the table.

"Genn-tle-mennn, mmmay I bbbring."

The eyes of the spectators focused on him.

No flush of enthusiasm existed.

Bodies bent forward from the benches.

The clergy exchanged sly looks with one another.

His father shed a tear.

Patrick took a deep breath and closed his eyes. He smelled the sweet scent of the forest, the sounds of birds chirping, sighted squirrels racing up and down a tree trunk and his words ran out.

"The Act of 1758 shows every characteristic of a good law. It is a law of general utility and is consistent with the original compact between the king and people."

His body clenched as he paused to take another breath. Words appeared on the edge of his mind. Forget the facts, the reasons, the answers, he thought.

A member of the jury thought him ready to depart port.

He declaimed, according to Captain Thomas Trevilian, a member of the audience, "A great deal about the benevolence and holy zeal of our reverend clergy, but how is this revealed?

"Do they manifest their fervour in the cause of religion and humanity by practising the mild and benevolent precepts of the Gospel of Jesus?"

Anger crisscrossed the hearts of the 20 clergymen.

"Do they feed the hungry and clothe the naked?"

He looked across the courtroom and sneered his question.

"Oh, no, gentlemen. Instead of feeding the hungry and clothing the naked, these rapacious harpies, with their power equal to their will, snatch from the hearth of their honest parishioner, the last hoe-cake from the widow, and her orphan children and her last milch cow. The last bed—nay, the last blanket, from the dying woman!"

The weasel-like eyes of the clergy hardened into red-rimmed slits.

"Damn that man," uttered several of the gang of 20. They hissed softly.

"The only use of an established church and clergy in society is to enforce obedience to civil sanctions and the observance of those which are called duties of imperfect obligation. When a clergy ceases to answer these ends, the community requires no further need of their ministry, and may justly strip them of their appointments. The clergy of Virginia, in this particular instance, refused to acquiesce in the law in question."

The fear that churned in his stomach earlier gone as a Thanksgiving goose.

One juror, a blacksmith, thinking justice glowed like the flame from a forge.

"Therefore, instead of good members of the state, they stand as enemies of the community; and that, in the case now before them, Mr. Maury, instead of countenance, and protection, and damages, very justly deserved punishment with signal severity."

Maury blinked tears, and his lips curved downward. With his fist clutched and his spirit weakly on the floor, he gasped.

Another juror, a baker, observed liberty rising like the proofing dough of bread.

Henry stepped back. Funny he judged, never before in his life did he feel as good.

He gazed at the jury.

"That excepting that you desire to rivet the chains of bondage on your necks, I hope you will not let slip the opportunity that now is offered, of making such an example of him."

He pivoted to Maury, who wished to clip his sails. "You might, hereafter, take this as a warning to yourself and your brethren, not to have the temerity, in the future, to dispute the validity of such laws, authenticated by the only authority; which, in my conception, gives force to laws for the government of this Colony, the authority of the legal representatives!"

The audience sensed that Patrick's words commanded enough power to overcome the opposition. He turned to the gang of 20. "It is the clergy's work in life to safeguard the people in high matters unregulated by the secular laws. If they failed in this, they failed in everything and were of no use in the great body politic. Should not a clergyman set an example of selfishness; to want more than his lay brother; to become a grasper, a worldling. Should not such a clergyman serve God or should he serve himself? Shame upon greed— shame especially upon pulpit greed!"

The twenty members of the clergy loathed the apostate and looked as pale as the ghost of Judas. With a warm gaze fixed on the jury he said, "Never forget gentlemen, a King . . . ," the courtroom focused as paused. The hearts of the spectators beating as fast as a hummingbird's wings. An awkward silence filled the room. Patrick let it boil for a moment.

"I repeat, a King, by annulling or disallowing acts of so salutary nature from being the Father of his people, King George III has degenerated into a Tyrant, and forfeits all right to his subjects' obedience."

A handful of gentlemen in the crowd murmured, "Treason, Treason!"

The word treason infuriated Henry's father. Hundreds of eyes blinked in unison. Patrick gleamed like a sunset.

Mr. Lyons, his face bursting red, called out aloud to the Bench, "This gentleman speaks treason, and I am astonished that the worships' could hear it without emotion, or any mark of dissatisfaction."

A member of the jury's heart hammered in approval of Henry. The judges sat patient and steady. No curves, dips, swells or angles on their faces. The thoughts of Henry and the jury locked in a shared understanding. A hush hung in the room.

Henry broke the silence, "You must seize upon the opportunity," continued Patrick, "now on hand to sustain the liberties of the Commonwealth. I hope the pages of your minds are ruffled open and seen the corruption of the clergy exposed."

Hearing a roar in the courthouse's direction, Sally Skelton Henry looked up from the skillet in the kitchen at the Tavern. Henry bowed and took his seat. The jury withdrew and returned within minutes. Patrick confident, opened the door for their decision.

"We," said the foremen of the jury, "find for the Plaintiff, one penny damages."

The rotund Mr. Lyons wobbled towards the bench, "As the verdict is contrary to evidence, the jury must reconsider its decision. Void it!" "The case of the plaintiff thumped to submission," Henry whispered to his co-counsel.

Three days later, Rev. Maury attended a musical soiree given by Governor Francis Fauquier at the Raleigh Tavern. Thomas looked at his teacher as a child might appear when their candy falls to the floor.

"The court ordered a select jury summoned," the Reverend offered, "but, how far they who gave the order, wished or intended it, you may judge."

Jefferson sighed, then stuffed his fiddle back into its case. He lifted his face before receiving a glass of cabernet by the Governor. Maury snorted before savouring his wine. Jefferson half-listened as the Reverend continued in a matter-of-fact way. "The Sheriff went into a public room, full of gentlemen, and told his errand. One excused himself (Peter Robinson of King William) as having already given his opinion in a similar case. On this, as a person then present, told me, the sheriff immediately left the room, without summoning any one person there. He afterward met another gentleman (Richard Sq. Taylor) on the green, and, on his saying he did not feel fit to serve, being a churchwarden, he took upon himself to excuse him, too, and, as far as I can learn, made no further attempts to summon gentlemen."

"From what I know of Henry, said Jefferson, "He credited the sheriff with securing a good, honest jury of twelve adult male persons."

With a glance at his pocket watch, the Governor interjected, "Feeble endeavours to comply with the directions of the Court in that particular."

"The sheriff," Maury continued, "went among the vulgar herd and selected and set down on his list about eight or ten of these. I met him with it in his hand, and on looking at it, I observed to him that they were not such jurors as the Court directed him to get, being people of whom I never heard before, except one. I sought him out and said, As party in the cause and one of the Collector's Securities, the law says 'you must excuse as a juror on this occasion.' This man's name remained and even called in Court, and, he excused himself, but was probably admitted. I cannot recollect, that the Court expressed either surprise or dislike for summoning a more proper jury."

Jefferson's eyes moved apart before he mumbled, "The law lost on the grassy slope of obfuscation."

"I objected against them," said Maury, "yet, as Mr. Henry insisted, they were honest men, and, therefore, unexceptionable; they were immediately called to the book and sworn. Three of them, as I learned afterwards, nay, some said four, were Dissenters of that denomination called New Lights, which the Sheriff, as they were all his acquaintance, must have known."

"What about the evidence?" asked Wythe.

"Brief and to the point," replied Maury. "Messrs. Gist and McDowall, the two most considerable purchasers in that county, were called in to prove the price of tobacco. They swore that, during the months of May and June 1759, tobacco sold at 50s. per hundred, and that himself, at or about the latter end of the last of those months, sold some hundreds of bhds. at that price, and, amongst the rest, one hundred scheduled for delivery in the month of August, which, however, were not delivered until September. That of the latter only proved, that 50s. represented the current price of tobacco that season and the sum of the evidence for the Plaintiff."

Thomas glanced back over his shoulder thinking, he heard a familiar voice at a nearby table. A woman shot him a graveyard grin. He turned away; his face burned with embarrassment. Maury scowled at his ex-student as he finished relating the evidence. "A receipt to the Collector, to the best of my remembrance in these words: Received of Thomas Johnson, Jun'r, at this and some former payments, £144, current money, by James Maury."

Simultaneously, Wythe and Fauquier uttered, "Really, nothing more!"

Maury released a sigh of disappointment. The men continued to sip more wine.

"The lynchpin for their defence," related Maury, "besides the oratory of Henry, constituted a witness for the defendants. He observed to the jury that they must find or if they must find, I am not sure which (but think the former) for the Plaintiff, but need not find more than one farthing."

Jefferson lost in space. His heart pounding for the girls he desired: "Becca," "Sukey," "Judy," and "Belinda"; oblivious to the fact that Justice, unlike the North Star, never stays fixed. "How long," asked Wythe, "did Henry speak?"

Maury stepped down in time. "I seem to remember he spoke for near an hour with wonder-working fancy, and through the tones of his voice clothed his images in a peculiar phraseology."

Anger leapt into the Governor's eyes. "Jurisprudence fails to keep order in society if men like Henry compromise with the law."

Wythe was thinking that the Governor was unable to fathom Henry's eloquence that blasts like a storm.

"How long did the jury deliberate?"

"They returned in less than five minutes and announced, "We," said the foremen of the jury, "find for the Plaintiff, one penny damages."

Wythe pictured Lyons trying to fly towards the bench like an arrow from Henry's bow.

"Lyons asserted," said Maury, 'The verdict is contrary to evidence, sent the jury out again, but the Court ignored his words. Thoroughly disgusted, Governor Fauquier, with a smile, scanned his guests and said, 'The ready road to popularity is to trample underfoot the interests of religion, the rights of the church, and the prerogative of the Crown.'"

"After the Court adjourned," continued Maury, who before sipping his pinot noir savoured its smell. "Henry apologised to me for what he said, alleging that his sole view in engaging in the cause, and in saying what he did was to render himself popular."

Jefferson swooped into the present and spilled his drink on the table. His mouth twisted in a harsh grimace. "This unexampled, unexpected, instantaneous verdict is an appearance of supernatural inspiration."

The nineteen-year-old student failed to realize that the germination of Independence occurred because "the lazy Virginian" painted to the heart with a stroke that almost petrified it.

"Life becomes very complex in a brief period," remarked Wythe.

The governor's face locked in shock. He rose before he thought and spoke before he left.

"This pleading of such supremacy for the assumption of power to bind the king's hands by provincial Legislatures, is inconsistent with the dignity of the Church of England and manifestly tends to draw the people of these plantations from their allegiance to the king." The words stormed into Jefferson: making him uncomfortable, unsure of the scent of its direction. He held up both hands as if surrendering. Spite dispersed from his face like witchcraft.

"Wait a minute," he mumbled. "Whose side am I on?"

CHAPTER 9

Henry's Tyrant

George III's premature birth occurred on June 4, 1738. His grandfather, King George II, could not have cared less, for he hated George's father, Frederick, who just did not get along with his parents. When his mother died on November 20, 1737, her parting words were, "At least I shall have one comfort in having my eyes eternally closed and shall never see that monster again."

The future King, George III, developed into a healthy but introverted boy. At four, he was described as fat and "lovely child."

He was loved by his father, who told him on numerous occasions. "I want to be your best friend."

Though he possessed faults, such as his mistresses' overwhelming debt, Frederick wanted his son to be part of a loving family(free of political differences) and have an excellent education. He devised a program: George woke at 7 AM, and classes began at 8 to 12:30 PM. Then an hour of play, more classes until dinner at 3 PM, and more classes until supper at 8 PM. Between 9 and 10, he went to bed.

"Son," he told George, who matured as a shy and reserved young boy, "I know you will appreciate learning Latin, Mathematics, French, history, geography, German, art and architecture, science, dancing, and fencing."

"Father, I look forward to being competent in reading and writing English. Will you play the cello when I study?"

"When I have time, it would give me great pleasure. I will play the music that Handel composed for my wedding,"

His competence blossomed, and he corresponded with his father in German when he turned eleven. At fifteen, he translated Latin and studied algebra, geometry, and trigonometry but lacked enthusiasm. He studied to please his father and was the first Sovereign to learn science.

It all started after another falling out with his father, King George the Second, in 1747. Frederick wanted his children brought up with the pride of being British, not Germans from Hanover. The King confronted Frederick.

"What do you know that is important," his teeth fixed in place.

"I have great knowledge."

The King's eyebrows contracted, and his mouth's lower corners showed anger.

"You will find it is not the same as Hanoverian intellect."

Thinking him Dunce the Second, the Prince of Wales said, "I prefer to be a patron of the arts and not akin to an oligarchy of aristocratic Whig relatives."

Frederick and his wife, Augusta collected Van Dyck and Rubens. Having grown tired of being lectured, he decided to use Cliveden, England, as life away from the royal court for his wife, Augusta, and their children.

"Never am I going to have the king say that to me again," he said to Augusta, "nor will I feel small or useless"

At the Italianate mansion and estate set 130 feet above the River Thames with grounds sloping down to the river, a violent rainstorm interrupted his favourite outdoor game, cricket. Prince Frederick abandoned the outdoors, knowing whist would relieve the boredom of waiting, but the game required a fourth to make up a rubber. A tall, charming, and excellent talking unknown nobleman, John Stuart, the third Earl of Bute, sitting in a gig conversing with Frederick's family doctor, accepted an offer to join as the missing hand.

His mind opened to the opportunity; he changed into a waistcoat for comfort. Glancing back over his shoulder as he walked indoors, he said goodbye to his past without knowing it.

"You know, Prince; you do not pick a partner like you choose a tie."

The Prince laughed. "Of course, but a man who treasures whist has no choice."

Bute pressed a card in his hand and laid it down. It was the winning trump and won the favour of Frederick. Ludicrously delighted, the Prince of Wales invited him to dine. Stuart feasted on seven varieties of meat, served with warm vegetables and champagne.

"How long did you sit in the House of Lords?" queried Prince Frederick. "I served as one of the sixteen Scottish representative peers from 1737 to 1741," answered the Scottish nobleman.

"Lord Bute, did you experience," asked the princess, "anti-Scot sentiment among the English people?"

"Yes, I have observed a widespread fear that your country fears being swamped by Scots."

"To what do you attribute this?" asked the prince.

"Because Scotland continues to develop faster than England."

The Scotsman folded his arms and shifted, feeling uncomfortable.

"There appear, unfortunately, Prince, a nascent anti-Scottish nationalist movement celebrating Englishness and an Anglocentric Great Britain."

"I hope," said Princes Augusta, "your Scottishness will not hinder you from giving more service to England."

"I will toast to that," said Lord Bute.

He knew he made valuable friends as Augusta gave him a steady look.

"Lord Bute spoke with me," Augusta announced to Frederick a few weeks later, "Not forced to deal with others' needs, he feels our son is socially and emotionally immature because of his upbringing in isolation from others of his age."

Displaying ability and just shy of his sixth birthday, George escaped the nursery and was placed solely under the care of his first tutor, the Reverend Francis Ayscough.

"I am astonished, Prince, that you learned several verses and passages out of plays and poems."

The tutor pulsed. An easy pay, he thought.

George glared at him, racking his brain for what to say. "I do not want to read any more religion from you." With raised eyebrows and red-faced, he yelled, "I know enough and want my privacy."

Wanting to be on the high ground, the tutor withheld a dirty look on his face.

"I am not a child, old bones."

The instructor sent him a quick grimace thinking him short of decorum. "You are of average ability and lack earnest effort."

The next day as the tutor put on his coat, he thought he smelled tar, but the sticky substance adhered to his arm before he could stop. Satisfied with his tactics, George sneered at him and refused to study with Dr. Francis any longer.

After Frederick's premature death in 1751, George became the Prince of Wales and heir apparent to the throne at the age of twelve. King George II ordered the bowels to be pit in a box. Three days later, the body and bowels remained lying in the room, the smell from the rotting corpse sickening young George. The country received this notice of Frederick's death

Here lies poor Fred, who was alive and is dead,
Had it been his father, I had much rather,
Had it been his sister, nobody would have missed her,
Had it been his brother, still better than another,
Had it been the whole generation, so much better for the nation,
But since it is Fred who was alive and is dead,
There is no more to be said.

"Prince George," addressed the king, his voice colourless like his skin, "I want you to learn the political status quo and rule like myself."

Born in Hanover, Germany, George II was the last British king to fight in battle. The privilege was bestowed on the French at Dettingen in 1743. George, terrified to say anything, eased back from his German grandfather.

"My instructors tell me you are an uninspired pupil and an uncommonly indolent one, wanting of application, averse to politics, and err on the short side of brains."

His hair tied back, young George seemed like a statue in the dull light. He tried to open the door of his mind but only gawked at his grandfather, who gave him a long, stern glance and then struck the boy's ears so hard that the incident resulted in George never living at Hampton Court when he reigned as king.

In 1755, the widow, Augusta, asked Bute, who had served as Frederick's chief adviser and confidant, for an interview.

"Draw a stool, Lord Bute, and sit by the fireside."

Adorned with a hat and feather, her makeup intact, the servant poured him a brandy.

"Will you become Prince George's tutor?"

Lord Bute looked startled. He stopped sipping and took a swallow, reflecting that a smart man would guard his expression.

"The total of his book-learning is adequate," she said. "But I question whether he recognizes the general course of things."

"I sense, Princess, his instructors in their efforts have failed to arouse his interest and inspire him with greater ambition."

"As George will be king and given his grandfather's age and health, sooner rather than later, something should be done.

"Very true," he said, as she nodded to the servant, who poured him another brandy, "if his stagnation continues, it will be his ruin."

"His instructors have wanted my son to accept the political status quo and be a king like his Hanover grandfather."

"I will encourage the prince to introduce reforms."

She blinked before lifting a hand to her face, considering herself pleased to ask him to come.

"What would the reforms be?"

"He should reduce the national debt."

"His father always advocated this but excuse me for interrupting you."

"And he should," Bute continued, "sever the connection between Britain and Hanover, put an end to corruption in political life, and free the Monarchy from the control of the Whig ministers."

Looking around her chamber, she realized her son would be the first British monarch from the House of Hanover to speak English as his first language. Her eyes lifted. Satisfaction entered her, pierced her, filled her.

The summer evening was quiet and of few words until the seventeen-year-old Prince of Whales said to Lord Bute, "I miss not having someone to guide me."

"How sorry I am."

"I see life around me but feel alone."

"Pray, do not concern yourself about this. That is the past. Be satisfied, knowing you are free to choose your destiny."

"I will try to be optimistic."

"The road will be rocky, but with my planning and your persistence and hard work, you will learn the attributes of a good king."

They talked in this way long, and successfully, George became excited to expand his mind.

"Mother," said the prince, "the Earl and I have been friends for a month. I understand, worldly wisdom never substitutes for learning the first principles of government, politics, and finance."

She wondered, *could this be a dream?*

"You are on the way to becoming an exceptional king."

"History reveals; mother, a Prince's education often determines, for good or ill, the fate of his people."

She laid out her hand on his shoulder. Her blood skipped frantically through her body, knowing Frederick would be pleased in George's development.

The Prince took a quick look around his mother's apartment.

"Lord Bute," he said, "often reminds me, I must continue to master Latin well enough to read the classics, Montesquieu, and Hume. To study French and German; delve into history, geography, and the British political system; master mathematics and elementary science; appreciate art, architecture, and music."

She realized her plans were working and asked. "What brings a smile to your face, Prince?"

"Perceiving the world can be mine."

Augusta could see that George lusted for ambition, an abiding ambition for the first time in his life. She viewed him reigning as the British monarch as she ran a steady hand through his coarse hair.

"The habits of serious study and political virtue will make everything easy, my son."

He unchecked any impulses he held.

"Mother, I am pleased we have the confidence and friendship with Lord Bute."

The next morning the prince arrived at work early. While waiting for Bute, he delved into his studies and dreamed of being king.

"I am proud," Bute told the prince, "to have supplied you with a purpose that kindles your ambitions and energies."

"A King's honour, honesty, and virtue I have learned are more valuable than being worldly-wise, for virtuous princes can change nations for the better. And Britain needs reformation."

"Look at the future from the view of the country, not the court," said Bute. The Prince sat satisfied that meaning and purpose now nestled into his thoughts. Ambition took centre stage over indolence. He felt a stab of pain. Would his subjects love him?

Cherishing that he knew Bute, he cocked his head, his face bright.

"Corrupt people," his mentor said, "whom law cannot correct may be restrained and corrected by a 'Patriot King,' who would begin to govern as soon as he begins to reign. He would espouse no party but manage as the common father of his people."

"When I ascend the throne of Great Britain, a standing miracle will come to pass when I refuse to make corruption an expedient of government or to countenance subordinates who do so."

"A Patriot King can reform the whole tone of British politics and curb the threat to individual freedom by the aristocracy."

"Knowledge can take us," said the Prince, "on an expedition from the dark side of authority."

A shiver ran thru his heart as he handed Lord Bute his essays on the *Original Nature of Government* and a *Short History of England*. The next day Bute stepped back and said, "I see you fully understand the monarch must defend the people against a corrupt aristocracy." Bute saw in George's eyes freedom from doubt and freedom from turmoil in politics.

"Nothing depresses me more, Prince, than the double-dealings of inferior minds. The accomplished intriguer makes the truth more deceptive than falsehood, and his lies, a confession of failure."

"My dearest friend, I feel affection and gratitude to you for instilling in me a desire to free the Monarchy from ministerial control and the political world in general from corruption. We will reduce the national debt and retrench the nation's finances and avoid the entanglements with European conflicts from George II's attachments to Hanover."

A slight smile extended from his mouth, but his eyes looked warm and moist.

"I am sure," said Bute, "you were born to cleanse political life."

"I appreciate you telling me." He wet his lips. "I am full of the idea that we need a new broom."

The King and George sat in silence, drank coffee, and occasionally peered at each other. The next day, Prince George folded his arms as he watched his grandfather for a moment. Unintentionally, running his fingers along his head's side, he thought it eerie to sit with George II.

Each sported flame-red hair, blue eyes, distinguished with lantern jaws, and stood six-foot-three.

A vase, by the king's high-backed chair containing some tired-looking flowers, distracted him.

"What do you wish?" asked the Prince.

"Explain to me your beard."

"I thought I needed to look more dashing."

"Kings-in-waiting are dashing."

Touched, the Prince studied the king's face.

"We always think we will have more time," announced the Sovereign. He sighed. Slowly his eyes closed, and he drifted off to sleep.

The Prince smiled slow and easy. The slap of George II's death echoed throughout England.

In his accession speech to Parliament in late October of 1760, the 22-year-old monarch played down his Hanoverian connections.

"Born and educated in this country," he said, "I glory in Britain's name."

"Lord Bute, I need you to review all eligible German Protestant princesses."

"Why, Sire?"

"It will save me a great deal of trouble, as marriage must sooner or later come to pass."

In a sharp tone, Bute said, "Your public duty is to procreate."

He chose sight unseen, the seventeen-year-old Charlotte Sophia of Mecklenburg-Strelitz and married her on September 8, 1761. The marriage lasted more than 50 years, producing 15 children.

The new king needed not remind Lord Bute, "The hour that we so long wished, I mean entering a reformation in Government, strikes. I want you to take the office of Secretary of State."

"Before such a decided step takes place, I have to win for myself a party so I can play a prominent part in politics."

"Well, in that case, I understand your wisdom to refuse."

George III turned away, then turned back, contemplating riding forth to kill dragons and the monsters of corruption and immorality.

Bute stretched his arms to the ceiling, and a glint appeared in his eyes.

"First, I must be admitted into the privy council and then appointed groom of the stole (a secretary to the king)."

The King's heart swooned then raced.

"Good. Good. By becoming groom of the stole, you will gain a seat in the cabinet."

"This will allow us to begin to purge the corruption of Pitt and Newcastle. It will mean, my King, when we are both dead; our memories will be respected and esteemed to the end of time."

In one quick moment, George understood. He thought of a new Great Britain, with subtle curves arrowing to the edge. He opened his mouth, shut it, then laughed.

"My dearest friend, I vow to sit upon the throne with the hopes of restoring my much-loved country to her past state of liberty; and of seeing her in time free from her present load of debts and again famous for being the residence of true piety and virtue."

"Your Highness, our task to reform the public and private morals of the politicians, stand before us, and to inaugurate a new world in which a just king and minister will reward merit alone, instead of bribing the venal and the factious."

George's thoughts triggered explosions inside his head; satisfaction convulsed freely inside him. He realized Lord Bute prepared him to rule.

'The groom of the stole allows you to enter the political contest between the Whigs and Tories."

"Actually, between the Whigs in office," informed Bute, "and the Whigs out of office. We must sort out the various brands of Whigs: The Big, or Revolution Whigs, the Bedford Whigs, Grenvillites, and Chathamites."

Bute believed he would be ready for them, his ambition raw, impatient, and primitive. He noticed some fear in his Sovereign's eyes.

The king's dream hissed loudly – wildly – piercing into him – dragging over reality.

Bute took the king's slender hand as a lover, bowed, and kissed it.

"Politics," Bute said, "smacks of personalities, prejudices, and local affiliations than of intellectually grounded principles."

The candles burned around them to their wicks. The delicate fragrance of power splashed on the king's face and the musty scent of pride. "My concern sees the opposition putting forth that I have sinister designs on changing the Constitution."

With a laugh, Bute stood straight, "Sometimes in life, ignore the worry." He paused, measuring his words. The silence swelled for several moments filling the space between them.

"No trace of enthusiasm exists in you for centralized absolutism that obsesses the minds of so many European rulers."

He thought of the king's needs – needs he ignored until they met.

Both men understood and accepted that. The conversation veered as Bute's words were deliberate. "Our plan must appear to side with Newcastle and leave Pitt with nothing but the popular support. It will help us end the continental war against France and our alliance with Prussia."

"I hope so."

An honest reply, he believed.

Clearing his throat, the king said, "If my dearest friend sides with Pitt, Newcastle will look forward to a speedy retirement."

His eyes opened wide.

"Exactly," said Bute, "our policy must excite and irritate the passion that already exists between the two ministers. Let it leap out and take control."

With muffled music heard from above, flickering candles before them and the art of seduction, they hoped to widen the breach between the ministers to make room for Bute.

With his hand tapping against the polished stone wall, Newcastle said to Bute, "At first, the king spoke cordially with me and chilly with Pitt."

Your suspicions of relations between myself and Pitt are unfounded."

Bute nodded a dismissal of Newcastle's fears as his mind focused on deception.

"The king speaks with little civility to me, treats me with marked reserve, and you and Pitt concert about measures without me."

"Mr. Newcastle," said Bute, "if I become Secretary of State, you and I will make a formable team. The King welcomes any opposition as long as you and your friends support him."

"How does he view Pitt?"

"As an enemy."

"And me?"

"As a friend."

A day later, Pitt demanded to Lord Bute in a clipped tone filled with a sad edge, "I must insist on having some share in the patronage belonging to the Secretary of State."

Something fluttered inside Bute at the thought. He would evade a further discussion. "I must discuss that with King George."

The energy fed on energy, desire on desire.

Delighted, Bute played the game.

That evening he leaned closer as Newcastle told him in a soft voice, "A far more important question: what is his Majesty's real wish and intention towards the war with France?"

Seriousness hovered around Bute's mouth. "The king adheres to the declaration in his speech at the session's opening that the honour of England remains of paramount importance."

"Does the king wish to carry on the war, to obtain a good peace?"

Though his anxiety passed, an air of both victory and defeat entered Bute's consciousness. "Let me say this; his Majesty will carry on the war as long as it seems practicable to carry it on."

The following morning Pitt's tone remained clear as he informed Bute, "Newcastle will withhold the necessary money to bring the war to a successful conclusion."

Bute, his look direct and calm, realized they were treading on dangerous ground. Informing Pitt, "The king admires you," the plot thickened.

"Then, we remain allies and friends."

A forced smile crossed the face of Lord Bute.

Standing by the throne, he detected the sound of children playing in the adjoining chamber. The light seemed low as he took a deep breath, biding his time as the king sucked cream from an eclair.

He strolled to an open window and smelled the honeysuckle from the garden. Turning to the king, he said, "Our new friendship with Pitt should widen the breach between him and Newcastle."

"Have you spoken with Newcastle?" asked his Majesty, his lips white.

"Yes, the real cause of Pitt's attack on me constituted my daring to join and act with him. Mr. Pitt hopes to drive me out and thinks you will not dare to support me, and then he will be master of his lordship ever after."

"Well, we were successful."

"Our obstacle to an alliance of Pitt and Newcastle, a union of aristocratic influence with the popular support, we dissolved," said England's jubilant leader.

"Yes, we separated Newcastle and Pitt. The former thinks we are less determined upon peace and more disposed to give in to and support Mr. Pitt."

Thinking of awakening with the sun on his face, the Monarch said to Bute, "It will be easy to deal with Newcastle."

Standing with conviction, Bute replied, "Freedom from Mr. Pitt and his warlike notions and dispositions."

He paused.

"I beckon you to proceed," said the king.

Bute then announced in a quiet tone, "We must take upon ourselves the burden of the war."

Lord Bute became silent, glancing around the room as if the walls possessed ears. He considered how men could have been so blind and foolish to think the king supported their evil ways with all their political life experience. It would be their ruin.

"My Majesty, politicians always want more than they have, and we must punish treachery, perfidy, and disloyalty."

King George III, by nature a conservative but not a Tory, believed no vital difference existed between them but brought Tories into government, rejecting the Whig leaders who were the family of the men who ruled Britain a century earlier. He strove for non-party government, remembering his father's words, "Never give up your honour nor that of the nation. His critics said, "He wanted to restore royal power and reject the constitution."

Through Bute's efforts, the king granted the Tory, Dr. Samuel Johnson, an annual pension of £300. Afraid the pension would force him to promote a political agenda or support various officials, Johnson asked Bute the king's position.

"With an arched eyebrow, Dr. Johnson approached me, Sire, and asked me about the pension."

"Tell him for me, my dearest friend; he receives it not for anything he must do but for what he has done."

Their eyes blinked in unison.

Not a pinpoint of doubt existed in the king's mind regarding Bute.

Pleased he could help Johnson, Bute walked over and eased down on a chair, bringing up the issue that pained him the most. "Our next goal must be to address the national debt."

George stood up from the chair with a fixed expression.

Bute observed concern on his face.

With authority in his voice, the king said, "We must reduce it!"

The mentor looked at his student with a bold look. He smelled his desperation.

"Do it soon," said the king, "the war with France drains the monies in the treasury."

"We must spend less," Bute said quickly, "and enhance revenues through wiser excise taxes."

The King's eyes lit up briefly, but then Bute shrugged and stared off into the distance.

George III and Bute tried to go on in a secure, practical way for the next four months, the king attempting to laugh, but the pain from politics flashed in his head hard and hot. His mind went blank after realizing his first tour of the policy under the guidance of Bute bombed. Opposition came forward and crushed their aspirations. They tasted the heat. Waves of accusations increased against the tapestry of their reform. The disgruntled Whigs filled the press with allegations: the aims of King George, unconstitutional, the royal favourite, an alien, an intruder, who monopolized the king's confidence and abused his power. And Bute and King George's mother, lovers.

"The tale holds merit with many," said the king, "and petticoats hanging together with enormous boots, a familiar sight at the public demonstrations, denotes a pun on you, Lord Bute."

"Political change, unlike the April sky of spring, stands still, resisting our efforts."

"I hope, my friend, you can bear the strain of incessant attack and criticism."

CHAPTER 10

Burr Confronts a Challenge

"Tell me everything!" Sally said upon Aaron's return from his
ill-fated attempt to venture to sea.

H er brother pointed to the river and smiled. Lightning snaked
across the distant horizon, thunder spoke, but the rain slept as
they strolled to the water.

With a warm gaze fixed on his anxious sister, he pointed to a log.

"Be seated."

With a glint in her eyes, she leaned forward. "Well."

Taking his time, Aaron glanced up at the black streaks, about a dozen,
in the grey sky.

A rush of emotion came over him.

"The captain of an outward-bound ship granted my request to journey to sea as a cabin boy. Despite the putrid, salty scent of the vessels shooting up at me, I focused on the glistening waves rippling under the intense sun, wondering where the sails of fate would land me. Then I espied Uncle walking down the dock looking for me. His head scanned everything in sight."

She giggled. "What did my quiet, serious, sensitive, kind brother do?"

"I clawed my way to the top of the masthead."

Sally felt his fingernails clinging to the mast.

"Come down immediately, Uncle yelled."

"Not until we agree on the preliminaries of a treaty of peace, I said."

"Did he possess that look?"

"Yes, his glare shot up at me, but I held my grip."

"OK, no whipping, and in return, you promise to refrain from such excursions."

"Returning home, I wondered if my future profession should be the law. Uncle told me I displayed all the essentials of lawyering in my debate with him."

Timothy enrolled Aaron in the Elizabethtown Academy, a prep school for the College of New Jersey that Francis Barber and Tapping Reeve started. Reeve observed a sense of wonder in Aaron as he stood upright. His mind open to all points of view.

Carrying a tray with a pitcher of mint tea, Aunt Rhoda set it down on the dining table. The baking smell of cookies that wafted from down the hall tortured the boys more than the girls. Ten eyes locked on the cookies like a magnet.

Aaron, clad in a simple brown shirt, stood aloof. Since learning that his uncle considered sending him to the College of New Jersey, his thoughts centred on his father and mother. Through the window of his mind, he imagined the highs and lows of a conversation between them on the lawn by Nassau Hall. He needed to find a connection to them, and the opportunity came when an essay on Jonathan Edwards by Samuel Hopkins landed in the hands of Uncle Timothy.

Twenty minutes later, after hanging up his memory, not a cookie remained.

"Children," announced Timothy, "assemble by the fire, and each of you will read aloud about our family heritage."

Logs crackled and adrenaline raced. Red and yellow flames shot from the hearth, reflecting on Sally's face.

The reticent Aaron turned from the fire and looked at Sally, who spoke in a calm, unhurried voice, "President Burr ordered on his death bed, that his funeral should not be attended with that pomp and cost, which is an extravagance that is becoming too customary."

A welcoming, raw-edged admiration gripped Aaron. His black eyes radiated a fierce desire to capture the memories of the past. Sadness raced through his heart, absorbing her words as she continued.

"Especially at the funerals of the great and rich, and that nothing should be expended but what was agreeable to the dictates of Christian decency. And that the sum that must be expended at a modish funeral, over and above the necessary cost of a decent one, should be given to the poor."

He held a hand to his eyes. His fingertips wetted by tears. "Why did you die, father?"

During the next hour, in an unbroken stream, other chapters of the book flashed past him. Aaron was lost in retrospection, asking himself if he should stand proud as such a man's son? He found it difficult as his father seemed so different. He wanted to walk in another direction.

When handed the book, Aaron's thoughts drifted to the tree's leaves, turning vivid red. He liked winter and welcomed it. Almost letting the book slip from his hands, he smelled anticipation surrounding him. The ten-year-old's heart skipped a beat before announcing, "A Brief Account of Mrs. Burr."

A memory of her shot through him with frightening intensity – a glare with her upper lip curled.

"She exceeded most of her sex, in the beauty of her person, and her behaviour and conversation. She discovered unaffected and natural freedom, towards people of all ranks, with whom she conversed. Her genius was much more than common."

Aaron hesitated drew a long breath. Uncle Timothy, with haughty eyes, humble heart, and misty-eyed, looked at Aaron, admiring his elocution. Aaron adjusted his position.

"She possessed a lively, vibrant imagination, a quick and penetrating discernment, and a good judgment. She possessed an uncommon degree of wit and vivacity; that yet coincided with pleasantness and good nature; and she represented a playful and sportive nature, without trespassing on the bounds of decorum or of strict and serious religion."

Aunt Rhoda wished she knew her, remembering her through Timothy's glowing terms.

"In short, she seemed formed to please, and especially to please one of Mr. Burr's taste and character, in whom he was exceedingly happy. But what crowned all her excellencies, and was her chief glory, RELIGION."

That wicked word, Aaron thought.

"I want the freedom to choose," he later told Sally, "No matter which way I turn, religion glares at me."

By the end of winter, Uncle Timothy decided the next path for Aaron.

"Succumb or succeed, Aaron needs a challenge," Timothy told Rhoda as he looked at her over his Bible's top.

Unstrained, so at ease, Timothy understood why he fell in love with her – she opened her heart and arms to him and calmed his soul. Taking a deep breath, he said, "While, in his mother's womb, no doubt existed as to his education. He must attend the College of New Jersey."

"Yes," she said, "his fate must stand unaltered, the Burr-Edwards family are to the College of New Jersey as red leaves to fall."

"I graduated in 1757, Jonathan Junior in 1765, Pierpont will in 1768, and Aaron Burr Senior, founded the college and served as its president."

She started to reply but then stopped, weighing her words. "Most of all, I hear – change charges forward in its curriculum.

"Pierpont, informed me a broad program lies in wait to supplement theological studies."

This new curriculum, in a short time, would be forged a cauldron of sedition. It was to take a step forward and crowd the king. Nineteen percent of the signers of the Declaration of Independence graduated from the college.

At the round dining table in the centre of the room, his family members assembled, waiting for breakfast. A weak light shone over the conversation. Aaron swivelled back and forth in his chair before he rose slowly and walked outside. His nerves were up in the air but not his determination.

An eagle glided over him in Princeton's direction, its wings still, the rising hot air acting as a thermal current that created lift. As he possessed no wings, he decided to stretch his legs along the thirty-mile trek from Elizabethtown to the College of New Jersey.

In May of 1767, his eleventh year, on the pre-dawn day, sultry and calm, he left home to visit his uncle, Pierpont. He desired to solicit his help in applying for admission.

When he reached the rutted, red road, not yet baked from the sun, it exhilarated him as he strolled towards his destination. He enjoyed a chorus of sparrows, darting from all directions onto the branches of budding maple trees. They serenaded him as he savoured the sweet smell of prosperous farmlands, enticing fruit-laden orchards and windmills grinding the bread of life. He did not mind that wildflowers no longer grew as they pleased in the fields along the road. The familiar route took him through thriving little villages peopled with men who produced proudly in the sweet and clear air.

"A flower, please," he said.

"For you," he handed it to a child playing by the roadside.

A more giant smile never occurred, he thought.

He continued seeing labourers, mechanics, and servants, who were well clothed and thought of Pierpont's words of, "The lure of American liberty flourishing and commonplace. The curse of taxes not having taken root as in England."

As he neared his destination, the wind caressed the trees with a gathering whisper and began to cool the air. Clouds foretold an assault of rain, and then blackness obscured the sun. He relished the transformation and the declaration of a storm. A hard, massive boom emanated, and long, jagged white streaks sliced the sky. Like a rapid waterfall, rain slashed the ground, and the dry, dusty earth turned quickly to red mud.

He took refuge under a stunted oak. Strings of water slapping the earth around him.

Proud of his choice of shelter, he enjoyed the storm, glad it ended quickly.

Entering Princeton's village, a tavern, a general store, and a few other shops that lined the single street caught his eye.

He stood and watched the sun's light reflect a rouge tint on the windows of the fifty houses surrounding the main street.

Not one slouching in disrepair, he observed.

He thought he smelled fresh paint, and the soft lace curtains that hung at attention on the houses caressed him. The town spoke to him, and he wanted to talk back. Its faint sound riveted him.

In front of him on the broad green lawn on a ridge above the high road, rested the recently built Nassau Hall, a beacon towering to the sky. "The campus," as President Witherspoon later called it, covered 4 1/2 acres.

A strange sensation ran through him. He turned and looked in all directions. Something familiar rang in his ears. The edifice from the basement to the top third floor featured one hundred windows. Aaron stepped back and sat on the moist ground. He shielded his eyes from the light reflecting from the windows. Surveying the massive stone structure that faced north on the high road, Aaron admired a row of young buttonwoods in front of it.

He then focused on the red brick house, home of the president on the NE corner, and felt that he wandered the structure, hearing conversations, laughter, music. Turning to the east, he observed a kitchen building and steward's house that also seemed familiar. To the south, the college outhouse and shed that housed the fire engine and the necessary leather buckets brought back memories.

As he leaned forward, he cast a curious eye at the front entrance where Homer's bust stood, the ancient Greek poet of Iliad and Odyssey fame. *Can I be a pure warrior like Achilles?* he thought.

"Or," he said to the statue, "like Odyssey, a hero who enjoyed an inquiring, evaluating mind and acted with reason, and showed bravery when needed."

The shadow of the imposing building covered him. He blinked several times, and a haunting overcame him. Faint, distant threads, unconscious memories dangled like ornaments from a Christmas tree. I have been here before.

He remembered being shaded by the same shadow. His thoughts turned inward, and he heard his mother and father speaking. He recalled the inside of the building.

"Yes, sometime before, of course, during my infancy," he said to himself.

He felt long, stiff fingers playfully running through his thick hair.

"Aaron." The voice of his Uncle Pierpont, revived him.

He looked up and asked, "Did I ever live here?"

"Yes, in Nassau Hall for about a year."

An image appeared of his Uncle sitting and drinking port on the very lawn; they were now on.

"You gave me a sip of wine, and mother glared at you."

"Get up," said Pierpont, "you need dry clothes."

As they entered the room, Aaron asked, "Whom do I see for admission?"

"The college rests between presidents."

Aaron wondering if that boded well for him. He hurried to freshen up.

The next morning Pierpont took him to the acting president, Mr. Tennent. A shallow, conventional, portly man, with thick eyeglasses resting on a tiny squat nose, was Aaron's first impression of Tennent. The president blinked, wanting out of the airless office. The thickest fingers he had ever seen, thought Burr. He believed him a pig that escaped from one of the farms he passed on his journey.

"Why are you here?"

"I have mastered the requirements for admission."

The acting president listened, but Aaron realized that his mind relaxed elsewhere. Wallowing in the mud of outdoors, he thought, and unhappy being behind an uncomfortable desk having to speak with more than a grunt or two.

"Yes, I know your family's history of the college and your proficiency in admission requirements."

Tennent closed his mouth and walked to the open window.

Annoyed, Aaron mumbled, "Back to wallowing among your papers."

The president turned.

Aaron shot him a half-smile.

The next afternoon Aaron returned to the man-pig's office. His cold gaze fixed on him, resentful that this man determined his future.

"Due to your tender age and small, frail form, you are considered unfit to attend at this time."

"I thought a schooled, prepared mind adequate!"

"You are dismissed!"

Disgusted, Aaron tried to toss his rejection out of his mind, but he believed he heard a chorus of grunts outside the office door. Returning home, he stood at a window looking out, wishing that birds could sing all winter long and that the trees never lose their leaves.

Hearing the Ogden boys and Jonathan Dayton horsing around, he turned to them, studying them with a lover's relentless attention. Hope shook in his head. He ran out and jumped up on Matty's back.

"Glad to have you back, Aaron."

The Ogden boys tackled Matty. Promptly, he dropped Aaron on them and then fell on top of his companions, draping them like an octopus.

He told Sally, "I am determined to show them they made a mistake with a suppressed yell."

"Hmm," her stated opinion.

"And your plan?"

With considerable care, he took two steps back. His pride hurt too much. "For the next year, I will master the subjects required of the freshmen and sophomore students."

"What are they?"

"More Greek and Latin, an absorption with Horace, Cicero's Orations, the Greek Testament, Lucian's Dialogues, and Xenophon's Cyropaedia, the Roman literary critic Longinus and then the ancient languages, especially Homer."

'You just re-read them."

"Yes, with delight, this time, I favoured Odysseus to Achilles.

Then, I will examine science, geography, rhetoric, logic, and mathematics."

"Aaron, I have a plan for you when you are not studying."

He smiled. "What?"

In a voice aloof but clinical, she said, "To undo what the pig said about your frailties and grow you in height."

Disgust raced through him upon hearing an illusion to Tennent.

"Interesting, and how shall this happen?"

"Accompany me."

She led. Aaron followed.

He admired her dark, defined features and her natural and refreshing beauty. Quiet, kind, and conscientious, he knew he could depend on her to follow through with harmony and cooperation. She stopped. He stood beside her, listening to the sounds of nature, wobblers chirping, grey squirrels chattering.

Sally glanced right then left . She pointed. "Notice this pile of rocks."

"Yes," seeing that some were big.

"See this incline?"

"Yes," a 45-degree angle, he thought.

"You carry," she pointed to the rocks, "up the mound and then back down."

"This will make me stronger?"

"Yes!"

He thought of writing a story, but his fingers became so scratched and bruised that it pained him to write, and the tale was abandoned.

"Plants grow after a good rain, followed by the sunshine."

"That seems reasonable."

"When the summer showers release their minerals into this bucket, the water is saved."

"That also sounds logical."

"You will sit in the full sun, letting the sharp noon rays strike your body. You must think, and please note an important point little brother, that you are like a plant."

"Oh," replied Aaron

"Holding the bucket over your head, I will pour the water over you."

Aaron, keeping a straight face, asked, "Any other ideas?"

"Lastly, I think you should climb a tree, and with your hands, hang from a limb as I tug on your feet."

Concerned about his admission to the College of New Jersey, Aaron dug his hands into his pockets as they returned home. They adhered to the regime, several days a month.

"The results, quite un-amazing," he said to his sister.

"I know," she said. "In six months, all your clothes still fit, and you grew only an inch."

A smile, softening his features reflected on the time spent with Sally.

If friends were like a peach, to find one as good as Sally, you must try a hundred, he concluded.

CHAPTER 11

Bute's Letter from a Friend

Bute had spent his nights restless and wakeful. His first reaction was that nothing could remove him from his place at the king's table, but his stern, no-nonsense tone wavered.

Not up to the politics of lies, he informed the king in April of 1763, "The well-organized ill-mannered, and unscrupulous press campaign, despicable like old age, has turned the people against me."

Mobs threatened him with assassination in the streets, hissed, and pelted him with rotten fruit. He read, "if awards exist for misleading, mismanaging, and misappropriating, then Lord Bute would be worth his weight in gold."

All the leading politicians of the day rejected him as violent, distrustful, manipulative, and deadly.

A favourite quip stated, "As dogs bark, Bute lies."

He resigned.

Left without his "warmest friend," George III called in evil men to govern bad men. His new minister, George Grenville, informed the king, "You are obstinate in your prejudices, with a tendency to let your anger turn into a sulkiness. You behave like a child, unforgiving to those who oppose you. You are quite unable to see any merit in a view other than your own."

"You," George said with a glare like a bear at a depleted beehive. He started to object, then slipped his tongue back, thinking himself unprepared for the coming jousting between kingly and Parliamentary supremacy that lingered in government councils.

Grenville, who trained in law but left the profession to enter Parliament as a member of the House of Commons, desired power. Demanding an influential political family, he differed in ambition from many eighteenth-century politicians who wished royal favour. He sought success and approbation in the House of Commons. It became his world.

Without his Lord Bute, George III refused to argue nor possessed the strength to do so. Mainly content with silence, he yelled at Grenville, "I resent your aggressive behaviour towards me."

"Why do I lack the king's confidence?"

King George scowled at him then grunted, shifting his eyes to a spider on the wall, Grenville waiting for him to become more obnoxious than a drunk.

"Your opinions," informed Grenville, "are seldom formed from any other motives than such as may be expected to originate in the mind of a clerk in a counting-house."

His Majesty gawked at him, not letting his new insults result in a wound to his ego.

"Remember Sire; your Bute could not deal with the city's moneyed men whose support funds the government requires. I have been successful in such a negotiation."

The King struggled with his temper and understood. He should have expected it. "You came to the Cabinet, I thought to preserve the Constitution and to prevent any undue force thrust upon the Crown by any body of men whatsoever."

Grenville noticed the look in his eyes and heard it in his voice. He thought, too often, life and politics are tricky. He took a deep breath as he glanced at his watch and yawned.

"You weary me for two hours and then look at your watch to see if you may not tire me for one hour more."

Grenville's hands clasped tightly together. He focused on the king as he informed him. "When appointed to the two employments, First Lord of the Treasury and Chancellor of the Exchequer, which have ever, hitherto, constituted the Minister of Great Britain, I consider myself the Prime Minister and should be addressed accordingly."

Several seconds passed, and then ten and twenty, and finally, his face gnarled like the branches of an elder tree.

King George wanted to end the audience and write to Lord Bute, but they uttered word after word. Pauses dotted every sentence as their patience turned upside down.

"I expect Lord Bute to absent himself from Court."

"But I enjoy my warmest friend's advice."

"Not at Court!"

The wind rattled the windows, and the topic of conversation shifted.

"The times are hard for the common man," responded Greenville.

"For a king as well. Your acts of Parliament have deprived me of sources of income. You and the other ministers made me contribute my revenues from the sale of lands in the Ceded Islands in the Caribbean to the public."

"Rest assured, my goal requires an increase in the public funds under the control of Parliament, and your income does not interest me."

A lack of colour appeared on the king's cheeks.

"Your Highness," Grenville continued, "The total burden of British imperial taxation on our colonies in British America equals 1-2% of our national income, somewhat higher in the southern provinces."

"How many people live in the colonies? Asked the king.

"Over one-and-a-half million. The white colonists in America pay on the order of about 1% of the annual taxes."

The King adjusted his position on the throne, calculating the revenue received.

"We must keep soldiers in America to protect the colonists from further disputes with themselves, the Indians, and the French."

With a sigh, George III understood the drift.

Paying little attention to numerous failures in London, Berlin, and Stockholm and how these bankruptcies stressed an already debtor community in America, both men displayed an ignorance of the consequences to come. Grenville backed the king against a wall, and the ruler felt uncomfortable. He frowned at Grenville, who then elaborated a Stamp Act, with fifty-four sections.

"What do the colonial agents have to say about this?

"Franklin proposed a plan for a loan office that would not only provide income for the government but at the same time supply the colonists with much-needed currency. I paid little attention to it."

The conversation gave the king a headache. The pain ground into his temples.

"The American colonies' population," informed Grenville, "stands at approximately 1.6 million, one-quarter being slaves. They have a literacy rate of 71% among the free."

"They like to read their Bibles."

"Regardless," said Grenville, "they will understand they must shoulder their fair share."

The King, struck by the higher literacy rate in England, noted to himself to ask Bute about this. The long ordeal finally ended, and Grenville took leave.

George III rested his head in his hands and began to rub his temples. Rushing to his study's privacy, he wrote,

May 6, the year you very well know.

My Dearest Friend, Lord Bute,

Since the Treaty of Paris ended the Seven Years' War, the idea of colonial taxation comes as a surprise to none. I listened to discussions through the whole winter of 1763. With the increased burden of taxation on Britain totalling £1,400,000 for the war, every branch of government considered the question of taxing America

As you have undoubtedly heard, a growing general acceptance through our country condones Parliament's authority. Grenville and his ministers believe the prevailing mood in the American colonies favourable to imperial interference and feel the necessity to impose new taxes.

Filled with resentment and self-pity, Bute smelled politics, the tang of conceit, and heard lies. He wondered if George III forgot their discussions.

New taxes will diminish the revenue arising from old taxes and hinder the nation's capacity to meet its debts.

A smile galloped across Bute's face as he thought of Grenville trying to get the king's attention.

The idea of Britain imposing a stamp duty on the colonies, as you know, rests on precedent. Sir W. Keith, exchequer-deputy governor of Virginia, suggested it to Walpole in the wake of the 1733 excise crisis. "I have Old England set against me," said Walpole. "Do you think I will have New England likewise?"

In 1751, Henry McCulloh, a London merchant with land speculation in North Carolina, suggested a stamp duty for the colonies to Lord Halifax, the then-president of the Board of Trade. In 1757, he submitted a scheme for a poll tax and a stamp duty.

One of the secretaries I recently learned of the Treasury, Samuel Martin, in 1759, recommended to Newcastle the imposition of a stamp tax on the colonists.

Bute's stomach tightened. He imbibed a string of profanities through clenched teeth as he thought of the cider tax he advocated to the king, which produced enormous hostility in cider-producing areas of England.

A fortnight ago, Mr. G announced to me his intention to proceed with a stamp duty in the colonies in a year. He said by delaying the introduction of the stamp duty, he hoped the colonies would formulate alternative plans for raising revenue. He refuses to make this explicit to the colonial assemblies. In his opinion, the Stamp Act seems like a reasonable basis for Anglo-American relations, putting British and colonial taxpayers on the same footing and establishing that America should rightly contribute to the cost of its defence.

"His ministry," he announced in the best of moods, "did not proceed with the Stamp Act in ignorance of colonial opinion." He believed the measure would be accepted without protest.

*"The total tax expected by the bill," he informed me, "adds up to nothing big
or fancy, is quite small."*

He smiled. "Expect little popular resistance to these duties," he said.

Bute put the king's letter down. He knew George struggled to decide,
but he asked himself how often he told him to mistrust the Whig politicians. A hundred times, he mused. Wanting to scream or cry, he returned to
the letter.

*He then informed me a stamp duty existed in Massachusetts in 1755
and New York in 1757. "Besides," he told me, "The use of stamp duties in
the mainland colonies finds precedent In Jamaica. A stamp duty existed
from 1760 to 1763 to provide revenues to fund the militia in the face of a
slave revolt."*

*I asked him about a petition to the House of Commons. It pointed out that
there would be grave consequences for the commercial interests of Great
Britain and her colonies should the Stamp Act be put into effect. He sighed
and raised his shoulders before telling me, "I must achieve the final and
effective subordination of the commercial interests of the Americans to the
requirements of our Mother Country."*

He looked at his watch before continuing.

"Your Majesty, may I be blunt."

I interrupted him, "Are not you always?"

*"The bowels of the English treasury are empty and need replenishment." He
came to an abrupt stop and sneered.*

I tried to remember how many times I heard the exact words.

*I queried him. "What are you going to do about the excessive amount
just added to the debt, sixty-million spent in driving the French off the
American Continent?"*

Before I finished my sentence, Greenville asserted, "to hold the newly con-
quered colonies in subjection, and to retain the inhabitants of the Ancient
Provinces in a state of constitutional dependence upon Great Britain."
After rubbing his head for several seconds, Bute paced about his study, think-
ing of Charles IIII's words, "Taxes ought not to be laid upon the inhabitants
and proprietors of the colonies but by the consent of the General Assembly."
With sweaty palms, he continued to read.
"Parliament's right to levy taxes in America lies nearest his heart; I told
him. "If any man," Grenville related to me, "ventured to defeat the regu-
lations laid down for the Colonies, by slackness in the execution, he should
look upon him as a criminal and the betrayer of his country."
About him, an atmosphere of chill and gloom exists. I suggested that my
four principal ministers meet at dinner regularly once a week. Reluctantly,
he agreed, but no real harmony prevails. Grenville's sensitivity and his
suspicious disposition make it difficult for him to trust his associates and his
abrupt and ungracious manner hinders intimacy.

Bute craved a cigarette; something to relax him. A drink would not do
as clock's hands just struck noon.

He realized that dangerous men surrounded his king. "Grenville lacks,"
he said to himself, "those good attributes that should be associated, at least
in my mind, with success in politics and have always been helpful in welding
together a successful party. Yet again, he advised me of his incorruptibility,
resoluteness, devotion to duty, and a strong sense of public responsibility."

I stared at him for several moments before he commented, "You look like
you have seen a ghost." Before I could answer, he said' "I prefer to trust to
sincerity rather than to civility in my relations with other."
I remembered your advice to me all too well before you resigned from Court.
Grenville will try to whittle away at the personal power and influence of
the king.

He told me to my face; God forbid that we should ever give power to the king without Parliament.

I feel the stiffness in his opinions and believe them always in the wrong.

Your prescience shone when you said he wants the decline of the personal influence of the king and to the supremacy of Parliament.

He thinks himself smart and clever. Possessing all the vile traits of a commoner, he takes joy in reminding me.

"You hate to have me, yet in a genuine sense, you wanted me, begged me to serve, almost went on your knee to me."

Bute willed himself to recall Grenville's tight smile and limp handshake. The more the man spoke, he remembered, the more enjoyment he deserved.

I believed him genuine in this, and I wanted him to consent — for the simple reason that the available alternatives constituted a poor choice.

As you know, Lord Bute, my main displeasure with Mr. G stems when he uses violent language in endeavouring to extort anything from me. Upon every occasion when any point comes under deliberation, Mr. G. urges its necessity for carrying on his Majesty's Government.

It should be as he would have it.

When any office falls vacant in any department, he declares, I cannot serve you if the man I recommend fails.

He uses this very remarkable expression. If Men presume to speak to you on business without my leave, I will not serve an hour. I informed him, The king should be permitted to receive advice on public affairs from a private individual. He glared at me.

At just after three the other day, while resting in the Queen's chamber, he requested a word with me. He asked in what way he gave offense to me earlier in the day. Let me count the ways, I thought.

Incredulously, I replied. "I find you too much constrained, and that when you propose anything to me, you act no longer as my counsel but imply I must obey.

Am I out of line, my Dearest Friend, for bringing this up?

Bute sensed the weight in the king's walk; knew the wounds to his pride, sharp, and his anxiety beyond skin-deep.

In 1765, King George III suffered the first of five bouts of deep depression. For a month or two, he had trouble staying asleep and smelled "the bowels of his father not yet sewed up nor the body embalmed" pervading "over the whole house and into his apartment" at Carlton house on the Mall.

The smell hit him like a snowball in winter. For days after this, his appetite disappeared like the sun at night.

Guilt clung on him as morning mist and difficulty surrounded him when required to render a decision, and he felt terrible about not telling his grandfather he was a son of a bitch. Imagining a pack of dogs on a wounded bear, he thought he would be better off dead.

A cultured monarch who liked Handel, Mozart, and botany, he landscaped his gardens, collected scientific instruments, enjoyed taking apart and putting back together clocks and watches, supported penal reform, and had a 40-foot telescope built. He loved to ride horses, played backgammon, received the Transactions on the American Philosophical Society from 1771 to 1801; his topographical map collection included 50,000 maps, atlases, architectural drawings, and landscape watercolours. His library contained 300 books on the American colonies, and his library was open to any scholar who asked to use it. George paid 10 pounds a month for newspapers between 1763 and 1772, wanting to know what was said about himself and his family.

As his reign continued, he watched as the American colonies sought their freedom because they grew up and reached the age of political maturity and wanted independence. Taxation is the excuse, but freedom is their objective. He wanted the pride and glory of Britain and its constitution to personify political liberty, believing in the rights of the people. That kings were servants, not proprietors of the people.

"That's how we created the noblest constitution the human mind is capable of framing," he told his wife, "where the executive power is in the Prince, the legislature in the nobility and the representatives of the people, the judicial in the people and in some cases in the nobility, to whom their lies a final appeal from all other courts of JUDICATURE, where every man's life, liberty, and possessions are secure, where one part of the legislative body checks the other by the privilege of rejecting, both checked by the executive, as that is again by the legislature; all parts moving, and however they may follow the particular interest of their body, yet all uniting at last for the public good."

His beliefs centred on John Locke's social contract. He feared the aristocracy wanted to tip this delicate balance between the prince, nobility, and the representatives of the people, too far in their favour. George's education was classically Lockean.

"I consider the people as the greatest and most permanent security of my throne in Briton," he often said, "and stand for the rejection of absolutism."

But always in the back of his mind was that Britain's excessive debt needed a drastic reduction.

CHAPTER 12

Resolved!
The Spirit of Resistance

In the fall of 1764 the ill-dressed man rode his horse for ten hours on the up-and-down, twisting terrain to Williamsburg, Virginia, His mission was to represent Captain Nathaniel West Dandridge, who hired him to contest the seat of James Littlepage in the House of Burgesses. Proud, his friend, chose him to plead the case against Littlepage for bribery and corruption. He realized the law opened his eyes, lifted his mind in one long quixotic crusade. Glad he did not have to act differently, appear different, or be different, Captain Dandridge trusted him.

It is all a matter of perspective, he told himself. He shot the passing trees a broad grin as he approached his destination. With his plan of action jingling in his head and his horse's trot light, he entered the Capitol, an open square of buildings at the town's end shaded by sycamores, honey-suckle, and crepe myrtles. His sense of nature pleased, breathing the sheep-mint in the air as its mild smell filled the air, he observed foundation walls traced in masonry.

A huge "H" was marked out upon the grass for all to see. Walking through the full passage of the "H," a covered gallery in length, surmounted by a cupola and clock, he sensed his time was now. At dusk, he strolled through the connected wings of the central parts of the two-story brick edifice. It reminded him of the great buildings of antiquity. The hall on the House of Burgesses' ground floor in the western half and the Council Chamber above, with its many windows and a tall portico, evoked in him a wish of election to the House of Burgesses.

He stared at the fronts of each side, fascinated by the lofty colonnades, with iron balconies above. and double doors, each six-feet wide. He traversed the 50-foot long and 25-foot wide foyer floor of flagstone and observed a similar room on the other side, the General Court.

Wanting to address the court, to put his arms around the law, the ill-dressed Patrick, a stranger to everybody, spent two days maybe, three, in and out of the lobby, gleaming the surroundings, his eyes and ears on high alert.

Outdoors, he enjoyed observing robins flitting from one branch to another on the elm in the courtyard. "His observations," to quote his friend Samuel Butler "are like a sieve that lets the finer flour pass, and retains only the bran of things."

Nary a Burgess displayed any curiosity in inquiring his name; the edges of their vanity were sharp and treacherous. He frowned, trying not to feel too sorry. A thought circled through his brain. They will soon know my name. In his old worn coat and hemp apparel, his hand resting under his chin, he found himself wondering about the old establishment that ruled Virginia.

Ushered with great state and ceremony by the chairman, Colonel Bland, into the committee's room, he sat in a high-backed chair done in rich maroon velvet.

"There were some things he could say," wrote the Chairman to his wife, "in the space of a few minutes by a copious and brilliant display on the great subject of the rights of suffrage."

The Chairman's wife never recalled such praise by her husband.

"Superior to anything ever heard before within these walls. Such a burst of eloquence from a man so very plain and ordinary in appearance struck the committee with amazement, so that a deep and perfect silence took place during the speech, and not a sound, but from his lips, uttered in the room."

Relieved, he strode from the room, walked along the eastern corridor, and stood in the late morning light. The sun not very bright, he thought. The Burgesses denied Dandridge's appeal. When Patrick learned of the decision, he muffled a snicker of scorn, "The politics of the House of Burgesses . . . subtle and sneaky."

On his return to Hanover, Patrick realized he wanted to be not only a member of the Burgesses but one who led the crowd. He needed an issue to hang his hat on. To speak the words — and raise the cry.

In London, Benjamin Franklin stirred some milk into his dark tea. *Damn it*, he thought, when he learned of the passage of the Stamp Act. He wrote to Charles Thomson:

> *Depend upon it my good neighbour, I took every step in my power to prevent the passage of the Stamp Act. Nobody could be more concerned in interest than myself to oppose it sincerely & heartily. But the Tide was too strong against us. The nation was provoked by American Claims to Independence & all Parties joined in resolving by this act to settle the point. We might as well have hindered the sun's setting. That we could not do. But since it*

is down my Friend and it may be long before it rises again, let us make as good a night of it as we can. We may still light candles. Frugality and Industry will go a great way towards indemnifying us. Idleness and Pride tax with a heavier hand than Kings and Parliament. If we can get rid of the former we may easily bear the latter.

The Stamp Act law came in as just another purple-gold slant of news through the American colonies' windows. No echo of dissent, just a hush in the dark.

But the tax oozed discontent in Patrick, and his entire psyche became bruised. It wounded his sense of justice and ate at him from the inside. Slated to take effect the first day of November 1765, the colonies' various British officials said, "Did you not benefit & should you not help reduce the enormous British debt that occurred from the late war with the French?"

This sounded reasonable, but in truth, the English authorities feared a new tax on the British populace, like the one on cider, would lead to another round of riots in London and beyond. "All legal documents, permits, almanacs, documents in a foreign language, commercial contracts, newspapers, broadsides, wills, pamphlets, playing cards, dice, and calendars must require the stamp of the king," Gentleman Johnny Burgoyne said to some members of the House of Commons at a private gentleman's club before he joined his mistress.

At the courthouse at Hanover in late April of 1765, men grumbled when they read of the Stamp Act's passage in a Maryland newspaper. They resented that the Act reduced the profits of attorneys and those needing legal help and skilled labour. An apprentice had at least one-half of the weekly wage taken in taxes.

Patrick read in *The Pennsylvania Gazette*, "We hear the sums of money arising from the new stamp duties in North America, for the first five years, are chiefly to be applied towards making commodious post-roads from one province to another, erecting bridges where necessary, and other measures equally important to facilitate an extensive trade."

Men of importance nudged the Act aside and kept a soft voice.

Richard Henry Lee considered taking office as a stamp collector and enforcing the Stamp law. James Otis took a different tone when it came to Grenville's Stamp Act. He declared in 1761, "A man's house is his castle," while resisting the "Writs of Assistance," which allowed British officers to enter any house and brutalize life and make a mockery of freedom. At that time, John Adams had proclaimed to his wife, Abigail, that Otis stood as the child Independence. Now, in 1765, Otis preached it was "the duty of all humbly and silently to acquiesce in all the decisions of the supreme legislature."

Men of backbone and opinion hung back, unwilling to submit and yet afraid to speak out in the language of bold and open defiance, recoiling from the snake in their path. But as with wind and fortune, change lingered on the sideline, waiting. Patrick tried to absorb their way of thinking and swallow the injustice but spit it out.

"No matter what the reason," he said to John Shelton on a lazy Monday afternoon, "the colonies from fear, or want of desire to form an opposition, or from the inertia of some kind or other, accept the light and air of British intervention in their lives. The idea of resistance is absent as honesty is in a den of thieves."

Shelton picked up a mug of ale and downed it. "You pay attention, Patrick. You listen, and you reflect on what is said and written. You make me think."

Patrick held back a tear or two.

"My years of experience tell me," said Shelton, "having something to lose makes one move cautiously."

"Liberty requires us, as humans, to act."

Shelton studied Henry and grinned proudly.

"George Johnston informed me," continued Patrick, "that some of the conservatives in the Burgesses – Richard Bland, Peyton Randolph, Edmund Pendleton, George Wythe, Richard Henry – curb their tongues, talk in whispers when criticising His Majesty, and when sending their protests to the London government, write guardedly."

"It is easy, very easy," said Shelton, "to give in to the prevailing majority."

Patrick weighed his father-in-law's words as he devised a plan to combat tyranny, while locking the Shelton Tavern. By the end of the following week, he approached the mostly wooded area of Williamsburg after a four-day ride. Called Middle Plantation and settled in 1638, it became the village of Williamsburg, named in honour of King William III of England. Situated on the centreline of the Virginia Peninsula between the James and York Rivers, its grounds gradually declined to the shores of the rivers. He studied its location on the high ground and observed it is a strategic plus, halfway across the Peninsula.

A boom of thunder interrupted his thoughts. He hurried past the capitol building, built under a royal charter granted in 1722, to his lodgings at Lewis's Tavern. Bolts of lightning followed and pierced the night.

"Life these days is ever changing, as the face of fate," he wrote to Sally before joining George Johnston, the representative from Fairfax County. *"Learnin' arrived,"* he continued to Sally, *"when the College of William and Mary, named in honour of the monarchs of the time, obtained a royal charter in 1693. Classes began in temporary quarters in 1694.*

It seems, my dearest one, college teaches learnin' not thinkin'."

Though he suspected it, his failures still haunted him more than he realized but contentment swelled to fill the void within him. However, no knowledge bounced within him that he would be completely and irrevocably twined to history from this moment on.

Downstairs at the Tavern, Johnston handed him a glass of brandy. He drank it as parched land absorbs a fresh rain. "The seat of government," said Johnston, "after temporarily residing at Middle Plantation, twice due to fires, moved from the muggy and mosquito-plagued Jamestown, the original capital of Virginia Colony (upon suggestion and presentation of the students of the William and Mary), to here in 1699."

"A good place to advocate against tyranny, my friend."

Thomas Jefferson, knee-deep in research for his mentor, George Wythe, overheard John Fleming, a respectable member of the Burgesses, for the county of Cumberland, tell an anecdote about Patrick Henry, the newly elected Burgess from Louisa County.

"On his first day in attendance on May 20, he spun around to hear Speaker Robinson advocating a plan for a public loan office, to the amount of £240,000, from which might be lent on public account. Of this sum, £100,000 went to redeem the paper of prominent men, deep in contracted debts, which, if called, spelled ruin for them and their families. Of course, with a little indulgence of time the debts might be paid with ease.'"

Henry grimaced and glanced up to check the look in the Speaker's eyes.

They were empty.

"What, sir!" exclaimed Mr. Henry in an animadverted tone. "Is it proposed then to reclaim the spendthrift from his dissipation and extravagance by filling his pockets with money?"

Unbeknown to the members of the Burgess, Robinson knew that discovery of the deep well of his debt to the public, so enormous, loomed at any moment. His plan for the loan office allowed for money lent from the public account to erase his deficit.

Jefferson, his jealousy like a mental itch, a mosquito bite on the brain, left Wythe's office to attend the House of Burgesses. While walking to the chamber, his thoughts of first meeting with Patrick, the Christmas of 1759, rattled through the furrows of his mind. He still frowned on Henry because he engaged in the season's usual reveries and neglected the scientific conversation of Mr. John Campbell, a man of science, married to Mrs. Spotswood, the sister of Col. Dandridge. Henry's manners boarded on coarseness, and that his only passions were music, dancing, and pleasantry bothered Jefferson (and that Patrick excelled in attaching himself to everyone). The law student shook his head, still not understanding the uniqueness of Henry. It seemed, Jefferson reasoned, a matter of surprise, which even yet, amidst all those various struggles for subsistence, the powers of his mind remained stalled, and little surfaced to suggest to any friend the pursuit of his destiny. He seemed, at best, to have been a plant of slow growth, thought Jefferson, yet, unlike other plants of that nature, formed for a duration and fitted to endure the buffetings of the rudest storm. Thomas drew back, doubting Henry's survival.

When he approached the House of Burgesses, Jefferson's eyes went cold, and he let out a long sigh, observing three Negroes hanging from the gallows for robbing a Mr. Walth. Trying to soothe his guilt, he swore to himself he would attempt to undo this injustice if the opportunity presented itself.

At the Burgesses, Thomas stood at the door of communication between the house and the lobby, as there existed no gallery to scrutinize the members of the House – a large proportion of high-principled men, a memorable crop of brilliant men, an aristocracy pledged by its very nature to the general good. It constituted, by the advantages of superior fortune and education, the vigilant sentinels and faithful guardians of the common safety that stood as the natural leaders of the people in a crisis of public danger. They numbered one hundred and sixteen, yet these giants of Virginia society only required 24 percent of the body to constitute a quorum.

Jefferson stood between eighteen-year-old John Tyler and a man wearing a gold cross, probably a Frenchman and French government agent. Excitement circled the three men, Jefferson observing Speaker Robinson sitting with dignity upon the dais but desperate and blinded by his financial situation, oblivious to any formidable opposition to the Stamp Act.

A gilded rod upheld a red canopy above the Speaker. In front and below sat the clerk at a table, upon which rested a silver mace. Some of the Burgesses dressed in velvet and silk, with ruffles and powdered hair, others in rough cloth and buckskin.

Tyler declared, "Thomas, there are only 39 members in attendance."

"Enough for a quorum," replied Jefferson.

Calm and controulled, George Johnston rose.

"I move that the House resolve itself into a committee of the whole."

"I second the motion," said the plain dressed Henry, calm as a purring cat.

Some members sat yawning; others displayed a thorough look of boredom and all expected business as usual.

Nothing reflected in Henry's personal appearance to excite curiosity or awaken expectation. He gazed at his fellow members, their brows crashing and looking like tired children. For a moment, his mind went blank. A chill ran down his spine.

Jefferson was wondering if the fair feet of Henry would wallow in the weeds of his complacency? Then Henry's words appeared.

"The colonies, either through fear, or want of opportunity to form an opposition to the Stamp Act or from an influence of some kind or other, have remained silent."

He dug in his heels, and slowly, the orator of Virginia turned, about to go a bow-shot beyond John Adams, the speechmaker of Massachusetts.

"You know, I have been for the first time elected a Burgess a few days before and am young, inexperienced, unacquainted with the forms of the House and the members that compose it."

Instantly drawn to the words, Jefferson observed Henry's arms move slightly. His powerful, bold, grand, compelling language was picking up speed as his hands moved in broader gestures. His voice rose like that of Reverend Davies.

"Though the night is long and dark, the promise of the morning is sure. I have but one torch by which my feet are guided, and that is the lamp of history."

The members of the Burgesses slumped silently.

Henry gave a quick, man-like snort.

Jefferson emitted a slight chuckle.

Henry's head pulled back, surveying the members of the Burgesses.

"There is none righteous, no not one and we are selfish. Finding men of weight averse to opposition, and the commencement of the tax at hand, and that no person attempted to step forth, I am determined to venture and alone, unadvised, and unassisted. Let us not be like a sick eagle who longs for the sky."

The Frenchman was about to behold a nation's first crawl, thinking Henry appeared to speak as Homer wrote.

Henry's colour rose as he raised the law-book, *Litton on Coke.* "I cannot like the members of this House curb my tongue, talk in whispers when criticising his Majesty, and when sending protests to the London government, write guardedly."

Messrs. Randolph, Bland, Pendleton, and Robinson felt uncomfortable. Their colour turned pale as they leaned back in their chairs.

Jefferson observed a look in Henry's eyes as the latter pressed his hand on the cover of the law-book before reading from his notes.

Resolved, That the first adventurers and settlers of this, His Majesty's colony and dominion, brought with them, and transmitted to their posterity, and all other His Majesty's subjects, since inhabiting in this, his majesty's said colony, all the privileges, franchises, and immunities, that have at any time been held enjoyed and possessed by the people of Great Britain.

Mr. George Johnston seconded the resolution.

Johnston, a friend of liberty, lost in the membrane of historical recollection, lawyered in the Northern Neck. Highly respected in his profession, he was a scholar, distinguished for his vigour of intellect, cogency of argument, firmness of character, and devotion to the cause of rational liberty – in short, precisely calculated by his love of the cause, and the broad and robust basis of his understanding.

Resolved, That by two royal charters, granted by King James the First, the colonists, aforesaid, are declared entitled to all the privileges, liberties, and immunities of denizens and natural born subjects, to all intents and purposes, as if they had been abiding and born within the realm of England.

Mr. Johnston seconded his resolution.

Resolved, That the taxation of the people by themselves, or by persons chosen by themselves to represent them, who can only know what taxes the people can bear, and the easiest mode of raising them, and are equally affected by such taxes themselves, is the distinguishing characteristic of British freedom, and without which the ancient Constitution cannot subsist.

Mr. Johnston seconded his resolution.

Resolved, That his majesty's liege people of this most ancient colony, have uninterruptedly enjoyed the right of being thus governed by their own Assembly, in the article of their taxes and internal police, and that the same hath never been forfeited, or any other way given up, but hath been constantly recognised by the king and people of Great Britain.

Mr. Johnston seconded his resolution.

Resolved, therefore, that the general assembly of this colony have the sole right and power to lay taxes and impositions upon the inhabitants of this colony; and that every attempt to vest such power in any person or persons whatsoever, other than the general assembly aforesaid, has a manifest tendency to destroy British as well as American freedom.

Mr. Johnston seconded his resolution.

"Your flammable resolutions, Mr. Henry," roared a smirking Pendleton, "do little more than reaffirm the principles advanced in our memorial, and remonstrance of the preceding year; that is, they deny the right assumed by the British Parliament, and assert the exclusive right of the colony to tax itself."

Henry replied, "There is a significant difference, Sir, however, between those state papers and my resolutions, in the point of time and the circumstances under which they were brought forward, for the address and other state papers were prepared before the Stamp Act passed!"

"Your resolves are not for law-abiding citizens," added Bland, "with roots, family or even distant friends."

"I beg to disagree, Sir. They do nothing more than call-in question, by a course of respectful and submissive reasoning the propriety of exercising the right, before it had been exercised of addressing the legislature of Great Britain."

"No, Sir," exclaimed Randolph, "your clever calculations predominate with miscellaneous clichés and idiomatic expressions."

"The Stamp Act has been forced upon us by a sick king," replied Henry. "The act is, in my humble opinion illegal, unconstitutional, and unjust."

"Must I remind the members of the Burgess," said George Wythe, "it is our duty to accept humbly and silently the decisions of Parliament."

Henry absorbed the words of the opposition, swallowing their insults, then spoke, "Every attempt," he countered, "to vest the power of taxation over the colonies in any person or persons whatsoever, other than the general assembly, has a manifest tendency to destroy British, as well as American freedom."

The key to liberty warmed in his hand. His eyes flashed, but he remained calm.

Never allowing anyone to stir the ship of their state, the pleasure disappeared from the faces of the Burgesses' conservative members.

Jefferson angled his head, taking in the cold gaze of his relative, Peyton Randolph.

Every word from Henry sends ripples of disgust through him, Thomas thought. "I should have known my mother's family took comfort in his allegiance to the king," he whispered to Tyler.

Randolph stood up, the light on his wrinkled face, "Sir, I do not see the act that has passed as an encroachment on the rights and liberties of the people and amount to a direct charge of tyranny and despotism against the British king, lords, and commons."

"And, Sir," added Bland, "they are a one-dimensional harangue reeking of contrived pedantry. You, Sir, suffer, and we endure," informed Bland, "from excessively heavy prose. Any pleasing moments were clouded by your long-winded failings."

Henry took a deep breath, his eyes again surveying his colleagues. He spoke to the barrage of ministerial pomp as natural as a summer breeze. "Parliament," his voice as soft as first love, "wants to lay on the American Colonies, which they call or style Stamp Dutys."

Feeling his way, he spoke deliberately as his words soared to a crescendo.

"In former times Tarquin and Julius produced their Brutus, Charles begot his Cromwell, and I do not doubt, but some good American would stand up, in favour of his country, but in a more moderate manner."

He watched the rush of motion that came into his foe's eyes.

Before Henry continued, the Speaker of the House, John Robinson jumped up, one of the most opulent man of the colony, the landed aristocracy's acknowledged leader; who chaired the House with great dignity for twenty-five straight years and the colonial treasurer.

"He, the last that stood up spoke treason, and I am sorry to see that not one of the members of the House possessed the loyalty to stop him before he traversed beyond propriety."

Henry shook his head. He knew who buttered Robinson's bread. He stood with a look, trying to catch the meaning of the Speaker's words.

"If I have affronted the Speaker or the House, I am ready to ask pardon, and I would shew my loyalty to his Majesty King George the Third, at the expense of the last drop of my blood, but what I have said must be attributed to the interest of my country's dying liberty which I have at heart, and the heat of passion might have lead me to have said something more than I intended, but, again, if I said anything wrong, I beg the Speaker and the House to pardon me."

Delighted, George Johnston whispered to a colleague, "Messrs. Randolph, Bland, Pendleton, Robinson understand him now, perhaps too well for their good. They fear for their place under their thick arch of power and their right kind of power that brought satisfaction to the British." Several members stood up.

"Hip, hip, hooray!"

Proudly, the plainly dressed man smiled. He took a deep breath, absorbing their energy. He focused his eyes and sighted freedom's face hovering over the assembly.

"I repeat that the Authority of Parliament and the king are abominable. His Majesty is a Tarquin, a Caesar, a Charles the First, and I wish another Cromwell would arise!"

The bodies of the members of the Burgesses stiffened. Henry knew he made an impression and wanted to toy with them and did nothing to hide the fact. He continued with incessant lightning and thunder, with the look of a god, thought John Tyler.

"At the heart of this obnoxious act is the absolute tyranny of George the Third!"

He paused as he said the name of George III.

"Treason!" cried the Speaker, whose lips curved against his cheeks.

Patrick, standing as solid as the principles of geometry, looked him straight in the eye.

"Any person that would offer to sustain that the Parliament of England has a right to impose or lay any tax or Dutys whatever on the American Colonies, without the Consent of the inhabitants thereof, should be looked upon as a traitor, and Deemed an Enemy to his Country."

"Treason, treason!" echoed from one part of the assembly.

Henry faltered not for an instant, but rising to a loftier attitude, fixing his eye on Robinson, and with a most determined fire, finished his sentence with the firmest emphasis, "... may profit by their example. If this be treason, make the most of it."

Peyton Randolph (the attorney-general) came out into the lobby and, while passing Jefferson, Tyler and the Frenchman, uttered, "By God, I would have given 500 guineas for a single vote."

The Frenchman was confused by the statement as Jefferson informed Tyler, "One vote would have divided the house, and as Robinson sat in the chair, he knew he would have negated the resolutions." The Agent of France noted in his journal that night, "The resolutions passed by a very small majority, and the Fifth, the most radical by perhaps of one or two only."

Henry, who unleashed the springs of passion, left town that evening. The next morning before the meeting of the Burgesses, Jefferson and Tyler observed, "Col. Peter Randolph, then of the Council, in the hall, sitting at the clerk's table till the house-bell rang, thumbing through the volumes of journals, to find a precedent for expunging the vote of the House."

Breathing between his slightly parted lips, Jefferson informed Tyler, "A vote took place while he served as a member or clerk."

Randolph continued to turn over the pages while Jefferson thought of Shakespeare, "Words, like daggers, enter in mine ears."

Jefferson slipped the event around his persona and apprehended "prose" uttered in expressive ideas allowed the capable man to make a name for himself.

"Yes," he told Tyler "words can make you immortal, are more powerful than the sword and on the right occasion can silence the thunderclouds of despotism."

The unnamed Frenchman recorded in his journal, "The timid members, who voted for the strongest resolution, the fifth, became alarmed; and as soon as the Burgesses convened, a motion carried to expunge it from the journals, but the "Resolutions" spread by newspaper throughout America with astonishing quickness."

Pierpont Edwards, spending a weekend home from college with his family, looked face-to-face into their eyes with a level gaze. Inspired by Patrick Henry and the Virginia Resolutions, he said, "Patriots took protest to the streets against the Stamp Act slated to take effect in America on All Saints' Day, the First of November 1765, which happens to be the anniversary of that dreadful and terrible earthquake that destroyed the city of Lisbon."

Young Aaron Burr wondered would he be brave enough to fight against England? See smoke billowing across an open field, smell the scent of cannon fire and burning ashes? To stand up in the face of adversity to defend freedom?

"The heart of resistance to British taxation rushes full force in the colonies, an alarm bell bellowing like bursting thunder," announced Timothy. The "Resolutions," were adopted everywhere with increasing variations, and Patrick Henry's name crackled everywhere. His voice was regarded as the great champion of colonial liberty. Its burst created turbulent times. Though common sense, which was not that common, sought to remain in charge, Henry's explosion of words released a spirit of resistance that became bolder and bolder until a majority stood in mob defiance. The colonies put their arms around Henry's resolutions, and the men favouring the Stamp Act stood backed against a cliff.

Patrick stood behind the bar at the Shelton Tavern, listening to his father-in-law read John Dickinson's "Address on the Stamp Act."

"Men cannot be happy, without Freedom; nor free, without Security of Property; nor so secure, unless the sole Power to dispose of it be lodged in themselves. But if when we plow – sow – reap – gather – and thresh – we find that we plow – sow – reap – gather – and thresh for others, whose PLEASURE is to be the SOLE LIMITATION how much they shall take, and how much they shall leave, WHY should we repeat the unprofitable toil?"

Shelton looked up from his seat. "You inclined the ball of liberty into motion."

About to respond, Patrick just shook his head in the affirmative and wondered what next. The light in the tavern changed as the fiery red orb vanished beneath the horizon.

He poured some brandy into his father-in-law's glass and refilled his, imagining the last threads of light lingering for a few moments in the background of his new life. A throng of patrons burst through the door. His spirits shot to his torso. He jumped on the bar, shuffling his feet as he sang a ditty:

> With the Beasts of the Wood, we will ramble for Food.
> Lodging in wild Deserts and Caves;
> Living Poor as Job on the Skirts of the Globe.
> Toward dusk and the welcoming night.
> Before we'll submit to be Slaves.

CHAPTER 13

Alexander Accompanies Nicholas Cruger

In the decade before the American Revolution, Caribbean planters of English St. Kitts and Nevis benefitted from sugar's high demand. Parliament curbed the foreign sugar trade and expanded the protected home market for the planters. This enabled Nicholas Cruger to set up a business in a house rented from Dr. Robert Mears at King Street #8 Christiansted, St. Croix.

Impressed with the young, intelligent Alex, he approached the boy's mother, Rachael.

"Can your son accompany me to the mercantile firm of Archibald Ingram in Basseterre, St. Kitts?"

"Say yes, Mère." Alexander's eyes opened wide.

Alexander queried Nicholas Cruger, "What business do we have on St. Croix on the boat to their destination?"

Cruger observed his light eyes casting a fierce, inflexible brilliance. "Have you heard of the term mercantilism, Alexander?"

The boy's baby blue eyes widened, fascinated by a new word.

"No, what does it mean?"

"The British believe that by statutes and policies, they can controul, regulate, restrain, stimulate, or protect their colonies."

"In what way?"

"By procuring raw materials, a favourable trade balance, and an ample supply of precious metals."

"Sounds like a good way for order to prevail over chaos."

Cruger frowned; his eyes flashed past Alex as the boat docked. In need of food and spirit, employer and employee found themselves at Noland's Tavern on this night, Halloween, 1765, a few hours before the Stamp Act took effect.

A giant of a man with thick, heavy hands, spiked hair, and a red beard turned to Alex, who stood outside the Tavern observing a crowd. He confronted him in a blaring voice, "What are you doing here, baby face?" Alexander locked eyes with the man until the brute became insecure enough to turn away. Upon returning to the Tavern, the youngster informed Nicholas, "There must be 300 to 400 people swarming outside."

The businessman downed his drink and walked with Alex towards the rabble, who continued to build up steam outside. Hearing a man yelling at the crowd, "Lord Greenville says the money will be raised to pay for our defence," they watched the throng hoot and holler. The smell of cheap liquor surrounded their nostrils.

"We must destroy the stamped papers of John Hopkins."

"Who is that, Nicholas?"

"Deputy of William Tuckett, the stamp distributor for St. Kitts and Nevis, and a merchant in town."

Suddenly, the crowd began to march in an easterly direction to the beat of a drum.

Alexander returned to the Tavern. He tried not to think about the disorderly crowd and turned to Cruger.

"What do you know about the Stamp Act?" Alex asked in a squeaky voice.

"A tax on all legal documents, permits, almanacs, documents in a foreign language, commercial contracts, newspapers, broadsides, wills, pamphlets, playing cards, dice, and calendars to help shoulder part of the cost of the late war with France."

"How is it administered?" asked Alexander.

"Documents must bear a tax stamp provided by commissioned distributors who would collect the tax in exchange for the stamp. Some of the revenue would maintain British soldiers' regiments in North America to keep the peace between the colonists and Indians."

"I read," Alexander said, "that violators of the Stamp Act will be tried and convicted without juries in the vice-admiralty courts."

"Parliament rationalizes that too often smugglers are not found guilty of their crimes."

"We are Englishmen, Nicholas, and if Parliament wants to garrison troops or tax, is it not our duty to obey their edict?"

"I often wonder," queried Cruger, "why our leaders accept Parliament's authority to regulate our trade. I prefer to manage my affairs in my way. I side with the soundness of the ordinary individual judgments. To paraphrase, Adam Smith, it is best to fend off attempts, by philosophers and policy-makers, to replace people's judgments with supposedly better systems invented by government."

He winked at his young friend, "I am not averse to a little rebellion now and then."

Alexander pondered the word *rebellion*. Excitement passed over his eyes.

"I do not favour the Stamp Tax," said Cruger. "Bad precedent. Humanity, blessed with natural liberty, is entitled to act on their judgments."

A new world opened up to Alex. His face stiffened in concentration. A state of alertness appeared in his eyes. He yearned to learn about commerce, government, and philosophy.

"The question is," continued Cruger, "who constitutes the legal authority to levy direct, internal taxes, such as the one imposed by the Stamp Act?"

"Is it not the first responsibility of every law-abiding citizen to obey the constituted authority?"

Cruger lowered his body so he could look Alex in the eyes. "Government is three-fourths bloodsucking and the other fourth, at best, bumbling."

"The irrationally of a mob rule scares me, said the orphan, his eyes open wide with fear and realization. "They make decisions that are dangerous to society."

"The Act threatens the standard of living of too many people, my young friend, and wipes the slate of goodwill clean."

A fortnight later, Alexander read in the *St. Croix Gazette* an account of that night's event and the many protests in the Caribbean and North America. He recalled the ever-boisterous crowd as he read, "They marched to the House of Mr. John Hopkins. Once there, they shouted three huzzahs, demanded the stamp papers, and broke into his house. After stealing the stamps from a storage chest, and in an open and Public manner, set fire to 4 or 5 quires of them at the door and watched as the blaze consumed them entirely.

The mob then forced Hopkins to swear to have nothing further to do with the stamps. They forced him to accompany them about three-quarters of a mile out of town to a house where Tuckett rested recovering from a fever. With drums still beating, the mob seized Tuckett and returned with him on horseback to the public market, where he dismounted and was knocked to the ground. The rabble yelling "THE STAMP ACT: High vice, corruption, an unholy stain, SUPPORT IT and your blood will be shed! THE HEADMAN'S axe waits to behead!"

He faced was being murdered but for the help of some Negroes who knew him and rescued him from the enraged populace. He attempted to leave Basseterre, but his escape was short-lived. "A mob of 500 white people" came after him and made him walk back to town. He pleaded with their leaders for the sake of his weak health but was gibed with "gross insults" and obliged to resign his office. He promised to announce his resignation in the newspaper "to avoid being suspended," presumably by hanging.

The crowd then rampaged through the Basseterre's streets to the office of the island secretary, Mr. Smith, without meeting any resistance. They threw bottles and stones and broke windows before pulling down the building's door and ripping some shingles off the roof. They burnt another four or "five quires" of stamped paper.

After accompanying Smith home with great acclamations of huzzas, they went on to the deputy provost marshal office, where they burned "one quire" of stamps. Disorder continued throughout the night with many "Violences and Disturbances," especially against supporters of the act who received "low and public Threats" and taunted with insulting language. Finally, they surrounded the custom house, yelling, but begrudgingly left after the collector declared "over and over upon his word and honour" that no stamps gathered dust inside.

During these episodes, Tuckett fled across the seven-mile channel from Basseterre to his native Nevis. There, he again began on November 2, the day after the Stamp Act took effect, "to distribute those badges of slavery." The St. Kitts "Sons of Liberty" followed him and, joined by other supporters, resolved that they would by "some stratagem, get and burn, or tuck him up," but Tuckett escaped their clutches. They burned two houses in a trail of destruction and hauled up a long navy boat that they loaded with stamps and "set the whole on fire."

Violence did not subside in St. Kitts. "Hardly a Man among them from the highest to the lowest," the Boston Gazette reported, "does not openly show his hearty Abhorrence of the Stamp Law."

On November 5, in Basseterre, a crowd reassembled to parade effigies of the stamp master and his deputy that soon burned in a common pasture. The evening concluded, "with an elegant supper, Drums beating and the French Horns playing, and the last Toast – Liberty, Property, and No Stamps."

In late November, opponents of the Act prevented a new supply of stamps from being landed and intercepted the stamp distributor's correspondence. Tuckett feared revenge and even assassination. He failed to find anyone in St. Kitts willing to serve as his deputy or let him a house. Defended by a small bodyguard, Tuckett reneged on his oath and clung to his office in Nevis, where he remained a ridiculed figure long beyond the Stamp Act's repeal.

In North America, Andrew Oliver, a fourth-generation resident of Massachusetts and in this instance a more or less innocent victim, vigorously opposed passage of the Stamp Act and then, to help enforce it, reluctantly accepted the job of a distributor. On the morning of August 14, he swung in effigy in Boston, on an elm known afterward as Liberty Tree. By evening his effigy burned, and a building of Oliver's thought to have been intended for the stamp office razed to the ground. He resigned the next day.

Early in September, a mob forced the Maryland distributor Zachariah Hood to flee for his life. He escaped over the top of a house at midnight in nothing but his breeches and shirt.

On October 3, 1765, some two hundred New York merchants decided not to import any more goods from England. And they resolved not to sell after the First of January until the Stamp Act met repeal. Within six weeks, 650 merchants in Philadelphia and Boston reached similar agreements.

At Wilmington, North Carolina, William Houston, Esq., Distributor of Stamps, came to this town on the 16th ult., upon which three or four hundred people immediately gathered together, with drums beating and colours flying, repairing to the house of said Stamp Officer and insisting on knowing, "Whether he intended to execute his said office or not."

He replied, "I should be very sorry to execute any office disagreeable to the people of the province."

"That is an inadequate answer."

Carried into the Court House, he signed a letter of resignation satisfactory to his distractors.

On All Saints' Day, November 1, Nicholas Cruger, with a warm gaze fixed on a quiet Alex, announced, "The Stamp Act according to its provisions failed to go into effect because its execution became utterly impracticable."

Alex said with a half-smile. "I guess business will continue as usual without the stamps and without any duties collected."

"I heard from an acquaintance in New York that Benjamin Franklin, caught by the first light of protest, swept away his pragmatic stance of accepting the Stamp Act. He decided upon hearing his acquiescence to the Act put a mob, torches in hand, in front of his Philadelphia home, threatening to set it ablaze."

"Who is Benjamin Franklin?"

Cruger responded absently, "That is a long-winded story; perhaps another time."

Ships cleared from both islands with unstamped papers.

The governor offered a reward for information about the riots but met with no success.

Young Alexander left with the impression that a mob making decisions means an abandonment of rationality and a danger to society.

INTERLUDE II
THE LOYAL SUBJECT VERSUS THE PENNSYLVANIA FARMER

The rain drummed down on a crowd of people gathered on the dock by the ship slated to leave for London, England. Benjamin Franklin peeped through his thick lenses and waved to his friends. His first visit in 1724 as a young man bolted through his mind. He squinted, downing an impulse to laugh. Going back to London evoked the same pleasure as it did thirty years ago. The passengers stared at the man with the Cheshire smile on his face. They noticed the thick calluses on his fingers. He stood for several seconds, a pale wet statue, remembering Sir William Keith's voice, the Royal Governor of Pennsylvania.

"Pick out and bring back printing equipment. I will make sure a letter of credit awaits you." No alarm bells sounded then; he trusted the governor, who gave him an amused look. Calling up the silliness of his hopes and dreams that he would return and open his shop and start a newspaper, he chuckled.

His ship landed on Christmas Eve. He now thought he heard those singers tolling. But then he remembered how his heart sank to his midsection when learning that no letter of credit, nor any money for the printing equipment or to pay his expenses existed.

Left stranded at the age of 18, in a foreign land, he reminisced how he joined a band of carollers and sang to his heart's content. At the same time, oil lamps sparkled in the dark, cold streets.

Befriended by Becky and her gang of performers, he slept at their flat. Two days later, he sought out Samuel Palmer, a famous and prestigious British printer, and took a job. For eighteen months, he worked to earn money to pay for his trip back to Philadelphia. During this time, James Watts, another well-known London printer, employed him. "A character-building event," he told a well-shaped female on board the ship of his present voyage. "I learned every angle of the newspaper trade from type to headline. My residence in Little Britain, a centre for printers and booksellers, and a lively hub of political and religious debate schooled me like I was at Cambridge." He went on like this, exactly like this, for hours.

"Pennies compounded turn into dollars earned," he told a group of female listeners." He tightened the belt at his waist with an easy tug so that his pants rested on his hips. "I returned home with Mr. Thomas Denham, a shopkeeper who hired me when we returned to Philadelphia on October 11, 1726. I soon set up my own printing business and published, may I say, one of America's most successful newspapers, the *Pennsylvania Gazette*." In 1733, he began *Poor Richard's Almanack*, and for twenty-five years his homespun wisdom attracted the imagination of his countrymen, delighting him.

Sleep came easily for Franklin, the first night of his present voyage. He dreamed of the magnet of politics and how it drew him in as a councilman, a Pennsylvania Assemblyman, and a Deputy Postmaster General. Tossing and turning, he could not get local citizens' views in the legislature passing laws and print that the Penn family overrode the government.

He yelled out, "What right have you to exploit the governed's rights through your interpretation of the Royal Charter?"

He remembered his second trip to England. He was hired by the colonists in 1757 to represent their concerns about the Penn family's arbitrary authority, their failure to uphold the guarantee of popular liberties in the Charter of 1701 to King George II, and their exemption to pay taxes on their enormous landholdings. He talked, the British authorities listened; all drank, nothing happened.

Home from London in 1762, he smelled the fresh breath of Philadelphia and thought as the ship docked, we each must define ourselves. Friends gathered at his residence, and bottles passed freely. Crows swooped by the house, annoyed by the chit-chat of voices. They took flight into a nearby tree, squawking.

"We should do this once a month," said Joseph Galloway.

Franklin blinked, felt his just shaven face, yawned, and thought of sleep. Catching himself, he announced to his guests, "You know that I do not love the proprietary and that he does not love me, so I decided to tell him to his face. He laughed and walked away, but I followed."

"You violate the ideals of the colony's founder, your father. Our Civil Union begets our Civil Safety and the sound Principle of government."

Franklin's body shook as he conceived of his contempt for Thomas Penn, more than he felt for any man living.

"Penn's eyes fixed on me," said Franklin, "with a strange mixture of hatred, anger, fear, and vexation."

Annoyed with himself for letting his hair down to his guests, he announced, "We should consider putting the colony under England's controul. I do not foresee any major obstacle."

Dimples flickered on his cheeks. He sat down with a pint or two of beer, not thinking of John Dickinson.

The two men butted heads the following year over the colony's Western parts' politics and the issuance of paper money as legal tender. Franklin backed a compromise through the Assembly that linked an allowance of paper money with a provision that allowed the Penns to require sterling for payments to them.

"This accommodation signifies a fundamental injustice," pleaded Dickinson, "a precedent for propriety prerogative, and contradictory to the maxims of equity and the spirit of liberty."

As often would be the case, his voice fell on deaf ears.

The agreement passed, but Governor Penn rejected the legislation, and Franklin informed his political machine, "All hopes of happiness under the Propriety Government have evaporated."

At his wife's estate outside of Philadelphia, Dickinson read with amusement that the compromise failed, biding his time for the Assembly to next meet. A report with twenty-six resolves endorsed by Franklin reached the legislature. It denounced the propriety system and wanted the government lodged in the hands of the Crown.

Swaying in his chair in the Assembly, Dickinson sprang up. "The present time demands no divisions of any kind in his Majesty's colonies; but for the closest union."

A majority stared at him, and a member asked, "On one hand, you say you are against hasty innovations, but on the other, we must fight against past errors."

"From my point of view," explained Dickinson, "society lives in a continuing state of ferment. Agitation and controversy, a necessary part of life, implies that the spirit of freedom remains active in people."

He stopped and paused, thinking that he missed the tranquillity of the countryside.

"Why?" Asked Dickinson, "would the king believe the colony desired to come more immediately under his command when they do not obey those royal commands already signified to them?"

"Your concerns towards the royal government, Mr. Dickinson," said Franklin, "are like a child not wanting to open the door to his room because he thinks a monster waits on the other side."

"Sir," retorted Dickinson, "I believe rule under the Penns less odious than seeking allegiance to the home country of King George III."

"What do you base that on, Mr. Dickinson? The whim of a woman?" asked Joseph Galloway.

"Sir, the history of government denotes something of a cycle, in which those who repeatedly govern extend their power and must be beaten back – of necessity by violent means. England, since the Glorious Revolution of 1688, experienced a giganick increase in royal power. In 1756, the monarchy allowed German mercenaries to garrison on English soil. A precedent for the Crown and Parliament to strengthen their authority and gratify every desire of Ambition and Power at the expense of truth, reason, and their country."

"Mr. Dickinson, to quote Shakespeare," said a man from the Western part of the Colony, "'methinks you make much ado about nothin'.'"

"Sir, the ministers of the Crown are mere sycophants, and the members of Parliament are often the most ordinary men elected through widespread corruption, the buying and selling of votes, the employment of alcohol and coercion to disable hostile electors, and the use of perjury to gain the vote of unqualified friends. Virtue and talent lack in the Commons, with the Lords and in the ministry."

Dickinson stopped and took a deep breath. He smiled, thinking of patience and perseverance.

"For these reasons, I am against the change of government meditated before our assembly. I find much offense in proprietary policy and dislike the Penns' government and its evils. They interfere with our legislature, prevent it from appropriating money for defence. I would end it if it could be done with the security of the province."

Franklin rose but not before pouring some cream into his tea. "I believe American and British interest to be aligned, and the danger of Ministerial or Parliamentary action would not open the door in Pennsylvania to schemes of taxation."

"May I point out," said Dickinson as he gave his chin a little poke with his thumb. "The Crown attends to vest the government in Pennsylvania advantageously to England and establish garrisons in our colonies. I do not lightly go against a plan sponsored by Benjamin Franklin and Joseph Galloway to replace the colony's proprietary system of the Penns with a royal government. If this change could take place with all our privileges preserved, let it instantly take place: but if they must be consumed by the blaze of royal authority, we shall pay too great a price. The moods in London are changing, and we must be aware. Royal Liberty is an oxymoron."

Dickinson looked across the Assembly, perceiving blank eyes and men in a trance. He wished to feel their pulse. "I choose to side with the people and against any man or plans subversive to their rights. Our rights must remain unaltered by the royal government unless b y the consent of the governed."

Mr. Dickinson," replied Franklin, "I do not like that Pennsylvania remains 'owned' by the Penn family. They are the final rulers of the colony. I believe in the great faith and the goodwill of the authorities in London to undo wrong."

"The Colony's legislature made up of local citizens needs to pass its laws."

"The Penn family can override any legislature if they chose to do so."

"Then the citizens must petition, protest in a non-violent manner, refuse to buy imported British goods, and then, if necessary, stand in open disobedience to the offending laws."

At the upcoming Assembly elections, Franklin met defeat, and Dickinson gained re-election. The proponents of the royal government in the Assembly appointed Ben as their agent to plead their cause for the "blessings of royal liberty" before the British ministry.

"Yes," Franklin said aloud as the ship neared England in early December of 1764, "this Dickinson stings like a thorn in my side. A real pain in the ass."

To think, recalled Franklin, he dared to publish the pamphlet, *The Protest Against the Appointment of Benjamin Franklin as Agent for the Colony.*

"Does he display respect for my popularity with the voters of Philadelphia and Royal authority? No! He demeans my years elected to a seat in the Assembly, even though I did not campaign for office, and my duties required absence from the province. He turns his head to the fact my defeat came from the hands of the Rabble, who lied when swearing they met the property qualifications to vote. And to imply I am out of favour with the British Government, when I constantly have and uniformly since used my influence in the Province promoting the Measures of the Crown. Does he not see, I am a man who holds a profitable Office under the Crown, and can expect to hold it no longer than I behave with Fidelity and Duty that becomes every good Subject?"

The light turned dull and dark on the still water. "For sure!" Franklin said to the Atlantic, "1765 will be the year Royal Liberty comes to Pennsylvania."

The Penns' rule continued because a slew of laws passed by British authorities silenced the anti-proprietary plan of Franklin.

As he did on his previous trip, Franklin enjoyed comfortable lodgings at the widowed Margaret Stevenson's house at 36 Craven Street. She and her daughter Polly became close friends to Franklin; family is a better name. Polly enjoyed teasing him, "You have become less a lodger than the head of the household."

"Because I enjoy living in serene comfort and affection!"

She handed him his cup of tea without cream.

He stayed in London, representing the colonists of Pennsylvania before the king. He later became representative to His Majesty from the colonies of Massachusetts, New Jersey, and Georgia. Franklin resided eleven years in London. He set up a laboratory at Craven Street investigating topics as diverse as the common cold, magnetism, and lead poisoning.

In Pennsylvania, Dickinson continued to preach, "Parliament possesses no more right to tax the colonies than the colonial legislatures have to tax the citizens of England."

In 1768, Dickinson wrote *The Letters from a Pennsylvania Farmer*.

I am a farmer, settled, after a variety of fortunes, near the banks of the river Delaware, in the province of Pennsylvania – The Dictates of my Conscience command Me boldly to speak on the naked Sentiments of my Soul – The colonies and Britain, form one political body, of which each colony stands as a member. Their happiness remains founded on their constitution and is promoted by preserving that constitution in unabated vigour, throughout every part – The colonies are parts of a Whole as limbs that must bleed at every vein if separated from the body – I am surprised that little notice has been taken of the Townshend Act. It is as injurious in principle to the liberties of these colonies, as the Stamp Act –I must conclude it is, first, a misunderstanding of the legitimate reach of government – Millions entertain no other idea of the legality of power than it is founded upon the exercise of power – They voluntarily fasten their chains, by adopting the pusillanimous opinion that there will be too much danger in attempting a remedy or another opinion no less fatal that the government's right to treat them as it does.

His essay ruffled the colonies smooth and peaceful calm and turned it into a popular disorder wave. *From a Farmer* became a toast from Massachusetts to Georgia, "The friend of Americans" and "The Benefactor of Mankind." His essay spoke the general sentiments of the American people of the time. Constitutional opposition, not rebellion, was the method of Dickinson's *Pennsylvania Farmer*. Still, by the summer of 1775, the conversation steered towards armed rebellion, leaving Dickinson to decide how to proceed.

CHAPTER 14

Jefferson Levels a Mountain & Builds a Foundation

T homas Jefferson watched Rebecca Lewis Burwell weave her way through the dance floor, leaving an image as stark as a funeral procession. A mortal wound of sadness pierced his heart.

"Why me?" he said.

His teeth chattered as he tried to think of words to say. Striving to put her out of his mind helped some, but he realized his future was ripped from under him. Blending into the crowded dance floor and disappearing from his view, he pined for her, as a songbird does a branch. He wanted to go after her, but a net draped over him. "Why are you leaving me?" he mumbled.

A ripping headache tore against his forehead as he thought there must be other means than matrimony to soothe the flames of desire. Returning to his lodging at William and Mary College, life, without her, ate away at him. He could not forget his first love. As the days passed between reciting Greek and Latin and reading Locke, he realized slaves would do as a device to extinguish his concupiscence. "Enjoy the moment," he repeated to himself.

Watching one friend after another became engaged, he took his mind off "what he was doing wrong." While paddling the Rivanna River, wild and romantic memories of being in a canoe with Rebecca were forefront in his mind; he realized that the river prohibited boats from carrying crops from Albemarle farmers to markets; he decided to proceed downstream to see if the situation allowed correction.

Discovering that the rocks below Milton Falls hindered the river from serving as a vital route for his and neighbours' crops, he successfully solicited private money to remove the stones. The colonial Assembly noted Thomas's "laudable and useful" project and granted "the clearing of the grand James River's grand falls, the river Chickahominy and the north branch of the James River."

He raised a glass of wine to his lips, it revived him, and the regret of Rebecca left his consciousness. Following in the footpath of his father, Thomas exuded mirth. While in Williamsburg, he liked to run the mile from his lodgings to the law office of George Wythe, whom he studied under.

"Clears my mind," he told his friends.

Behind his desk, Wythe looked up at his apprentice.

After huffing out a breath, Thomas asked as he stepped forward, "Was the slave hanged?"

"Yes," said Wythe in a stifled voice, "yes, he was hanged."

"And what," inquired Thomas, "became of his younger brother?"

Hopelessly, Wythe lowered his head.

"He was hung too, for abetting in the theft of the cow."

The blood drained out of Thomas's head; Wythe watched each drop flow out and his red hair contrasting with his pale cheeks. A long silence followed.

"He was only ten," said Thomas.

In 1764, at the age of twenty-one, the conditioned, toned bachelor inherited 40 plus slaves, 16 horses, 45 head of cattle, 135 hogs, and 5,000 acres of prime land along with his father's desk, bookcases, cherished books, maps, original surveying notes and journals, surveying instruments, and his account books as Albemarle's Surveyor. More delighted than he could remember, with Rebecca not stabbing at his heart, a feeling of contentment settled over him. He found he could indeed relax and, in the shadowed light of dusk, began to categorize his father's books.

After listening to Patrick Henry address the Burgesses, Thomas knew the skill of oratory beyond his ability. Embarking on a study of the political arts, he hoped to reach his fellow men's hearts and minds. Through the effort of Governor Fauquier, "the ablest man who had ever filled that office," according to Thomas, son and mother reached a rapprochement.

"Mrs. Jefferson and Thomas," said Fauquier. "Peter loved you both; honour his memory, and be a family."

Jane rose and laid her hand on Thomas's shoulder. "The past stands firm," she said. "But is not the future open?"

Thomas mulled the matter over in his mind and said, "Yes."

Sunshine flooded Fauquier's soul.

"As Shadwell is a convenient stopping place to and from Williamsburg," Jane said to her son, "have your friends and acquaintances spend a night."

She soon observed his skill in engaging others, listening, and not being the centre of attention.

"His voice, his articulation, his actions have blossomed," she wrote a relative. "And I feel in some small way: I contributed to his writing with grace and conviction."

As his mother sealed the letter, she recalled a dinner party she attended with her son. The hostess, an intelligent and dignified Virginia matron of the old school, was famous for her cuisine. Jane remembered the glow that adorned her face. Boasting that Thomas inquired with great particularity how her best dishes were compounded and cooked, a glow adorned her face.

"I know," she said, smiling to Jane, "this was half to please me but, he is a nice judge of things, and you may depend on it; he won't throw away anything he learns worth knowing."

Jane knew her late husband; Peter would be proud to know Thomas observed this rule regarding all facts thought worthy of record. Thomas decided to set out in the spring of 1766 to Philadelphia for inoculation for smallpox by Dr. William Shippen Junior. He recalled when his father sent him out to the woods with a rifle when he was ten to see if he could survive on his wits in the wild.

"Yes," he said to himself, thinking back, as he walked through the foreboding forest; everything scared him: the low hanging branches, the jagged rocks he climbed over, the swiftly moving river, the sounds of creatures in the thickets. The frustration ate at him, but did he not carry on? *Yes*, he remembered, and then that "a wild turkey caught in a pen." He gleamed with joy as "he tied it with his garter to a tree, shot it, and carried it home in triumph."

His father beamed with joy as he presented him with the trophy.

He realized not as the woodsman of his father, but how hard a trip could be through the civilized land, he thought.

With his shoulders back, his spine straight, and his chin high, Thomas, accompanied by Juniter, rode alongside his one carriage horse.

Juniter, born in 1731 in Conakry, Guinea, was the oldest son of a prince. Taken as a young child by British traders who supplied slaves for the Spanish and Portuguese colonists in America (80,000 a year), he, at first, ended up on St. Croix bound by a Doctor Fawcett. Bought by a member of the Randolph family who visited the island, he ended up at Shadwell, as Thomas's personal slave.

"Master Tom," said Juniter on the first day of their journey, "you goin' too fast."

With a lopsided smile and tightness in his eyes, Thomas turned his head towards Juniter before letting out a yell as his horse run away with him. Quickly, his slave curtailed the runaway horse, preventing the breaking of his master's neck. A slight smirk draped on the slave's face as he attached the horse to the carriage. Unfazed, Thomas whipped his stead and raced ahead. Later in the afternoon, Thomas experienced the same problem; his horse ran away with him and greatly endangered his neck's breaking.

Towards evening, he observed Juniter sticking out his tongue, and he realized, from experience, this meant the slave was in deep thought.

"Feels like wet weather comin'."

"Yes, yes, I am sure it will," laughed Thomas, "Just like the last time you predicted rain."

Juniter's mouth twisted into a vivid semblance of a grin.

Thomas went to bed early, his enslaved servant thinking rich folks must have their way.

At sunrise, they started and proceeded into a copious storm.

"Never seen a downpour this hard," said Juniter with a straight face.

Thomas glared at him. For two hours, they trudged forward without meeting with a single house to which Thomas could repair for shelter.

On the third day approaching the Pamunkey River, Juniter said, "Looks like it deep at the ford."

Ignoring his observation, Thomas rushed forward, the water so deep as to run over his cushion as he sat on it.

"Master Tom, look a rock."

Before Thomas could react, one wheel mounted the boulder, which was as high as the axle. Juniter threw his whole weight on the mounted wheel. With all his skill in the doctrine of gravity, he prevented the centre of gravity from being left unsupported, allowing his master to escape the danger.

Thomas thought of taking Juniter by the arm and looking into his soft brown eyes and curly hair and thanking him but did not want to give him any satisfaction. The trip continued as a nightmare. Thomas wanted for a moment wanted to chuck it, but his instinct was to dominate.

On this occasion, he confessed to himself that violent hydrophobia seized him.

Stopping at Annapolis," he wrote to Dabney, "the houses incredibly beautiful and better than those in Williamsburg. I visited their Assembly that happened to be sitting at this time. Their upper and lower house, as they call them, sit in different rooms. I went into the lower, sitting in an old courthouse, which, judging from its form and appearance, was built in the year one. I was surprised on approaching it to hear as great a noise and hubbub as you will usually observe at a publick meeting of the planters in Virginia."

Continuing to Philadelphia, he admired William Penn's city, which was the first to codify freedom of religion, individual rights, trial by jury, and a democratic assembly as the pillars of a constitution amendable by the people.

Being that blacks, he believed, secrete less by the kidneys and more by the skin's glands, he decided inoculation for Juniter. After his vaccination for smallpox, he proceeded to New York, where he boarded in a house with Elbridge Gerry of Massachusetts, educated by private tutors. He entered Harvard College at the age of fourteen.

Juniter was always a call away, minding his own business, Gerry, thinking it a mistake to interfere between a master and his slave. With a B.A in 1762 and an M.A degree in 1765, Gerry joined his father's merchant business.

By the 1770s, they numbered among the wealthiest people in Massachusetts.

"What do you know about the Virginia Resolutions?" said Gerry.

Jefferson stretched out his arm, his face barely visible in the afternoon light filtered through the hemp curtains. "I was present when Henry spoke."

Gerry's face lit up like a jack of lantern.

He leaped up, "Tell me about Henry and Virginia."

"Very well," said Thomas.

"You will get a peep into all. After several hours of talk and bottles of Madeira, Gerry turned to Jefferson. "I would be pleased if you made notes on the customs and manners of Virginia and sent them to me."

"Feeling as I do about Virginia, I think I will."

Upon returning home, Jefferson was admitted to the bar in 1767, and he addressed the grave of his idol. "I am ready, father, to make my mark in society." One of his cases involving the thief of a bottle of whiskey and a shirt.

In or out of the courtroom, Thomas never hesitated to obsess on Elizabeth, the attractive bride of a close friend, John Walker, whose connections ran deep with the Jefferson family. Walker's father, Thomas, a doctor, was an executor of Peter Jefferson's estate and watched over young Jefferson.

John and Thomas boarded at Maury's school, and they attended the College of William and Mary. They often darted out of their rooms and talked along the hallways about life, death, and love. Both men were rising stars in Virginia politics.

Agreeing to join a delegation on route for Fort Stanwix, in New York, for Indian negotiations, Walker made Thomas first among his executors, considering him his best friend. Living a short distance to the Walker residence called Belvoir, Thomas visited Elizabeth. While her infant daughter napped, the twenty-five-year old's heart was racing, or maybe he thought it was hers, his hope soaring, he tried to make love to her. Her rejection unfolded like a flower, and on another attempt and another, the result was the same. Unabashed in his shortcomings, he stood tall when he should have hung his head low. Before the sun rose, he mounted his horse, Gustavus, and rode the 2 miles from his mother's house at Shadwell to his little mountain, Monticello.

He noted it took eighteen minutes this Sunday of May 15, 1768.

A t the base of his mountain, he observed the man who had agreed to level the mountaintop.

"A good morning to you, John Moore."

Moore's head cocked back at a 45-degree angle staring at the top of the mountain.

"And to you, Mr. Jefferson."

"You appear quite blissful this chilly morning," said More.

"With your help, my life-long dream climbs towards reality." His eyebrows lifting, Moore studied Jefferson. "Well, let us ride through the thick forest and ascend your steep, savage hill."

Reaching the swirls of mist at the summit, Moore surveyed east, west, north, and south, thinking the mile ride up as slow as Satan's ascent to Paradise.

"The House must be situated on the very summit of the mountain, on a circular level."

The blue and misty mountains, now lighted up with the sunshine.

"I want a commanding a view of all the surrounding country, Charlottesville's small town of the winding Ravenna River."

Moore took notes.

"It must have a view of the blue ridge and the distant mountains from the north side of the house."

"I can see why," said Moore, "how much of an area do you want levelled?"

Two hundred fifty square feet at the northeast end by Christmas.

Moore scratched his chin with the forefinger and thumb of his right hand. "How much are you prepared to pay?"

"80 bushels of wheat and 24 bushels of corn, 12 not to be due until the corn is harvested."

"What if solid rock has to be dug?"

"Then we will ask indifferent men to settle the part between us."

Elected in the winter of 1768 to the House of Burgesses as a representative from Albemarle County, he would serve with Dr. Thomas Walker, Elizabeth's father-in-law.

While waiting for the Burgesses to convene, he attended plays: Shakespeare's *Merchant of Venice*, Thomas Otway's *The Orphan*, and John Gay's *The Beggar's Opera*. He threw his heart and soul around the theatre, thinking nothing touched him the way it did.

He watched the farce by Henry Carey, *The Honest Yorkshireman* with his friend, Governor Francis Fauquier. He learned the next morning that he died that night, the veins in Jefferson's forehead showing. Shock and a feeling of unreality overcame Jefferson. For the first time in his life, he worried about his mortality. On the north side of Bruton Parish Church was the burial site. It was a short distance from George Wythe's house. There, Thomas learned his enlightened friend wished to have his body autopsied.

"He wanted to become more useful," said Wythe, "to his fellow creatures by his death than in his life."

Jefferson frowned at his mentor, knowing the governor's witty voice booming down the staircase of the palace was gone from their lives.

Not quite a delegate for ten days, the issue of supporting the circular letter of Massachusetts to protest the Townshend Acts came to the floor of the Burgesses. The new Governor, Botecourt, dissolved the Assembly on May 17, 1769. Jefferson walked with his colleagues to the Apollo Room of the Raleigh Tavern. They debated which "measures should be taken up in their distressed situation for preserving the true and essential interests of the colony."

The Virginians vowed not to consume or import goods from the mother country before leaving Williamsburg. Conflict and crisis now stared at Jefferson. He paused, smiling to himself, the rooms of his ambition waiting to be furnished.

Later in 1769, with the House of Burgesses about to reconvene, Richard Bland, a cousin of Jefferson, agreed to act as a surrogate for him.

"Cousin," said Jefferson, "I have observed that the whole commerce between master and slave is a perpetual exercise of the most boisterous passions, the most unremitting despotism on the one part, and degrading submissions on the other. Our children see this, and learn to imitate it; for man is an imitative animal."

Bland frowned at this ominous observation.

"The parent stomps," continued Jefferson, "the child looks on, catches the lineaments of wrath, puts on the same airs in the circle of smaller slaves, gives a loose to the worst of his passions, and thus nursed, educated, and daily exercised in tyranny, cannot but be stamped by it with odious particularities."

An hour later, Bland rose in the Burgesses, "I propose that this assembly grant the owners of slaves the permission to emancipate their slaves, thus transferring emancipation from the General Court to the owners of the slaves."

"You ask us to allow the individual slave owner the right to unilateral authority to free slaves?"

"Yes, this choice should be beyond the governor and legislature who decide, but be up to the planter, a request for freedom based on 'meritorious service.'"

Seeing Bland "treated with the grossest indecorum," Jefferson realized he stood to lose popularity if he pursued principle.

At the General Assembly, Jefferson and allies proposed an amendment as part of a revival of the laws, "the freedom of all slaves born after a certain day, and deportation at a proper age."

Deportation because free whites and free blacks cannot live together peacefully.

"The public mind cannot bear the proposition of emancipation and deportation."

"Yet the day is not distant when it must bear and adopt it, or worse will follow."

"Nothing is more certainly written in the book of fate than these people are to be free, nor is it less certain that the two races, equally free, cannot live in the same government. Nature, habit, opinion have drawn indelible lines of distinction between them."

The political animal in Jefferson realized that to pursue abolition, coupled with deportation, was political suicide.

"There is nothing I would not sacrifice to a practicable plan of abolishing every vestige of this moral and political depravity."

Jefferson never shied away from words, but it was deeds that hindered him. Robert Carter, a Virginia planter, freed his slaves in 1791, realizing the blight of slavery incompatible with the moral issue.

Mr. J elected to ignore the ethical issue and rationalized, "The revolution in public opinion which this cause requires, is not to be expected in a day, or perhaps in an age, but time, which outlives all things, will outlive this evil also."

In man, there is a mass of sense lying in a dormant state, and which, unless something excites it to action, will descend with him, in that condition, to the grave.
– Thomas Paine.

CHAPTER 15

Little Burr, Bigger Dreams

"It is human nature for the British government to want to pass the burden of taxes onto the colonies' shoulders," said Timothy Edwards. "It all started with the Stamp Act."

"They consider the American colonists more or less as tenants," responded Pierpont, "who are expected to furnish products such as tobacco, sugar, and ships' masts."

"And they," continued Timothy, "expect the colonies to refrain from producing for export certain products such as woollen cloth or beaver hats; to buy imported manufactured goods exclusively from Britain; and not to indulge in bothersome dreams of economic self-sufficiency or, worse, self-government."

"Since Parliament repealed the Stamp Act," said Pierpont, "it has been one tax after another."

"Life turned complex in a very short time," said Timothy.

"Boys, are you listening?" asked Pierpont,

The two Aarons, Ogden and Burr, and Matt Ogden nodded. "English authority burns around you. You will eventually have to put out the fire."

"Why are they always trying to pull the wool over our eyes?" asked Matthias.

Burr was thinking to follow the money. He dragged his fingers through his thick black hair.

"Since they passed the Declaratory Acts," said Pierpont, "they believe they have the authority."

"Even though Parliament failed to give the colonists representation in the Parliament," said Timothy.

"They think we are sheep," said Burr, "and expect us to enjoy their shears."

"Baaaaaaa, baaa-baaa," issued from the mouths of the Ogden boys.

Pierpont tried to suppress his chuckle but ended up bursting into belly-aching laughter.

The three boys continued baaa-baaing as they crawled around on the floor.

Timothy appreciated the boys' humour but, after several seconds, struggled with his temper that he wanted to vent towards the mother country, "Where do they find the nerve to think Parliament has absolute legislative power over the colonies."

A silence descended awkwardly. "And if that leaves our hair uncurled," continued Pierpont, "Parliament then passed the Townshend Acts in 1767."

The boys stood stern and proper, suppressing the desire to smile. Timothy nodded his approval of their present decorum.

He turned to Pierpont, "Their coffers are constantly in need of more revenue in the colonies to pay their governors and judges' salaries."

Pierpont, cut in. "I read in an English newspaper that the Chancellor of the Exchequer, Charles Townshend, the second son of a Viscount, hoped to pick up a sum of £40,000 for the English treasury."

Burr moved his shoulders a vigorous, uneasy motion, imagining the whoosh of soldiers marching.

"Well, it is too bad he did not concentrate more of his energy on farming," sallied Timothy. "He pioneered the use of turnips in crop rotation, earning the nickname Turnip Townshend."

"He died," informed Pierpont, who took a deep breath, "somewhat suddenly, on 4 September 1767."

"Choked on a turnip," said Burr. His smile widened for a moment.

Sitting back, Timothy appreciated his nephew's remark. Glancing down, he shook his head.

"These hounds of tax tyranny are rushing to the gates of the colonies. Their desperate murmurings triggered protests inside the colonies after they occupied Boston in 1768 with British troops."

"Dissent begins, like a small stream," added Pierpont, "growing as it runs, gathering its momentum from the undue reign of authority."

His brow furrowed. "Do not the colonies want to stay as Englishmen?" asked Aaron Ogden.

"They do, cousin," said Burr, "but more from inertia."

Resting his elbows on his knees and relaxing his head into his hands, Pierpont, then straightened and announced, "I sense a giant disorder rising like a sunrise."

Timothy waited a moment until he knew he could speak calmly. "Few, if any colonists, want the umbilical cord to Mother England severed."

Not wishing to leave this dire statement hanging in the air, Pierpont, quoted his valedictory oration on Civil Liberty. "It is lawful for every man, and often an indisputable duty, to hazard his life in defence of his civil liberty."

The two Aarons and Matty began whistling, out of tune, "Yankee Doodle Dandy."

As fresh challenges clouded an already blurry horizon, young Aaron Burr watched and listened, fascinated by all impulses. But he devoted every waking moment to gaining admission to the College of New Jersey, on his terms. In 1769, Aaron petitioned the College to grant him status as a junior at the age of thirteen. He glared with pent up anger as he read the letter denying his request but granting him admission as a sophomore. Disappointing news but not as frustrating, he would learn, as wet gunpowder.

In the summer of 1769, James Madison stood on the lawn in front of Nassau Hall with his slave, Billie, after an eleven-day trip from Virginia. He continued to stand, all five foot five of him. He expected the students to introduce themselves to him.

Three months elapsed before Burr met him and took his measure. Never once fantasizing how their destinies would rise like flour and yeast; Madison, a sweet loaf, Burr flat and stale. Madison held within him an image of superiority, but his classmates dubbed him "Jemmy." They all received nicknames. Aaron's was "Little Burr."

Madison and Burr, two differing minds pure and straightforward: Jemmy, grave, not a free spirit. Little Burr, light-hearted and a free spirit; these qualities determined their future.

Jemmy loved to bathe in the words of praise but not too much because he then wondered, "Why?"

Madison was the one man, James Wilkinson, failed to sweet talk with a bray of laughter and a slap on the back. The fresh stream of Jemmy refused to bathe in praise from Wilky. He heard the crunch of falsehood in the speech of Wilkinson.

The stone structure of Nassau Hall housed the president, tutors, students, a library, and classrooms. It stood in contrast to the two hundred acres of dense woods that surrounded it. Hear the bell, clang, clang, clang, and the man who rang it day in and day out – John Witherspoon, the Scotsman, recently arrived from England, who became the sixth president of the College of New Jersey.

Time, distance, and direction was never lost on Witherspoon. His ancestors fought to keep liberty alive. Quick as a lover's wink, he understood the situation in his new country and became involved in the American struggle for freedom. He worked a lot and dreamed a lot more. The common enemy, the British, reinforced his resolve. He would be a signatory of the Declaration of Independence.

The college teachers consisted of three tutors and President Witherspoon, who taught Classics, French, Hebrew, Theology, History, Eloquence, and Moral Philosophy, divided into Ethics and Politics. There, at the College his father nurtured, in the fall of 1769, the "Bell" became part of Aaron's life. When it rang, it sent reports of pain to his head that hurt much, and his body experienced tingling sensations.

There were seventy-five or so students, whose family paid twenty-five pounds to attend. They ate, slept, studied, played, and prayed within the one hundred seventy-seven feet long by fifty-three feet-wide Nassau Hall. On its walls hung pictures of British kings and Governor Belcher of New Jersey.

Past the front hallway towards the rear of the first floor was the Chapel, 40 feet square. The students experienced its coolness in the summer and its cold in the winter. On Sundays, when public worship commanded, they attended, except for sickness. There was one service in the morning and another in the afternoon. It seemed peculiar to Burr that one needed a constant reminder not to stray from the road to salvation. The corridors of heaven, he judged, stayed wide enough for both saints and sinners alike.

As the growing schism widened between England and her colonies, the students' anger started to swell like the tide coming in. The more radical ones, Philip Freneau and Henry Breckinridge, wished to hang George III in effigy between the kings' portraits but never could acquire the rope. Burr suggested that they learn to weave, but they just grinned at him with fixed expressions of amusement.

Instead, they decided to let their words promote revolt and created a satiric, poetic dialogue, "The Rising Glory of America," at the commencement in 1771. One particular refrain of their performance deserves mention, not for its lyrical skill but the irony it would portend for Burr's future.

> A thousand Kingdoms rais'd, cities and men
> Num'rous as sand upon the ocean shore;
> The Ohio shall glide by many a town
> Of note; and where the Mississippi stream
> By forests shaded now runs weeping on
> Nations shall grow and states not less in fame
> Than Greece and Rome of old.

Any ragged, small acts by Great Britain resulted in fresh wounds in the students of the College. Listening, little Burr took it all in and sensed a battle approaching. He dreamed of raising a sword. Nations grow, Burr thought, from men who dare to dream, the essence of a future expedition in 1806.

The second floor of the library sheltered at least 1,500 books. Whenever Aaron walked the library, he observed without fail; the snow faced Jemmy lost in Grotius, Puffendorf, Machiavelli, Locke, Sidney, Montesquieu, Hume, and others, never comprehending that action is worth a library of theory.

Little Burr's eyes visited Jemmy's treasure trove as he read them as part of Witherspoon's course on Moral Philosophy. But the cynic in him believed Government, no matter how many times a man tries to thwart its power, "yields not to the tug, but only nods," as John Dryden mused. Future generations attempted to punch holes in its plan, allowing it to grow in strength and "turn to sullen state," concluded the poet.

The third floor housed the students in a chamber, forty-nine rooms in total, each with a central study twenty feet square, two large closets for bedrooms, and a window. Aaron hated the notion of being confined there, trapped by his indecision. He kept an eye peeled for amusement, any amusement that might lift his spirits.

President Witherspoon, a strict disciplinarian, imposed a rigorous curriculum that started with walking through the halls at five o'clock every morning clanging the Bell. The loud, joyless, metallic sound woke Aaron from his Don Quixote dreams. Wanting to sleep through the clanging, he knew a servant would pound at the door, and if he remained in bed, an introduction to the floor would occur.

After the bell rang, the students dressed within thirty minutes, and then prayers happened in common. At six o'clock, Aaron marched with other students, straight-faced and without a smile, in seniority to the library for two hours of study in philosophy, history, science, the principles of public law, and rules of criticism and taste. At eight o'clock, the students retired to the cellar, where the dining room's food awaited them.

Teachers and students ate together by edict at three tables: seniors and freshmen, juniors and sophomores, and third-table grammar schoolboys. Those of the upper class sat in alphabetical order and moved up one seat daily so that each student might sit by a teacher.

As they ate grilled meat or fish and sipped tea, the tutors examined them on the previous day's lectures. On the other end of the cellar, the classrooms, and at nine o'clock, formal classes began lasting until the president's clanging bell at one o'clock.

The students then retraced their earlier footsteps and repaired to the dining room to choose soup, fish, meat, gravies, potatoes, vegetables, and sour fruit tarts, a Witherspoon favourite. The tarts were not a darling of Jemmy, and in their future years in politics, little Burr would bring him some, only to see his face drawn downward.

For two hours, from three to five, study hours transpired. Burr often strode the short distance to the tavern where the stage for the New York-Philadelphia route stopped. He sampled the menu of news from beyond Princeton.

After studying intensively during his first year and achieving praise, ennui overcame him. His ambition hissed softly, and his desire shifted. "The serious limit their freedom," he told Samuel Spring, a fellow student. Spring rolled his eyes to the left and spoke in a mild tone, "Oh, Aaron."

"Not work, but play will make me free," said Aaron.

The British edicts said too often and too loudly prompted the College of New Jersey students to develop an ever budding hostility towards their English cousins. Ignorant and unaware that their actions checked the colonies' impulses and plagued the new land of promise and opportunity, they cultivated disobedience.

In July of 1770, a letter, intercepted and seized on an alleged tip-off by Hercules Mulligan, became known. When the students at the College of New Jersey found out that some New York merchants would not abide by the non-importation agreement and invited Philadelphia to follow their course, rage crowed in their eyes. Burr suggested that they, in black gowns, march in procession to a place on the grass in front of Nassau Hall as the bell tolled. With Homer's bust staring at them, the letter went to flames by the hands of the hangman. The students then sat in silence for several minutes. Burr eyed Witherspoon, watching him from the corner of his eye.

A week later, Burr met two sisters in their early teens, not yet hardened and cynical of life at the tavern at the Princeton-Kingston Road. Their eyes peeked out from under eyelashes as Burr inspected them. Taken with his appearance, always in his favour, the sisters felt he possessed the best part of beauty, an elegant visage, a sleek figure, and charming speech. Impressed that he, so small, entered as a College student, they asked him to "lorn em some readin' and writin'."

The forbidden fruit of the establishment stimulated his palette, and he spent hours engaging and observing the most adamant and idle conversation about the politics of the day. The unaccredited institution complimented Witherspoon's course on Moral Philosophy.

"Men rise," he wrote Sally, "not from the book but the head of ale. The essence of humanity whiffs among the burning cigars, the spilt liquor, the steam of passion exhibited through friend and foe at the tavern. The concern for a stranger to someone in need and the general merriment of citizens socializing under a neutral roof intrigues me."

Here he developed a fondness for mechanics, tradesman, carpenters, coopers, tanners, millers, blacksmiths, and apothecaries.

"When reason rules," he said to the sisters, "the passions, like a musical concert, are in unison; but when emotion becomes excessive, it inflames the mind."

They felt nervous, he realized. Hearing these words in a smooth voice left them confused. He observed their hands trembling as they glanced at one another.

"In a polished society," he announced, "the passions are naturally moderated and made subservient to the rules of decorum."

He felt the angst in their hearts loosening just a little.

"Aaron, skittle off," the girls giggled, "or be late for your class."

Burr shrugged and smiled, and quiet love eyed Burr from the girls' hearts. Whatever he desired would have to wait.

He moved fast on foot from the tavern for the lecture by Witherspoon that began at three o'clock. With beads of sweat glistening on his red-cheeked face, he sat next to Samuel Spring, "Oh, Aaron, when will you become more solemn."

A grin flashed, child-like and fast on Burr's face. Drawing his class-mates and President Witherspoon's attention, Aaron dared his teacher to ask him a question.

"Plato, Mr. Burr, wanted to banish orators because their power is dangerous. What might you say?"

"I believe him in error. The same argument could be turned against the pursuit of excellence in any field. Learning of all kinds encourages virtuous men to defend themselves against the wicked."

"What types of activities are good and bad, right and wrong?"

"I believe Socrates would agree the study of human conduct and values teaches that the human condition is never permanent."

"What do you draw from that conclusion?"

"Well, Sir, enjoy your good fortune and be not too scornful in misfortune."

"Class adjourned," said the Scotsman.

During Witherspoon's tenure at the College of New Jersey, 21 of his students went on to become founders or presidents of colleges, 13 governors, 20 U.S. senators, 33 members of the U.S. House of Representatives, three U.S. Supreme Court Justices, one vice-President, and one a poet of some note, Phillip Freneau.

The curriculum clock necessitated that prayers begin before the students ate their buttered bread and drank hot chocolate. Burr did not like getting down on his knees and wanted to screw his heart shut to religion. It made him warm and cold simultaneously.

At six o'clock, the pupils dressed for the evening in a tailcoat and silk stock, satin breeches, white stockings, and silver-buckled shoes. Their heads adorned with powdered wigs as they strolled into the assembly hall to listen to another sermon.

Aaron pushed back the words and rubbed his face. "Well, heaven and hell are not that far apart."

At seven o'clock, they returned to their rooms studying and being monitored by the tutors. At eleven o'clock, the Clanging Bell of the indefatigable Witherspoon rang in all its glory, requiring the students to extinguish their candles and undress for bed. A fleeting, bitter smile touched Burr's lips. He tossed in bed, uncomfortably. "Stand ready," he told himself.

Despite the arduous study routine, little Burr and his fellow students felt the necessity to exert the joys and pranks of youth. On more than one occasion during the frigidness of winter, the president's bell disappeared, and when found outdoors, Burr volunteered to return it with flapper frozen in a block of ice to Witherspoon. With a harsh, suppressed frown, Weatherspoon received the bell. A loud silence followed before he dismissed Burr, who refrained from smiling.

The underclassmen's outhouse caught on fire all too often, and one better be cautious when using it on a cold night.

After some light-hearted banter about philosophy with Samuel Spring, gunpowder's sound reverberated through the third floor of Nassau Hall. Burr jumped up from his chair. He heard laughter and rushed towards it. He encountered Henry "Harry" Lee and his younger brother, Charles. Henry was laughing, but Charles was crying. He immediately knew that the fair-haired, blue-eyed, spirited, long, and husky lad from Virginia would be a friend, with an ironic sense of humour. The next day he joined with Harry as they placed a considerable amount of gunpowder in the room of the practical jokers who put Charles in tears.

Stargazing grabbed the attention of many students. Several telescopes landed on the topmost floor of Nassau Hall, and the students spent endless hours gazing through the barrel.

"The telescope is for scientific adventure, to focus on the stars, not peep into a girl's' bedroom," announced President Witherspoon.

Not able to suspend any student because the entire class, housed on the floor, gazed, he delivered an exhausting and severe sermon.

You know it is in vain to think

That men of sense and spirit

Will ever cease to swear and drink.

After this episode, President Witherspoon decided to encourage the formation of societies.

The roommates, Madison and Freneau, revived with their friends Hugh Henry Brackenridge and William Bradford, Jr., the extinct "Plain Dealing Club" as the American Whig Society. They advocated total independence for the colonies. For two years, Aaron debated with them, but then quit due to William Patterson's influence, who had remained connected to his alma mater, the College of New Jersey. He helped Aaron restore the Cliosophic Society, whose motto meant, in praise of wisdom.

Paterson, the future governor of New Jersey, planted a seed in Burr.

"The New-Englanders denote an inquisitive kind of being, prone to foolish curiosity and will open letters not meant for their eyes." He would, in time, realize this did not only apply to the curious New Englander.

Two decades later, as politics came to play a more significant part in his life, he conducted a good part of his correspondence in cipher. Like many prominent men, he wanted his words invisible from the peeping orbs of the Post Office.

The Cliosophic Society centred on legal philosophy. Paterson asked at the first meeting, "Do you defend a client for murder if you know they are guilty?"

Skirmishes between the two societies naturally came into play: poems and prose posted and retorts assigned – a subtle rivalry developed between Madison and Burr.

"Yes, I planned," stated Jemmy.

"Amazing," murmured Little Burr.

"Sorry," Jemmy said stiffly.

"Not good enough," responded Burr.

"You are wrong."

"Nothing new."

"What is it you want?" asked Burr

"To strip the flesh from society."

An angry colour flushed on Burr's cheeks. Words erupted from his mouth

"The bad granted," said Aaron, "but the good along with it?"

Madison's jaw tightened, and he walked away.

"To regenerate a new coating particular for your purposes is like eggs soon to turn rotten."

Burr walked around the campus, punching holes in Madison's attitude towards society. The course of his college education happened quickly. Aaron received first prize in reading English and attained second place in Greek and Latin in his sophomore year. The third prize went to Harry Lee, who placed first in translating English into Latin.

When the seniors Jemmy, Brackenridge, and Freneau graduated in September of 1771, Burr, as a Junior, received a first-place award in reading English, spelling, and reading Latin and Greek. In September of 1772, Burr graduated with first honours for reciting the English language and spoke at his graduation on "Building Castles in the Air."

"Man should not dissipate his tour of life on dreams. He should plough the earth and plant some hope so that future generations can enjoy the harvest."

"Well, father," Aaron said to himself, "point me towards my destiny."

He stayed at Princeton for a year after graduation, frequenting the library, poring over many books, notably the French philosophers and parliamentary rules of order. He pondered what path to travel and steered his conversation towards "the weaker sex."

"They have the same mental ability," he wrote Matty, "as men do, with less ego."

With an innocence that flowed like a stream through a dream, Burr knew a decision awaited. What should he do with his life?

Visiting Elizabethtown in the summer of 1773, he sailed, hunted, and talked about the coming war and women too, like young men do.

The choices for an educated and gentleman's son meant medicine, the ministry, or law.

With confidence in his abilities and judgment, none of the avenues left him smiling. Sometimes he scowled, not sure about life and what lies ahead.

As the full moon rose another fraction of an inch higher, Burr squinted out into the sky, and time dragged on.

CHAPTER 16

A Letter to James Hamilton

As a slight shower fell, the temperature was warm and humid outside the Cruger store in Christiansted. Suddenly, the drizzle turned to a hard rain that beat down on the roof. Alexander looked up; he liked the rapid succession of beats on the metal roof. Continuing to nibble on his middle finger's fingernail, he reviewed a prior shipment of sugar, rum, and cotton to New York.

His heart beat faster, thinking of New York. Nicholas Cruger's stories of the town left him with the desire to live there. He promised himself that he needed to find a way to go. He then checked the calendar with a cold gaze to refresh his memory of the upcoming week's exported goods. There must be more to life than being a clerk. He knew he must reinvent himself.

Done with his task, he strode over to sacks of flour and plopped down. His bottom felt comfortable, but his stomach shrank until it felt like a hard, cold rock. He knew what he thought would solve his problem. A jar of ink and sheets of papyrus resting nearby called to him. His hand found a nearby quill, dipped its tip into the open jar, and with an easy swirl, his wrist graced the paper with a stream of words.

Honoured Sir and Beloved Father,

I take up my pen to give you an imperfect account of my life up to the Fall of 1772.

In time, thrown upon the bounty of my mother's relations, the Lyttons, some of whom you might recall, were wealthy.

But riches can be as fleeting as the wind, and it blew like a hurricane through the family, leaving misery widespread.

I have come to understand that this world that binds us as a chain is selfish and rapacious. I sit here wondering how to tell you about Mère.

On February 10 of 1768, she and I contracted yellow fever, James miraculously spared.

The next morning a white woman, Ann McDonne, applied a cold compress to our heads. Mère's condition lingered.

She turned for the worse, and after a week, James appraised our situation to the nearest doctor, Agedius Heering.

He lives on Queen Street with his wife, two white female servants, and slaves.

He performed a bloodletting on Rachel and gave her "fever medicine."

An emetic and more fever medicine prescribed to her the next day. I received "cooling medicine."

Dr. Heering then gave Mère fever medicine with valerian, a decoction, and alcohol for her head on the 19th for «Elicks.» He ordered a chicken and administered a "clyster" and bloodletting.

I remember hearing the doctor explain to James, "By removing the "tainted" blood from the patient, the disease should be purged."

For your information, father, Emetics induce nausea and vomiting—another purgative.

Valerian: a plant-based drug acts as a sedative.

Decoction: the result of extracting a water-soluble drug by boiling.

Clyster: an enema.

The treatments ultimately killed Mère, my dearest friend.

On the night of February 19, 1768, at 9:00 PM at the age of 38, the light faded from her eyes. Buried the following day at the Lytton cemetery, reserved for their family when the plantation sold.

In black veils and James with new shoes, I watched our parent lowered into the g round, her coffin draped in black cloth.

Parish clerk, Daniel Oxley, conducted the services and recorded it in the St. John's burial register.

An island shower made its presence but, as usual, passed over in twenty minutes.

A rainbow then stretched across the rolling hills floating an arc of red through orange, yellow, green, and blue to violet.

Weakly. I smiled, knowing she would have enjoyed the colours. The memory still sends ripples of pain through me.

Mr. Dipnall provided bread, eggs, and cake, her favourite meal.

Though death grabbed my branch of support in life, and a strong wind surrounded me, I refused to succumb to adversity.

Loss is part of life's cycle. We live, we die. What grows must decay.

I thought you should know that the Dealing Court's review of her estate showed her as a competent businesswoman. They noted, "her bookkeeping in good order, and that she could apparently meet her payments."

Between you and me, sir, and the great divide that separates us, I did the books.

Our hard-earned belongings included 6 silver spoons, 7 silver teaspoons, 1sugar tongs, 4 dresses, 1 red skirt, 1 white skirt, 1 black silk sun hat, 1 chest of drawers, 1 chest, 1 bed with 1feather comforter, 1 long pillow, 6 leather chairs, 3 different tables, 14 porcelain plates, 11 cups and saucers, 3 stone platters, 1 porcelain basin, 2 irons, 1 iron pot, 2 metal candle holders, and 1 mirror in a brown frame.

In the following days, I did not think life could get much worse for James and myself. But that malicious vulture, Johan Michael Lavien appeared, (now a custodian at a Frederiksted hospital) with his divorce decree in hand. The famine of his vengeance, never-ceasing, he insisted through his crooked teeth, stained from Dutch tea, that we owned no legal right to any of our inheritance, being "whore children." (James did not speak or smile for a month.)

The Dealing Court agreed and awarded everything to his twenty-two-year-old son, Peter, who lives in South Carolina.

At the auction of our rightful property, Peter Lytton purchased our books and a few other items.

It became apparent to me, and I informed my brother, "The law, like a spider's web, uses us, as its nutrition."

I shall never forget that the welders of real power in society are those who can manipulate the law.

Someday I hope to tame the cold eye of privilege.

To refresh your memory, my relative, Ann, mère's older half-sister married James Lytton, a successful planter, who possessed a considerable fortune.

They departed for St. Croix, circa 1737, after a strange plant disease and drought left a large scar on Nevis' lush vegetation.

Three of their children, Peter, James Junior, and Ann, would affect my brother's and my life. As you might recall, James Lytton Jr. went bankrupt in 1764, creating a big scandal. He absconded with the family schooner and hijacked twenty-two slaves. He sailed for the Carolinas. His actions forced James senior to sell his estate and move back to Nevis in late 1765, shortly after our family moved to Christiansted from Nevis. His wife, Ann, my aunt, died within one year. James Lytton Senior, distraught over losing his wife and busy coping with his children's financial and legal problems caused became distant.

Life's harsh rust showed.

Fearing that we would be homeless as dogs in the street, James and I became wards of the thirty-two-year-old widower, Peter Lytton.

He lived with his Negro lover, who wore earrings as big as chandeliers and whose eyebrows resembled a bent bow.

They produced a son named Don Alverez (Don Valesco).

After living with cousin Peter for seventeen months, in July of 1769, we found him "soaked in blood in his bed."

Financial setbacks in several business ventures and his most recent failure in Christiansted's grocery business contributed to his suicide.

I had advised him and offered to help with his affairs, but he ignored me like green corn.

His father, Peter Lytton, became as lifeless as the grave he too would soon enter.

He died a month later and decided to change his will five days previous to his departure but failed to leave James and me a penny. We were crestfallen as Shakespeare's dried pear. As I faced the ground floor of poverty, fortune placed me with Thomas Stevens' family on King Street in Christiansted. His son Edward, a year younger, became my best friend. When he (I call him Ned) sailed for British America to attend King's College on Manhattan Island, I must admit that my eyes swelled and a tear or two wet my face. After turning down an apprenticeship to a carpenter, Thomas MacNobeny of Water Gut, James went off on his own. I have not heard from him.

My bright eyes turned solemn. I miss him dearly.

A few years ago, I wrote my absent friend, Ned, a heartfelt and honest letter. "Ned, my Ambition remains prevalent. That I despise the grov'ling condition of a Clerk or the like to which my Fortune &c condemns me. I would willingly risk my life though not my Character, to exalt my station. I'm confident, Ned, that my Youth excludes me from any hopes of immediate advancement, nor do I desire it."

I intend to prepare the way for my future. I am no philosopher you see and want to Build Castles in the Air. My Folly makes me ashamed and begs you will conceal it.

Father, I trust you will forgive and do understand my impatience, for I fear for the uncertainties that the future will bear on me.

Now, I must mention to you that on another day of warm weather and not much of a range in temperature, about 83°F, with a light ocean breeze at the L-shaped storefront I labour at (Beekmans' name gone, Kortright in by the way); I stumbled upon a week old *Royal Danish American-Gazette*, January 26, 1771.

For your edification, this semi-weekly first appeared on July 7, 1770, and is the only newspaper published in the Virgin Islands.

Having the desire to have a poem published, I browsed my competitors, and an article by a correspondent on a slave insurrection on Tobago caught my eye.

"They attacked Mr. Hamilton's house the night I left; wounded three white men desperately, two of whom are since dead; Mr. Hamilton received a shot through the thigh, but walks the road recovery."

I must admit to you that I shivered and turned as pale as the linen I inventoried. Having not heard from you for over five years, I presumed, the "Mr. Hamilton" must be you.

In the following months, I found myself depressed and relieved at the same time, until a ray of sunshine struck my jinxed life.

Anne Lytton, my cousin, returned to St. Croix after the suicide of her brother and the death of her father in 1770. Her kindness sweetened every beat of my heart.

I know you will be at peace in knowing that.

If you recall in 1759, she married John Kirwan Venton, who then bought a sugar estate. By 1762, his boiler house burned to the ground killing seven slaves, and he went bankrupt. His creditors took their home and effects. They left their daughter with her parents and sailed to New York.

In his will, Anne's father left her 2/7 of his estate and prohibited the predatory Venton, unfortunate in money, from having access to her wealth. When her husband learned of the terms of Mr. Lytton's will, he left his wife and went to live in Frederiksted.

She stayed at her late brother's house in Christiansted.

Frequently, I visited, and we consoled one another.

After the recent horrific hurricane, Venton filed for bankruptcy again and posted a notice to his creditors. "John Kirwin Venton forbids all masters of vessels from carrying Ann Venton, or her daughter Ann Lytton Venton off this island."

I helped (as I knew all the masters of the vessels), my cousin and her daughter flee.

They landed in New York free from the odious bullying man.

Before leaving, she entrusted me to collect payments from her father's estate. I completed one in May of this year.

Trust makes the soul pure. A friend strokes the heart when they believe in you, visit you just to say hello, forgive your mistakes, never judge you, understand you, and walk beside you.

My employer, another person who I consider a friend, is Nicholas Cruger, who shelters me from the crude insults of life.

On April 15, 1772, he married Anna de Nully, a daughter of Town Captain Bertram Pieter de Nully. He became a member of this respected St. Croix planter family.

I attended their marriage, performed in the Dutch Reformed Church in Christiansted.

At the reception at The Town Captain's estate, the Captain approached. Stared at me, not in a threatening manner, and said, "I know those eyes, they bring back memories."

His wife, Catharine, approached. He excused himself but not before inviting me to come for a visit and talk, but he died before we could meet. I often wonder what he wanted to tell me. Before I close, I must tell you about a remarkable man.

Though I am an Anglican, who attends the same parish as the Lyttons, my employers, and the Stevens' family, I befriended the Reverend Hugh Knox a Scotch-Irish Presbyterian pastor, physician, and journalist who opened his library of mathematics, chemistry, philosophy, and religion to me.

The pastor, whose grey eyes spark, and I took up a genuine interest in each other beginning in 1772. We have spent endless hours talking at his congregation at the intersection of Prince Street and Water Gut. He has influenced my education, spiritual welfare, and views on morality, propriety, and integrity.

He encourages me to write about the devastating hurricane of August 31, 1772. I think I will.

To quote from Benjamin Franklin's *Poor Richard's Almanac*, "Nothing ventured, nothing gained."

Franklin seems a man I would like to know.

May the precious fragrance of my prayers spring upon you.

Your Loving Son.

N.B.

I forgot to mention that when reading in the *Royal Danish-American Gazette* of March 6, 1771, I came across the following notice. On Thursday next at 10 o'clock forenoon, will be sold at Publick Vendue, at Mr. Roeder's tavern in Frederiksted, 3 houses, some lots of land, and other effects, belonging to the estate of John Michael Lavien deceased.

Immediately, it struck me that not all of his investments of my mother's inheritance turned sour.

As a youth without influential friends, I am powerless to get back what belonged to my brother and myself.

This, I understand too well, but I vow to take responsibility for my life and let no man block my way.

CHAPTER 17

The Clerk Takes Leave; A New Beginning

The two men admired Alexander Hamilton very much and considered him a friend. He was talented and possessed a pleasing, determined, appreciative personality, free from conceit, and wished to be counselled by gentlemen he admired.

"I pray the vessel survives high winds, storms, and crashing breakers," said Reverend Hugh Knox.

Nicholas Cruger grimaced, "Pirates and fire, too."

Fearfully, the two men looked out to the sea from King Street, cooled by the sea breeze while standing on Cruger's business dock. The air smelled of sugar, rum, and molasses from the horse-drawn wagons as men unloaded goods for shipment.

"His opportunity for a proper education lies in the colonies," said Knox, "away from keepers of enslaved wenches, rakes, drunkards, and night rioters."

"May he make the most of it."

"He will and burgeon," said Reverend Knox.

After a few moments of complete silence between them, the reverend, with a drape of sunshine covering his face, prayed Alexander would be forever free from the miscreants of the island who lacked serious religion and were Sabbath-breakers.

"The seed of greatness resides within our young friend."

Watching the trade winds pull the *Progenitor* away from the small Leeward Islands that arched from Cuba to Venezuela's coast in a chain of more than thirty tropical wonderments, they discerned they would miss the young man.

For several moments, on the stern of the vessel, Alexander's thoughts centred on his illegitimacy. Utterly unprepared for this journey, he promised himself again to look forward and not dwell on the past.

Gamesters, church neglecters, common swearers, and unjust dealers of society brushed his life's shoulders, weighing on his soul. While living on Nevis or St. Croix's Island, he often cursed himself when he fell into this self-defeating lapse. He brought to mind his mother's advice, "Never allow predatory tongues to cut your throat."

Usually soft and warm as melted wax to Alexander and his older brother, James Junior, she never minced words when giving advice. Alexander knew first-hand that a worm of a man preyed on her without conscience as he dropped his past into the sea and witnessed an enormous clanging echo. Contrary to the usual course of his life, animated tales and good reflections bubbled to the surface. The sea and the wind screamed at him, beckoning him to a new adventure.

He nodded and wanted to jump for joy, but experience slapped his face that happiness, like a blue sky, cannot be lasting. He laughed at his relapse. With no formal schooling and knowing no Greek or Latin, he sailed for an education at the College of New Jersey. Now, at the age of eighteen, he realized that he suffered under the guise of circumstances, the excrement of being poor throughout his life.

"No more!" he yelled to the sea.

Very coolly, very carefully, he brought up the words, "I will leave my past: no more pickpockets, whores, rogues, vagrants, thieves, and other filth and cutthroats. My future begins now."

A rush of exhilaration flowed through his veins. His heart raced, and his mind knew no bounds. He could not remember being so excited. To say leaving the West Indies in July of 1773 brought him joy would leave truth crippled.

His eyes then fixed on the receding men responsible for his departure, Knox and Cruger. A glow of warmth spread through him. He waved good-bye to the distant shore.

"The grov'ling condition of a Clerk or the like is no longer my destiny," he said.

A warm breeze soothed his face, and he drew it in, dreaming about what awaited him in British America as he recalled a line from Don Quixote, "Thou hast seen nothing yet."

With no savings, he trusted a beautiful woman would fall in love with him, or war would exalt his station among men. Willing to risk his life, but never his character, he entered the contest of his journey with a smile and a sharp chip on his shoulder.

With long hours of study, due diligence, and application, he would enrol at the College of New Jersey in Princeton and make a name for himself and surpass all in his path. With his letters of recommendation secure on his person, victory instead of defeat stood as his rallying cry.

At this moment, he believed he could walk on water, fly if necessary. Stepping forward, he barked, his lips pursued, "No steps back."

He looked upward and yelled at a luminous cloud hanging from the bluish-purple sky, "Get ready for Alexander Hamilton, the Great."

Birthed on the nine-mile long and five-mile wide island of Nevis, situated on the rim of the northeast corner of the Caribbean, he resided for the last eight years under Dutch rule on St. Croix. The days previous to his departure, his heart gushed with joy – all the way to the top – just the way his mother liked it. The vessel, the *Progenitor*, limited his movement, another minuscule island in his life, he thought.

He did not miss his past employment, overseeing incoming inventory and accounting for outgoing merchandise. Understanding fortune placed him on board as a kind of particular test; he marvelled at its ornate carvings, gilding, large windows, and its raised poop deck for the livestock as he inspected the ship with bright eyes. He discerned its construction that allowed it to carry an abundance of goods and not passengers. The ship, loaded with sugar, rum, cotton, molasses, and hardwoods, became his new home. He walked from stern to bow, noting the crew's habits – how much work they did from sunrise to sunset. He intended to write his observations to his former employer, Nicholas Cruger.

The voyage exhilarated him; it cleansed him of any trepidation about his new destination. He prayed that the time of sitting uncomfortably at a desk with a quill in hand as a clerk would be no more, knowing nothing of the future needs of George Washington.

The treatment of a black member of the crew brought a memory to him. He recalled walking through Nevis's tight, twisted streets, observing slaves auctioned at Market Block and Crosses Alley. He cringed at the whippings that took place in the public square against the backdrop of flaming sunsets and turquoise waters with horror.

He yelled to the sea beyond, "To hell, you bastard slaveholders. Someday . . . ."

A warm wind massaged his face as Nevis & St. Kitts became solitary peaks in midsea, a school of dolphins twisting and turning for his amusement.

"Yes, indeed," he said to them, "there would be no regret leaving behind these rejects of London's streets who came to make their fortunes exploiting the less fortunate."

Observing the plantations first-hand when living in the Caribbean, he gleaned that a shift in Europeans' dietary needs occurred. Wherever one gazed, sugar swam into tea and coffee and jumped into chocolates, jams, candies, and other sweets in much more significant amounts.

The lure of a pocketful of silver coin brought indentured servants, overseers, and sons of men of lineage, who hoped to have a sugar plantation – to mingle with the wealthy. Most wandered from island to island, hoping to make a fortune on the backs of others through the sweet draw of the White Gold, sugar. Indeed, James Senior, his father, fit the bill.

He explained to Alexander. "In 1537, the first sugar refinery took root in Germany. Numerous people touted it cured headaches, relieving childbirth pain, cleaned the blood, and strengthened the body and mind. It was excellent for the eyes and the common cold, healed wounds, and when mixed with wine and cinnamon invigorated the elderly."

Alexander cast an incredulous eye, shook his head, and stared at his elder with a fixed expression. "Really, father!"

Their eyes met, but Alex broke it off. James turned and wanted to hold Alex until all his son's doubt faded away. The business of sugar left a mark on Alexander's keen mind, and the money generated by the exploitation of slave labour in producing it left an unsweet taste in his mouth.

After attending church with Nicholas Cruger, he remembered telling him that, "In 1700, the average person consumed about 4 pounds of sugar per year. Sixty-five years later, it had more than doubled."

"How exciting," said Cruger, who knew his desire for sugar knew no bounds.

"Do you know the consequences of this?" asked Cruger.

Alex shot back, "Sugar generates more wealth for the British than all her colonies in North America?"

"Yes, its lure, my young assistant, creates an inordinate amount of riches for some."

"And an ocean of inequality and exploitation for black men and women," interjected Alexander, "bound face-to-face with chains till death."

Slowly, Cruger nodded up and down. Alex's imagery sent ripples of sadness through his soul, but he continued to profit from the white gold; like most men, he knew no other way.

"And the population of slaves increases daily."

"Doubled since my birth."

"That would be about how many years?" joked his employer.

The youth ignored the comment.

Born July 11, 1753 or 1774, he considered himself older than his eleven years.

"Too many of the white labourers," the boy continued, "prefer the scent of the blooming rose and wilt from the brutal heat, fatal fevers, and heavy labour of island life."

A ringing bell on the ship startled him. His memories were left dangling as the evening rays of the sun filtered through a dense mist.

"Come and git it!" echoed through the ship.

Firm footsteps sounded heavy. Alex was not in a state of hunger but followed the tattooed crew to the smell of food, eyeing men attired in an assortment of colourful thigh-length jackets cut close to the body and stopping at the waist where they flared. He thought them natives of Barbados. He counted eleven buttons on several sailors descended from a two-inch standing collar from the neck to the waist. He thought them from Jamaica.

While eating salt meat, hard biscuit, and red cabbage, his eyes gazed at the wild hairstyles, fit, he thought, for women. The red on their lips from the cabbage recalled his mother's image, who made a dye from it to use as rouge on her cheeks and lips. The jewellery made of shark bone dangling from the sailor's ears amused him.

His blue eyes pleading to shut, he slid off towards his bed. Passing between the tables, he heard a crew member say, "He delighted in pulling out their toenails, and ripping off their heads."

A momentary, debilitating sensation, quite uncomfortable, emanated from Alexander's upper abdomen to the back of his throat. He sneered at the man who occupied the seat, oblivious to him.

"Being a sailor," he murmured, "is not as wondrous as my imagination concocted."

Upon entering his berth and ready for sleep, he discovered his bed as narrow as a wink.

A neat, handy, and helpful boy of about twelve years with short brownish hair and round face appeared. In a squeaky voice, "Necessity requires I lash you in."

"The sea term for being tied, you mean."

"No fun falling out of bed."

The cabin boy's face squinched as if he ate a sour grape, saying, "Mr. Cruger would not be pleased."

"Your name, young boy?"

"Aaron Thorn, Sir."

"How did you achieve your present employ?"

Well, Sir, when my parents died, I became the ward of my uncle, and we did not get along. I decided to run away and asked the captain to take me aboard."

"How long have you been at sea?"

"Goin' on two years."

As he began to nod off, the cabin boy departed. No dreams nor memories, or thoughts entered his consciousness. After a few hours, he awoke, releasing himself from his bondage. His adrenaline screamed like a wild stallion as he strutted to the deck. Under the sheen of a sky full of stars and the moon's brightness, he controulled his excitement as he heard the sea wash the side of the vessel while heaven spoke.

He remembered walking with his mother and brother, James Junior, along the beach after a tropical storm struck St. Croix on October 7, 1766 damaging their store at No. 34 Company Street. They resettled down the street at No. 23, half a block from the Sunday Market.

October became November, and so the months passed. On most Sundays, Alexander's body glistened with sweat from a hike to a nearby bluff to watch the dark-skinned march of the slaves to the market. At liberty to sell poultry, fruits, and vegetables for themselves, he marvelled that they shuffled with delight in time in their white muslin, in a sort of poetic rhyme on the way to town with their Merchandise. Pained by the horrible vulgarism of slavery that offended his sense of justice, he thought, could he smile under such conditions?

He left his indignation on the hill and jumped to his feet, bolting to the men in loose drawers and waistcoats and black caps, women in jackets and petticoats with handkerchiefs of gauze or silk worn in the fashion of a turban. Both sexes balanced white wicker baskets on their heads that contained the various articles for the market: pineapples, grapes, oranges, shaddocks, water lemons, pomegranates, and granadillas.

In one basket, a child raised its head from amongst flowers of every hue. They shielded her from the heat and smiled at him. In another, a lamb, a turkey, or a pig, all covered up in the same elegant manner, showed their heads. The twelve or thirteen year-old Alex enjoyed marching with the men and women pinned by slavery in a sort of regular order with a resolute desire to forget their life of bondage.

By evening, he sang with them as they, sometimes a little drunk, returned to their existence, singing with merriment their stanza about hurricanes:

June, too soon,
July stands by,
August come it must,
September, remember,
October, all over.

A gust of the wind shook the island. The sea clapped as the moon, bold and bright, blasted from the hard night sky onto the emerald, rippling water. The ocean spread over his thoughts and drowned them, leaving, refreshing air and scents within his spirit.

Memories became hunched creatures crisscrossing his life. He drew his breath in. The cold shards of his childhood now pained him. He realized life stood so tall, so hard in night's coldness, as he felt the ship's floorboards, polished and smooth, not offering comfort or security. Seagulls swooped over the infinite ocean, through the moonlight, and then streaked off.

With his head down and eyes on the flat, bright deck, Alex thought of beginnings, endings, connections, bitterness. He fought off the resentful feeling of having lived on the underside of humanity, the patches of hate and ignorance, and being stained by the cloth of sin.

"Alone," he replied to the ebb and flow of the sea, "An orphan."

The sea left him isolated; its vastness scared him. Waves flopped as they pleased. Some emerald, others blue. His youthful pledge to cast the past away, losing ground, he fell into a fury of memories that hummed around him. His father, James senior, filled the sky; his odd hazel eyes stuck in his head.

He recalled the time they walked the mile-long narrow merchant-lined street of Dutch St. Eustatia, glancing at goods that any merchant with a hope of profit would have drooled over. Eight miles northwest of St. Christopher, the rocky island, a speck in the ocean, less than seven square miles, echoed with life and attracted like a magnet the vast commerce of every quarter of the globe. Free to the trade of all nations, it tolled the bell of prosperity.

He heard the chattering of people who strolled or rushed about that afternoon, as father and son enjoyed the ring of commerce, neither bothered by the fog of tobacco smoke.

With a smile, James Senior wrapped his arm around his son, "I am proud that you accept the challenges of life, and do not give up. I have never told you, but I respect your quest for knowledge and that you want to make a name for yourself."

Taking a long breath of air, Alexander blew out his insecurity, any angry thoughts vanished, and quiet ones tumbled in.

"Where do your aspirations come from?" asked James

"I get them when I read excerpts from parliamentary debates in London in the *Royal Danish American Gazette* and mother's books. They expose me to life beyond the walls of the horizon."

James opened his mouth, shut it, and decided the best thing to do was smile and listen to the faint sound of music from a rooftop above them.

"Your encouragement, father, makes me want to continue to achieve."

"Son, I want you to know that I will always provide support without pressuring you to focus on any profession. I look forward to you growing up and achieving your goals. Do not do anything that goes against your disposition."

His words rifled through the slim frame of Alexander – if one heard and observed the moment, they would have been surprised at the boy's age.

His father mulled over his advice to his son and thought, *he's not like me.*

The son frowned as he remembered his father; he never spent much time with him.

The whiffs of the sweet smell of tobacco massaged their nostrils as they viewed goods of different uses and qualities. The murmur of Alexander's name on James's lips seemed more delicious to him. The breeze whispered across his face. The sun stung his moist eyes. Birds called to each other.

"Father, have you noticed that your long, silver-embroidered waistcoat attracts attention from one to the other?"

"You can thank your grandfather for that."

"The Scottish Laird?"

His father smiled. "I do not know what your mother tells you about your heritage."

"She tells me I should stand tall like the native bamboo trees, but I would like to hear about it from you."

"Well, son, you tread on this earth as the heir of a blue-ribbon Scottish family. I am the fourth of eleven children, nine sons and two daughters. Born in Stevenson Parish, Ayrshire, your grandmother, Elizabeth Pollock, the daughter of a Baronet, married my father in 1711."

James stopped and gazed at the rich embroideries, painted silks, flowered muslins. He pointed to one in particular. "Reminds me of my youth.

Your grandfather, the fourteenth Laird in the Cambuskeith line, possessed a coat of arms that went back to the fourteenth century."

"What kind of house did you live in?"

"I used to live in a thirteenth-century Castle bought by my father in 1685 who renamed it the Grange. It sported a fogbound view of the island of Arran across the Firth of Clyde."

"Anything like here?"

"As different as night and day. It stood on a windswept hill above Stevenson's little seaside town that looked over rolling meadows watered by streams and ponds. My brothers and I swam there. Cows and horses fed on treeless hillsides."

Alexander smelled the cows even though the scent of tobacco whiffed everywhere.

They stopped and observed sailors' jackets, trousers, shoes, hats before his father's eyes shifted.

"Your grandmother possessed silver plates," pointed to them "like these, and she wore French and English hats."

He looked again, "Like these."

Alexander pictured her sitting in front of a mirror, sipping a cup of tea while trying on her hats. French gloves for fourteen pence a pair made an impression on Alexander. He picked them up, associating them with his mother, but knew not to ask his father to buy them. They fought throughout the past week, their fists clenched, trying not to get violent but.....

"The estate expanded in all directions," said his father. "It encom-passed not just Stevenson but half the arable land in the parish. There were some weavers and artisans, but most people lived in cold hovels living on an oatmeal diet and subsisted as tenant farmers for my grandfather's family."

His son looked up at him, thinking he usually held his tongue and was not as happy as he appeared now.

"Did you sleep in the same room with your brother?"

"No, I slept in my own room, with beautiful arched Gothic windows with a view of the gardens below and a steep bank that overlooked a picturesque glen."

Alexander's world spun like a top. He started the day as an outcast in closed confines and now held giddy thoughts of a heritage that lasted till his dying breath.

His mind flashed to the Middle Ages and the thick masonry walls that enemies pierced earlier during the war. He watched the ivy drape the structure and light penetrate the slits in the stone as his father's youth unfolded.

"I like talking to you, papa."

James bent over and kissed his son on the head.

"Why did you leave all of that, father. I do not understand."

A degree of anger crawled into his voice. "The fourth son, as I was, would never come into possession of the property. The Law of Primogeniture bestows on the first male child the inheritance of the estate. The prospect of a career in the church, the military, or the government did not interest me."

James thought if I could only redo that decision. He looked back, asking himself what accomplishments rested under his roof. Nothing echoed in his ears. And now his son, here on a forsaken island – had he robbed him of the standing that the family name would have brought to him? But it did not sadden him because he possessed a lasting faith in the future, forgetting it sometimes arrives like an unwelcome guest.

Alexander took a quick, shallow swallow as a cloud blocked the sunlight. A chill slid up his arms and made him wish there were no clouds.

James winked at his son. "I turned down a profitable marriage for my name, the looks of the bride below my standards."

He fled to the West Indies to avoid fatherhood – he remembered, now.

"I do not understand why a father would do that to his sons," said Alexander.

"Life resembles a winding lane, with alluring fruits tempting our vanity, son. It often comes down to the luck of the draw."

English thread-stockings caught his father's eyes.

"Cheaper than in England," he informed his son.

"How do you know that?"

Giving a knowing smile, James picked him up and wrapped him onto his broad shoulders.

"Something, the son of a fourth Earl, knows."

James stopped to purchase excellent claret for less than two shillings a bottle, Portuguese wines of different kinds, pickles, and sweetmeats extremely fine.

"We did well. A bargain at ten or eleven shillings."

"Eight shillings five pence exactly."

"How do you know that?"

Giving a knowing smile, Alexander shrugged his shoulders.

"I am the grandson of a fourth Earl."

That night, as on many others, James drank, and as before, Alexander and James Junior heard:

"James! You promised me."

"Shut your mouth, woman!"

"And if I do not, what are you going to do?"

Upon reaching the halfway point of the trip to British America, the wind stilled as the vessel passed out of the warm climates and approached America's coast. The change in the air left goose bumps on his arms. A chill set on the deck of the *Progenitor*, and Alex decided to read in his berth. But his brother's words a month before his departure rumbled through his mind.

"I could tell he thought me stupid in the interview for the apprenticeship."

Alex frowned, knowing he could not take care of his older brother. What could he do? He said a hundred times to himself. *Stay and hold his hand?* He implored Knox and Cruger to find a situation for James junior but to no avail. He then remembered his mère's favourite saying, "feed the mind some Shakespeare – or some chocolate." Without any chocolate, he grabbed Shakespeare's sonnets and snuggled with the book.

He read from number 1, "From fairest creatures we desire increase, That thereby beauty's rose might never die," and concluded with number 154, "The little Love-god lying once asleep, Love's fire heats water, water cools not love."

Raising from his bunk, the sandy-haired, thin-nosed, attractive "foreigner" (as John Adams and Thomas Jefferson would call him) ventured to the deck. He watched the sky bleed as the fiery sunset fell from the cliff of the horizon.

As the Roman goddess of love and beauty, Venus appeared in the sky; he mused when would the mistress of love wave her torch and take possession of him, make him feel the cause and effect of sincere love, go beyond himself and stretch to someone else.

He sang a song for his love.

If I could wave a wand around the earth's shadow
Making all things special like a turtle-dove
I would swirl distress into melting snow

And water the dry fields with love.

Under the silver lining of stars and sky, blemished with joy, hope, and strength, he heard a "hello."

"I promise," as he looked up, a full moon lighting his face, "to pay attention to the present and give little thought to the past, for life is an ever-changing metaphor."

His tears spent, his thoughts turned to building "Castles in the Air."

It invigorated him to find the window in his mind susceptible to hope.

"You are not alone," he heard.

He could not withhold a brief laugh. His thoughts tightened as he dipped into his memory.

Nature, the catalyst that landed him on the ship to British America, was fresh in his mind. When discussing with Reverend Hugh Knox the "Great West Indian Hurricane," Knox tickled the brain and asked him to give an account. He swallowed the challenge and wrote about the storm of terror that killed thirty people and swept ships hundreds of yards inland.

In the *St. Croix Royal Danish American Gazette* of the Sixth of September, the Reverend introduced the author of the letter as "a Youth of the Island."

I take up my pen just to give you an imperfect account of the most dreadful hurricane that memory or any records whatever can trace, which happened here on the 31st ultimo at night. It began about dusk, at North, and raged very violently till ten o'clock. Then ensued a sudden and unexpected interval, which lasted about an hour. Meanwhile, the wind shifted round to the South West point, from whence it returned with redoubled fury and continued so till near three o'clock in the morning. Good God! what horror and destruction—I cannot describe—or you to form any idea of it. It seemed as if a total dissolution of nature was taking place. The roaring of the sea and wind – fiery meteors flying about in the air—the prodigious glare of almost perpetual lightning –the crash of the falling houses—and the ear-piercing shrieks of the distressed, were sufficient to strike astonishment into Angels. A great part of the buildings throughout the Island are levelled to the ground – almost all the rest very much shattered—several persons killed and numbers utterly ruined – whole families running about the streets unknowing where to find a place of shelter – the sick exposed to the keenness of water and air – without a bed to lie upon—or a dry covering to their bodies—our harbour is entirely bare. In a word, misery in all its most hideous shapes spread over the whole face of the country. – A strong smell of gunpowder added somewhat to the terrors of the night; and it was observed that the rain was surprisingly salt. Indeed, the water is so brackish and full of sulphur that there is hardly any drinking it.

Alex remembered the words came easy, in a stream of consciousness.

He thought his essay satisfactory for him but far better than anyone else's attempted description.

The day after the appearance of Alex's article, Nicholas Cruger, after dropping off supplies at Knox's Church at Water Gut Street, turned the conversation to Alex's letter.

Several seconds passed while Knox searched for words. His expression blanked as he gazed at Cruger.

"Nicholas, the boy needs to have a proper education."

"Of course, the same thought travelled through my mind. We must send Alex to New York."

"Better yet, to the College of New Jersey.

Cruger scowled and said, "Why not King's College?"

"I know no one there."

"Then write a letter of introduction for him to the College of New Jersey."

The conversation buoyed them even more. Knox removed his spectacles to eliminate a smear, and the face of Cruger became blurred.

"You must set up with your firm of Kortwright & Company the practical arrangements for the financing of his education.

Cruger contacted Hugh Mulligan, a prosperous merchant, whose brother, Hercules, ran a haberdashery business on Manhattan Island. Hercules promised to lodge the boy. Born 1740, in Ireland and brought over by his parents when about seven years old, Hercules would take to Alex as a mother does her firstborn child (except if the mother's name is Jane Jefferson).

The rain turned to drizzle as Alexander turned the corner by the wharf on his last day on Christiansted, St. Croix, in June of 1773. He observed an anchored boat, the vehicle to his future.

"My future lies yonder," he yelled, "and I will conquer it."

He dismissed the fact that at nineteen or twenty, he never sailed alone or been beyond the islands. Lingering on the dock, he waited for his benefactors. His mind and heart turned to Ann Lytton Venton, his eyes shining with delight. He fulfilled an obligation to her by retaining another receipt, as late as June 3, 1773, for a sum obtained for her from the Lytton Estate.

Whistling and humming, his mind centred on the time to come.

He mumbled, "I wish for war."

And a war waited for him.

CHAPTER 18

Jefferson in Love, Again

Throughout 1768, slaves dotted the twenty-five-old Thomas's Monticello mountaintop from sunrise to sunset. Inhaling deeply, he shrugged before barking out orders for the levelling of his mountain. He dropped his sextant to the ground. The thought of a quick levelling of his mountaintop vanished from his mind. He pressed his fingers to his eyes, hoping that the job would be completed when he dropped his hands. Thomas laughed, "I need a magic wand."

He dug past his savings as Monticello neared completion.

The next year, elected to the House of Burgesses, the foundation of his essence took form. The one thing he thought he could do without, Patrick Henry, turned him counterclockwise. The hand of fate seated him beside Patrick at the Burgesses. Thomas looked amused and ordered himself to get along with the son of thunder.

"I know of no way," said Henry, "of judging the future but by the past."

With a nod of his head, Jefferson reached over and tapped his forearm. "I guess we will have to read more of the past if we want recognition by the descendants of political democracy."

Henry let the remark pass as he did not want to disturb his sensitive companion. Jefferson marvelled, during debates in the Burgesses, at the words Henry brought to the chamber. Writing Dabney Carr, "I never heard anything that deserved to be called by the same name with what flowed from him; and where he got that torrent of language from baffles me. I frequently shut my eyes while he spoke, and when he finished, I asked myself what he said, without being able to recollect a word of it."

Upon Dabney's request, the Squire from Monticello made notes when Henry spoke on the Burgesses' floor.

"His brow lifts mechanically."

"Venom virtually pours out."

"After the Boston Massacre of early March 1770, his words swallow easily."

Jefferson shot a hot, jealous glance at Henry.

"They tell us, sir," Henry said, "that we are weak; unable to cope with so formidable an adversary. But when shall we be stronger? Will it be the next week or the next year? Will it be when we are totally disarmed and when a British guard lives in every house? Shall we gather strength by irresolution and inaction? Shall we acquire the means of effectual resistance by lying supinely on our backs and hugging the delusive phantom of hope, until our enemies shall have bound us hand and foot? Sir, we are not weak if we make proper use of those means which the God of nature hath placed in our power."

Unable to speak publicly, Thomas took a different course than discourse. He chose to hold the brush of history, to stroke words and put his voice on them, to achieve the scent of immortality.

"I can write, work hard in committee, and consume large volumes of information," he told several Burgesses members. They used his talents. He buried himself in human rights issues and burned through the pages of Locke, Rousseau, Montesquieu, Hobbes, and Voltaire.

"Hobbes' contention that people needed rule by an iron hand and that man's nature held the seed of evil, I reject," he wrote. "I prefer Locke's three natural rights: life, liberty, and property. I agreed with him that the citizenry must give up some of their natural rights to the government for the protection of their rights in return."

"Montesquieu's discussion of the separation of power through checks and balances remains a compelling read. His opposition to war, religious persecution, and torture remain the bible of liberty."

He wondered how to use Rousseau's polite society of heart and mind to set up democracy besides Locke, Rousseau, Montesquieu, Hobbes, and Voltaire. He wrote Dabney, "I will be the midwife waiting to deliver the child of independence."

Construction limped forward on his Monticello Mountain in 1769. Jefferson's let his gaze wander forward, but his muscles trembled and became unsteady. He frowned more often than not. The days nudged aside, but he leaned back with his glass. He smiled, nodded up and down, and drank another glass of Bordeaux.

"Master! Master! Shadwell burns!"

A bitter, dark ache sliced at him. He envisioned his birthplace, the one-and-a-half-story frame dwelling of Shadwell, filling the sky with flames.

He rushed to the smoking ruins.

"My books?"

"No master, all burnt, but we save your fiddle."

Despair whipped him as he descended to the underworld.

"On a reasonable estimate, he wrote Dabney, "the cost of the books burned must be £200 sterling, and I lost every paper I possessed."

Jefferson moved to the South Pavilion at Monticello and sipped hope again as construction proceeded. He cared not of the toll exacted on his slaves who maneuvered the various "everything" to his Shangri-La. Exploitation was lost in his intellection's whistling wind, as an ample supply of wine and excellent food moderated his despair.

Shadwell's jinx continued, for on May 26, 1771, the mill at Monticello was "wiped away by the greatest flood ever known in Virginia." Fires and floods let despair ran through the hills and valleys of Monticello.

Alone and his existence unwrapped, Thomas needed someone to share his life with but thought his awkwardness around women killed his chances of meeting the special one. In late 1770 or maybe early 1771, the lovelorn twenty-eight-year-old dreamed of a woman dreaming of him. He watched them slip over the horizon together. When he awoke to a grey, misty, cold morning, he wondered, would the missing ingredient of his life – love – ever appear on his plate?

At court, Thomas moaned that his witness never appeared. He left and walked dejectedly to the shade of the sycamores, the temperature approaching 100 degrees. He cursed that the judge refused a continuance and dismissed the case. He dreaded informing his client and knew collecting his fee would be unpleasant.

Approaching his destination, he noticed a petite woman with a homemade satin bonnet upon her head and her step light, carrying a young child. He envied the husband of the woman. The youngster dropped a small, embroidered hanky to the ground. Wanting to act as a knight in armour, he rushed over to the helpless woman, picked up the child's possession, and handed it to her mother. His heart glowed more golden than the noon-day sun.

"Thank you, sir."

"May I introduce myself?"

"Of course, Mr. Jefferson."

He blushed and was at a loss for words. She giggled. The sunlight shone on her tanned face as her large, expressive eyes captured his attention.

"You and my late husband attended William and Mary as classmates."

Jefferson's heart skipped a beat at the information, "late husband."

"My name," she informed as she smiled, "is Martha Skelton."

He remembered a Bathurst Skelton, an amicable fellow but one of the less serious students who preferred gaming and women. He also anted up his heart to Rebecca Bidwell, but like Jefferson, received a sideways nod.

"I am sorry for your loss."

A slightly pained grimace came and then left her countenance. Her fine figure was as sturdy as the trees surrounding them and her fragrance greater than the honeysuckle of fragrance. Their smiles were fast and spontaneous.

Delighted on his part, and soft on her part, even a little shy.

"Magic exists. How can one doubt it?" she said, "Have you gazed at rainbows and wildflowers, heard the wind's music, stood alone in the silence of the stars? Anyone who loved knows of magic."

He cherished the meeting and disregarded his rule of life – never leap into something without thinking it through. She liked him. That seemed elementary to him.

"May I suggest," asked Thomas, "that we retire from the heat and get something cool to drink. And if you like some food."

"Some cold milk for my son, John, would be appreciated, and I am famished."

They strolled along the Duke of Gloucester Street towards the college, engaging in conversation as if they knew each other for eons. His heart raced like never before. He gave her a long look and thought, I have landed in heaven. She wanted to hold his hand and thought of friendship, commitment, the coming of love, standing together.

Their afternoon passed at the Raleigh Tavern. She considered him fair looking and liked his height, air, address, and felt that his personality displayed a great deal of spirits and liveliness like her father. Wanting to spend more time with him, she feared that her widowhood and young child were hindrances.

Skelton, twenty-one, and an accomplished rider on horseback, played a musical instrument, danced, sang with more than usual taste and effect, and enjoyed literary tastes. Her eyes peeked out from under her eyelashes as he looked at her. He wanted to take a bite out of that peach, to bask in her warm, affectionate disposition but feared his awkward nature would drive her from him.

Love dropped from the sun, the moon, and the stars and surrounded Thomas, and he knew it. He wanted her for a wife but wondered would his good fortune continue as they rode together through the countryside, tasted the fruit from the orchard, performed duets together, he on the violin and she on a harpsichord.

On rainy afternoons, nestled by a fire, wanting to please her, he read Homer and composed a poem or two for his wealthy, beautiful, and accomplished hazel-eyed beauty.

Special love erupts upon my scene from nuance to light ready to apply even in a moonless night to be seen sparking my forlorn spirit to comply our love can soar over any mountain my thirstiness longing for your fountain.

He leaned towards Martha and shot her a good-natured wink.

A sprightliness and sensibility flashed on her face that promised to ensure Jefferson's greatest happiness.

She asked, "Another?"

Now our chapters drape from the autumn skies come dancing from the time our souls first stirred when an odyssey floated upon our eyes with future days waiting to be explored my heart upon yours pulsating as one balancing soul on soul under the sun.

The fire blazed and crackled in the library at the unfinished Monticello as Martha sat beside Thomas. A cauldron of desire boiled within Thomas. He pulled her against his chest, hoping she would not resist. He felt her hesitate for a moment before pulling him towards the settee.

He resisted not.

She kissed him.

He wanted more.

She leaned back.

He contented himself with a brush of his fingers against her cheek.

She thought this could be a mistake but kissed him again.

"You taste good."

His blood ran like molten lava.

She hovered over his lips, nibbling as the fire cast shadows through the room before pulling back far enough to admire his face.

"You are a handsome devil, Thomas."

He blushed and took her hands and kissed each. Martha and Thomas sat on an outdoor swing with her son, John, between them making plans for the four-year-old's birthday. But John died on the tenth of June 1771, a week before his birthday.

Thomas wanted to absorb her loss, swallow her pain.

"I loved your son and looked forward to raising him as my own."

She narrowed her eyes against the hurt as she thought of her son. "Let us cross the void together.

He pulled her into his arms and held her tight, hearing her low sigh straining to go forward.

Jefferson travelled from Monticello to "The Forest," the home of Martha's father, to sign a wedding bond on December 23, 1771. After quickly dismounting his horse, he skipped to the front door, but something seemed amiss.

CHAPTER 19

Marriage and the Four Percent Return

"Boo!" Martha let out, as he turned the house's corner,
poking her fingers hard into his midsection.
He flinched.

Martha enjoyed the practical joke she played on Thomas the day he arrived to sign the wedding bond. She let him knock at the front door, knowing when no one came; he would strut to the house's back.

She shot him a glance.

"You lookin' for somebody!"

Flustered, he stammered, "Ah."

She sighed, her face softened.

The face of a saint, he concluded.

He seized her by the waist and lifted her, so they were face-to-face and brushed his lips over hers. On the First of January 1772, Martha and Thomas said their "I do's to one another. Thomas then took hold of Martha Skelton, the twenty-three-year-old, widow of Bathurst Skelton, and daughter of John Wayles, and pressed her to his chest. Wayles, thought they looked tranquil, proud, and secure. Fourteen days of celebration at her father's plantation followed. They danced, sang, and played music together.

A flood of love washed over them. In the mornings, afternoons, and evenings, their eyes locked on one another like magnets; their bodies entwined in shared love.

"Joy, romance, passion, humour. I have it all. Never leave me."

"Silly husband, my place belongs by your side, forever."

As time idled, he noted a tip, to Elizabeth Hemings, a concubine of the bride's father in his account book.

Before sunrise, the newlyweds set off in Thomas's two-horse carriage for the 100-mile trip to Monticello. By late afternoon, they encountered a snowstorm. Near dusk, Martha was wrapped in a hemp blanket as Thomas turned to her, "We must abandon the carriage. Too much snow."

"The distance to Monticello?"

Thomas turned left then right.

"Eight miles."

"Deepest snow in memory," said Martha. "Horseback, my love."

Martha thought of a ride in the night that she will never forget. She sighted her eyes on his distant mountain and then turned to Thomas. "I would race you, but I do not want to leave you floundering in the snow." He gave her a mock scowl as she trotted off, contemplating how lucky he was to have her as his wife.

They arrived at Monticello around midnight and rushed to the "Honeymoon Cottage," a one-room 20-foot-square brick building. A chill ran through Thomas's body. He looked around for some wood for the hearth.

"Without fire, the newlyweds rested."

"You can light my fire, Thomas."

His cheeks matched his red hair.

The couple, upon investigation, discovered a bottle of wine and some oak logs for heat. Martha dropped down beside him and sang, words that echoed off the hard walls.

Oh hard, my fortune and hard, my fate
Controulled by my father so early and late,
And when I get married just to end all the strife,
Controulled by my husband for the rest of my life.

Jefferson's laughter, robust and raised, as the fire's warmth, penetrated their bodies.

His long limbs slide lay beside her small, slender figure. He held her close as he smelled the scent of winter in her auburn hair. Her glow complete as a sunset. Her hazel eyes aroused with pleasure. It took him a moment to find his words before whispering in her ear, "My beautiful spring's first budding rose."

Slowly and softly, she said, "I love you."

Her touch on his face was as warm as the blood flowing through his veins. He tasted desire and wanted her lips. He realized he worshiped her and pulled her closer. She put her lips against his and let his passion boil. He kept his peach in reach, warm through the night, and many nights afterward.

Intense and frequent abdominal cramps pierced Martha. Pregnant, she knew. (With one of her two children of six to reach maturity.) Playfully, she jabbed a finger at Thomas's chin. She took his hand and put it on her stomach.

With a flare in his eyes, he said, "Really?"

"Yes, my darling."

His thoughts turned outward, hoping for a son. Martha filled her hours supervising the house slaves and servants, concocting recipes and homemade medicines, making soap and candles, sewing, knitting, and even brewing beer when not acting as hostess.

"You act as my third hand," Thomas said in a calm, relaxed voice. "You make my life easy."

She giggled and then winked at him.

"What would you do without me?"

Pleasure danced in the sky as she catered to his tastes and whims; many, he knew.

"You bring a lightness to my spirit."

She heard the faint sound of his heart beating.

"Shall I sing?" she asked.

He began to play his fiddle

Red, red, red
The colour of my true love's hair
His lips like a rose so fair
And the most handsome face and the neatest hands.
I love the earth whereon he stands.
He with the wondrous hair.

His thoughts clamped on her, but before he spoke, she asked, "I have been reading Henry Fielding's, *Tom Jones*. It owes much to his personal life, I believe. Tell me your thoughts?"

"I learned that the death of his wife Charlotte in 1744 traumatized him deeply. His affection for her shows in the character of Sophia Western. Her gentility and resolve make her a fitting monument to true love."

Jefferson's eyes flickered when Martha dropped into topics that touched him.

On a Sunday evening, after returning from a ride about his mountain, he learned of Dabney Carr's sudden death. His heart trailed off, the conclusion inescapable – his best friend was gone. Every thought of Dabney sent ripples of sadness through his heart.

Thinking about his conversation with his best friend, he turned to Martha, "Time to honour my contract with him."

Standing near Monticello's ancient oak tree after the burial, his six nieces and nephews' fate rumbled within him. He knew he must shelter them, but what would Martha say, a migraine approaching at the back of his head.

"Well, Thomas, you have gone from a bachelor to having an extended family of nearly a dozen.

Twelve days after Dabney's death, his wife's father, John Wayles, who enjoyed being a slave ladies' man, died, allowing Thomas to inherit 11,000 acres of land and 135 slaves.

Martha shook her head and stared into the distance.

"The fair sex being far from 'fair' in the eyes of the law," she mumbled.

Martha leaned back and frowned. Thomas wondered what could be wrong? She then came directly to the point.

"Please sit down, my dear husband."

Thomas moved to the chair by the southeast window.

He noticed a heaviness in her walk.

"I am sorry I have disturbed your afternoon reading."

She observed the sunlight highlighting his red hair and ran her hand through it.

"I want to bring the offspring of the union," she grimaced as her body shifted, trying to keep her eyes on Thomas, "of the Hemings-Wayles intimacy, to the Monticello house."

A muscle above his left temple throbbed.

"You what?!"

A flesh wound of guilt oozed from her face.

With a sceptical eye, he asked cautiously. "You sure?"

He noticed the rush of emotion that came over her.

"Yes, I owe it to my half-brothers and sisters."

His head rose slightly and briefly.

One of her half-sisters, Sally, looked as white as Martha but was considered black and thus a slave.

By the fall, Thomas decided to section off some ground for his kitchen garden, and lawyering dropped from his agenda by year's end. With bright eyes, he spent time with his newborn daughter, Jane, never missing the law.

While riding to Dabney's grave, he heard a voice in his head, something to do with slavery, but ignored it. His feelings for his friend overcame his mental process.

That evening, while sniffing a glass of wine and savouring its earthy aroma, his earlier sentiment on slavery bounced back. He realized the voice he ignored stated a phenomenon he had perceived at Monticello. A profit existed on the birth of slaves, a bonanza, and a perpetual human dividend at compound interest. He sat and surveyed the situation for a few moments and then set quill to parchment.

"I know no error more consuming to an estate than that of stocking farms with male slaves almost exclusively. I consider a woman who brings a child every two years more profitable than the best man on the farm. She produces an addition to capital while his labours disappear in mere consumption. I allow nothing for losses by death, but, on the contrary, shall presently take credit four percent. per annum, for their increase over and above keeping up their numbers."

He considered himself nothing but shrewd, and his numbers supported his conclusion.`

From 1769 till his death in 1826, Thomas Jefferson owned more than 600 slaves. The first slaves inherited from his father and father-in-law. And the 20 or so he purchased, the rest, 400 or so, entered into slavery at his compounded 4% return.

He rode on the backs of his slaves while profiting from their birth and labour. They built and then rebuilt his lavish estate and plantation at Monticello. Though he drafted a Virginia law in 1778 that prohibited the importation of enslaved Africans and, in 1784, proposed an ordinance that would ban slavery in the Northwest Territories, he remained a slaveholder. Knowing he stood knee-deep in debt, his views on the "moral depravity" and the "hideous blot" of slavery sided with the "practical" and allowed his inconsistency about human bondage. By the middle of the next month, Jefferson sat sniffing and sipping another glass of Cabernet Sauvignon at the Raleigh Tavern after the Burgesses had adjourned.

"You have the look of a man who is enjoying himself," said Henry.

Jefferson smiled, trying to withhold any condensation.

"Do you not notice the earthy quality, especially in the aftertaste, Patrick?"

"I must admit Thomas that I prefer whiskey."

Jefferson swirled the wine centrifugally in his glass, held the glass up to the light, lowered it to his nose, closed his eyes, took a sip, paused in contemplation, opened his eyes, and declared, "Heaven."

Henry looked at Jefferson back and forth, with a blank look on his face as though he declared himself loyal to the king.

Jefferson said, "I find that most people drink red wine too warm."

Henry downed another glass of whiskey.

"What temperature should it be?"

"Between 60 to 65 degrees Fahrenheit."

"Why?" Asked Henry.

Jefferson detected an amused look in his eye.

"At that temperature, the wine's flavours will be sharp and fresh, and the wine's textures will find full expression."

A smile tugged at Henry's mouth as he rose with his glass of whiskey held tightly in his hand as he raised it to Jefferson.

Let dreamers proclaim
Of the pleasures of wine
For lovers of soft delight
But this is the song
Of a tipple that's strong
For men who must toil and fight.

Thomas laughed as he gave Patrick a quick smile.

After another drink or two, the conversation turned to how to deal with Great Britain.

"The pain to the colonies' pride sears like a pig on the spit," said Patrick who grabbed his thoughts and wondered what kind of game England contemplated. He recognized the time on hand to put into words the hope-fulness of a new nation.

"Considering the chain of Acts passed by Parliament," he said to Henry, "I find it surprising that armed conflict stands silent."

"The fuse of rebellion stretches through the colonies, waiting for igni-tion," replied Henry.

An arrow of reality pierced Jefferson. "Virginians owe several million pounds of debt to the mercantile houses of London."

"I have been readin'," said Henry.

Do miracles never cease? thought Jefferson, trying to picture Henry with a book.

"Since the British defeated and drove the Dutch from our borders, the only buyer for our crops have been the English merchants. Without com-petitive bidding for our crops, being denied the privilege of buying foreign goods and shipping services in the cheapest market, the Navigation Acts from the 1660s reduced the profits of the tobacco planters and forced them to cut the costs of production, namely labour."

Jefferson's eyes were fixed on Henry, whose jaw tightened.

"Yes, those bastards furnished the colonies with an ample supply of slaves, but only from English slave traders, and the planters were obliged to buy on credit, reducing them to a state of commercial bondage."

"And forbade," said Jefferson, whose eyes flashed heat, "the plantation owners from curtailing the nefarious traffic."

"Once a planter entered into debt with an English merchant, he was obliged to market his crops through his creditor to obtain new supplies."

The flesh wound of debt oozed through his pores, and thinking of his entire indebtedness gave Jefferson a headache.

"The British navy," continued Henry, "protected the tobacco ships sailing for England, and the Crown's expenditures for military purposes provided a circulating medium, money, to buy English goods, thus increasing our dependence on British merchants, vessels, and supplies."

"The ragged insults of mercantilism result in a new flesh wound daily. It requires us to employ British shipping, depend on British merchants, and look only to British sources for capital and credit. Virginia's debt," said Henry, whose features pulled downward, "equals the total owed by the twelve other colonies."

Jefferson heard the weight in his voice.

Tightly, Henry's hands clamped in front of him.

Jefferson knew the figures, for he continued to till a deep debt garden and did not know how to reduce it, despite a 4% return on his slaves.

Henry stepped forward, as Jefferson said in a hushed voice. "We must advocate in the House of Burgesses suspension of payments to the London creditors."

Their minds locked in a shared understanding. Jefferson pulled back, finding less fault in Henry, the man he considered lazy. They raced over the next several months, often shoulder to shoulder, attempting to achieve this end.

CHAPTER 20

From One Island to Another; Hamilton and Burr Meet

Quick to react to the smoke's smell, Alex rushed to the fire's heart outside the ship's galley. Looking up and down, he barked out orders to the stunned crew with a raw authority that crackled. The blaze did not destroy the ship but left his eyes bleary from the hour ordeal. As he fell asleep on the deck, the smell of smoke clung to him like the night mist.

Twice depicted on the east and west sides of the Mauritius River, aka the Hudson, on a 1610 map, Manhattan simmered with activity since the French and Indian War. The island of many hills sparkled in the afternoon; the charred *Progenitor* drifted towards the wharves on South Street.

With alertness in his eyes, Alexander focused on the right and left as the *Progenitor* passed New Jersey on the left side and New York on the right. His heart wanted to jump up, but his mind controulled his joy, his future a blink of an eye away. As the ship docked, a fresh breeze fanned his heated brow. Energy erupted within him. It thumped through his head, his mind, his fingers, his arms, his toes. His heart beat to the rhythm of a war drum as he surveyed the men assembled on the pier, looking for Hercules Mulligan. His eyes focused on a redheaded man who stood upright, whose head scanned the ship's deck searching for him.

"That must be him."

As Hercules took his arm, Hamilton flinched, believing that the tailor possessed a wildly romantic nature. Alex looked down, his eyes admiring Hercules's well-shined black shoes.

"Young man, I see that it is true that you do have sparks in your eyes."

Alex blushed ever slightly. Their faces became locked in a mutual understanding, Hercules, drawn to his hypnotic, magical personality. His new friend took hold of his arm. "Let us stroll," he winked, "by a circuitous route, to my home."

Alexander counted the many times the activity forced them from the sidewalk into the dangerous roadway by loads of merchandise that noisy cart men transferred from their vehicles to the stores.

"700 vessels cleared the port in 1772 compared to 99 in 1746," said Hercules.

Alex scanned workers of all kinds, applying their trade in rope, snuff, and an ironworks.

Vicious horses' bit at his elbows, their drivers grinning at his undaunted nervelessness.

Barrels of flour rolled against his shins, but he paid them no attention.

"Watch out me boy; you stand within an ace of commerce crippling you for life!"

"I am quite familiar with the hazards of a city. It invigorates me."

"A left here," informed Hercules, "takes you to a street that runs parallel with the wharves."

Alex took a glance down the street while wondering how they would get any further. An endless chain of horse-carts and wagons formed an impenetrable barrier as the rude cries of the unconnected drivers jarred upon the nerves and sense of civility.

They inspected each other's eyes several times before attempting to cross, but fear forced them to retreat. After much delay, Alex sensed a break and charged forward, his new friend on his heels. Mulligan slapped Alexander on the shoulders as they reached the other side, "I like your spirit, laddy. Would you like a pint of stout?"

Alex lit with life, said, "Certainly."

They entered McGahee's tavern. Alex observed men sharing a newspaper, perusing the latest broadside or pamphlet, and engaging in friendly and not so friendly banter concerning the latest news and gossip. They drank frothy stout and listened to the brisk, lively talk, of local affairs or distant England, by men dressed very gaily. Alex overheard that the fair sex was very obliging, and 500 prostitutes lived by St. Paul's Chapel, near the entrance to King's College.

Hercules winked at him and said, "Certainly a temptation to the youth."

"They all talk very loud, very fast, and altogether," said Alex.

"If they ask you a question," replied Hercules, "before you utter three words of your answer, they will break out upon you again and talk away."

Alex knew the page of St. Croix turned to a new chapter.

"The newspapers," said Hercules, "are delivered by post to taverns, and the literate patrons eagerly read them aloud to the illiterate."

Alex raised his mug, "Let us then drink stoutly and talk lively," he commanded.

Hercules observed his young friend's eye, thinking they could beam light through the fog. A few hours later, Alex counted many lots of unoccupied land before reaching Mulligan's white house. He liked the picturesque roof.

"This is your new home."

Already soaked to the skin with happiness, he grabbed Hercules' arm. "Thank you."

When not attentive to his books or exploring the bustling city, he lived there briefly and sat with the family in the evenings enjoying the lighthearted banter. The noise of the children laughing roused him.

"Alex," asked Hercules' youngest daughter Ailene. "Recite a poem."

Gold rested in her eyes, little specks of it. He never noticed it before.

"It tests me when among new friends. Why should I not tell the truth about such manners? I repeat. It thrills me to converse with a wonderful friend. Even though we talk nothing but nonsense. The roar of visible friendship is both stimulating and delightful."

He enjoyed the frantic pace of his new life. He went days with little sleep and did not feel tired. After some light-hearted repartee about the enacted Tea Act, Hercules turned to Alex.

"Designed to help the struggling East India Company, it created a monopoly on the sale of tea, and a sea of controversy erupted in the colonies."

Alex scrutinized Hercules before laughing at himself.

"I read it in *The Public Advertiser* of September 11, 1773."

"Ah, yes," said Hercules with a muted chuckle, 'Rules for Reducing a Great Empire to a Small One,' by Benjamin Franklin."

"I enjoyed its brevity, playfulness, and comprehensiveness," replied Alex knowing he wanted to meet the legend.

"It challenges the reader to see British policy through colonial eyes and takes a fresh look at the American problem."

"Are we not Englishmen?" asked Alex.

"I considered myself one until the British dissolved the New York Assembly and required new delegates favourable to British interests."

Hercules took a deep breath and tilted his head down to look into Alex's blue eyes in a grave and sober manner.

"As a member of the Sons of Liberty, I helped construct a Liberty Pole on the Bowling Green. About the middle of January 1770, an assortment of arrogant British soldiers toppled the pole, cut it into pieces, and stacked it in front of Montagne's Tavern. A conflict followed, called the Battle of Golden Hill, we, with swords and clubs, the Brits with bayonets. An armed melee, my boy, and I have not considered myself a British subject from that day forward. The fire of liberty, like the sun, sheds light in shadows."

Slowly, Alex exhaled and cleared his throat, "I held no idea England wanted to lose its empire."

The next morning Hercules and Alex arrived in the dawn of morning and stood for a few minutes, waiting to board the boat to take them across the Hudson River. Alex narrowed his eyes at the dark, deep and radiantly green-blue river.

Armed with his letters of introduction from Hugh Knox, he found himself on a visit to Elizabethtown as heaven's bright eye danced forth from the East. "Thanks to a leather treatment enterprise," informed Hercules, "Elizabethtown is a prosperous village of 800, and already a century old."

"Do you know Francis Barber, the headmaster of the Elizabeth Academy?"

"Yes, he is six years your senior, a graduate of the Academy, and a recent graduate of the College of New Jersey. He will tutor you in Greek, a requirement for entrance to college."

Alex closed his eyes, hoping when they opened, he would be a student at the Academy. As he and Hercules crossed an old stone arched bridge that spanned the Elizabeth River, he observed spinning among the salt meadows and the militia parading near the courthouse. For a second, Alex thought of Don Quixote and then Julius Caesar.

After passing two churches: the red brick St. John's Anglican Church (for the pro-English citizens), and the wooden First Presbyterian Church, Alex marvelled at the 400 buildings mostly of weathered grey cedar shingles placed on five tree-lined streets of gardens and orchards.

He turned to Hercules. "This town lives in a garden."

"And a flora ripe in political thought," responded Hercules.

After the interview with Barber, he walked for a mile beside Hercules to the north of Elizabethtown towards William Livingston's home with a shower of thoughts, "Tell me about this Livingston fellow," said Alex.

"The Sons of Liberty say he is no public speaker, but very sensible and learned, and a ready writer."

"What did he write?"

"His Sentinel essays, which declared that that the Crown wanted to subvert the right of trial by jury, left New York up in arms. The Stamp Act then added fuel to the fire of a plot against American liberties."

"I know first-hand that the revenue act of 1764 imposed strict curbs on trade with the West Indies and the Currency Act prohibited future emissions of paper money as legal tender. Powers of the Admiralty courts was increased, and the Acts of Trade were strictly enforced."

"Correctly," Hercules said with a deep smile, "Livingston let out that specie payments demanded by new tax laws pointed to a period of deflation and business depression."

Approaching the east side of Morristown Road, Hercules pointed to the doorsteps of their designation. He informed Alex that "Livingston urged a boycott of British goods as early as 1762, and he foresaw the end of the wartime prosperity, urging economic retrenchment and discouragement of social extravagances."

If only his stomach would stop grumbling, Alex thought.

His letters of introduction held tightly in his small hand.

"Relax, laddy," said Hercules.

"Fighting off nausea," Alex smiled.

The door opened, and a tall, thin man with bright skin looked down on the pint-sized Alexander.

"Hello Hercules, it is a pleasure to see you again."

Alexander said in a firm voice, "Sir, my name is Alexander Hamilton."

Livingston studied him; his bushy eyebrows rose.

"Yes, the young man from the West Indies. Please come in."

Alex's eyes surveyed the interior of the sprawling mansion.

"I am going to call it Liberty Hall," announced Livingston.

"Do you enjoy retirement from your New York law practice?" asked Hercules.

"Have not the time. The family just moved in. Let me escort you to my library."

Like old friends, they sat on the settee. Alex's eyes fastened on the books with a resolute intelligence.

"To answer your question, Hercules. The law's deep well of knowledge no longer interests me. My pursuits now lie with liberty."

"I am sure," said Hercules, that it will become the headquarters of freedom in New Jersey."

"It would be an irony," said Hamilton, "being the first permanent English community in New Jersey."

"Known as the free borough of the town of Elizabeth," rebutted Livingston.

Hamilton smiled and recognized that Livingston possessed unusual talent. For a moment, the men in the Livingston library said nothing. They drank tea and occasionally looked at each other. Alex shifted positions until the silence ended. Livingston noticed Alex's eyes fixed on the books in his library.

"Feel free to spend time reading Locke, Pope, Swift, Addison, Steele, Ben Jonson, and Spenser."

Alex's heart fluttered on the wings of a songbird. The near twenty-year-old knew fate looked over him favourably. When not in class at Francis Barber's two-story Academy in Elizabethtown, he enjoyed reading Greek and Latin under a cupola on the First Presbyterian Church's grounds.

Through his friendship with Catharine Livingston, he socialized at Liberty Hall with outstanding leaders of the mounting opposition to Great Britain. Quickly these men understood the truth of what Hugh Knox wrote about Alex – a light shining brightly. Sitting in William Livingston's library with John Jay, William Alexander, aka Lord Sterling, and Elias Boudinot, Livingston was absent with Hercules Mulligan as the tailor took measurements for a suit for the upcoming wedding of his eldest daughter to John Jay.

Alex leaned forward, resting his elbows on the cluttered edge of an oak desk, listening to a discussion on English rule.

"Parliament refuses to deal with the political differences that distress the colonies," asserted William Alexander, Livingston's brother-in-law.

"Britain refuses," informed Boudinot, "to consider Americans as British subjects and to have the political rights as anyone in England."

Boudinot added, "As a scythe sweeps off the stalks of wheat, so do the laws of Parliament sever our liberty."

"Remember a pebble can make a spiritless pond sparkle," informed John Jay, "and freedom is the pebble of the soul."

"Civilized society must have an absolute right," said Lord Sterling, "to legislate, adjudicate and levy taxes through their elected representatives."

Hamilton's sleek, undersized hands, loosely grasped, tightened as he prepared to speak. The protégé could not shut down his regard for the British government, thinking the men's view of protesting taxes, petty and inconsequential.

"Does not English mercantilism deserve some credit for the phenomenal growth the thirteen colonies experienced during the 150 years in which they were subject to England's policies?

"I will concede," said Boudinot, "that shipbuilding flourished in the North, and New England shipbuilders and owners participated in the trade of the whole English empire."

He hesitated, and Jay said, "England prohibits our meats and cereals."

"But fish, meats, cereals, livestock, lumber ship to the various foreign markets," said Alex.

"For now," said Lord Sterling, "but our ships sail at England's mercy when they war with the French."

Alex stood, hands on his hips, trying to hide a smile.

"Potential crawls here, waiting for you to forget about the past and turn to the future."

A hush in the library as the faint sound of music spoke.

"We turned to manufacture," said Jay, "but the English authorities frowned upon this."

Alex shook his head, thinking, the men, eternal pessimists.

"They enacted statutes," said Boudinot, "restraining our woollen, iron, and hat industries and prohibited mints and the establishment of commercial banks – necessary institutions to grow to manufacture."

"We lived with these restraints before 1763," said Jay, "because the British military expenditures supplied the people with the funds to pay their debts and purchase needed supplies in England."

"You must understand, Alex," said Lord Sterling, "after 1763, the easy money from military expenditures from the war with the French vanished. The English proposed to tax the colonies to maintain defence establishments in America."

"And enforce prior restraints the Crown choose to ignore."

With a majestic turn of his head, Alex contemplated the men.

"And they initiated new taxes," said Jay.

"Making it difficult to pay for the manufactured goods we need from England," concluded Boudinot.

Alex took it all in. "I agree," he said, "that the policies of the British are restrictive, injurious and detrimental, but I admire their use of mercantilism but not the men who implement it. *Dura lex, sed lex.*" (The law is harsh, but it is the law.)

Outside, the wind roared. Spending the night at Liberty Hall, Alex read till late evening, did some writing, and settled into bed. After dawn, he sat up and cupped his chin in his hand; thoroughly satisfied, his preparation for the College of New Jersey was complete. With Hercules by his side, he strutted to Dr. Witherspoon's office, and the then president of the College, who Mulligan knew.

Sitting in an uncomfortable chair in the President's office, Alexander observed a portrait of Aaron Burr Senior, late president of the college. He let out a sigh that ended in a muted chuckle. Witherspoon sensed the flame of the young man's ambition.

"Sir," said Hercules, "may I introduce you to Mr. Hamilton."

The interview proceeded until Witherspoon held up his hand.

"I have examined you to my entire satisfaction and am well impressed, particularly with your knowledge and determination."

"I wish to enter the classes to which my attainments would entitle me but with the understanding that I should be permitted to advance from Class to Class with as much rapidity as my exertions would enable me to do."

The president impressed with Alex's confidence that sparkled on his face. He gave great attention to so unusual a proposition from so nervy a youth.

Witherspoon shook his head. "I have not the sole power to determine, but I shall submit your request to the trustees who must decide."

"I do not believe," concluded Hamilton, "men should not be like bricks placed high or low by chance."

Witherspoon thought, what a vigorous and sassy youth.

"Good to have met you."

Hercules and Alex boated back to Manhattan. Alex looked back every quarter mile, his eyes always trailing off, unsure about his future. In about a fortnight, a letter arrived from the president.

"Your request cannot be complied with because it is contrary to the usage of the college. I regret this because I believe you would do honour to any seminary."

Nearly a week later, Livingston received a letter from Hercules.

"As you and Boudinot reside as trustees who adore Hamilton and know first-hand of his intelligence is it not surprising that the College negated his request?"

N. B. "Did not James Madison's similar claim a few years earlier gain approval? He completed his education of four years in two."

After reading the letter, Livingston sat still for several moments, musing, "The College will regret this decision."

Sometime in the fall of 1773, in the gold and red-stained woods of Elizabethtown, they met. Before Hamilton enrolled at King's College to ascend the stairs of ambition, Aaron Burr went northward to Bethlehem, Connecticut. Burr was contemplating to study with the Reverend Joseph Bellamy and try to commit to his grandfather's contention.

Hamilton and Henry Brockholst Livingston, while going on an errand from Liberty Hall to the apothecary for Henry's mother, Susanna, observed Burr advancing towards them. Livingston, a friend of both, smiled as if he discovered a cure for old age.

"Well, you finally meet, by happenstance after all, and me trying to set it up." He hesitated and foresaw a future tragedy as the faces of his two friends exhibited fraught with disdain. Both thought they would lose something if they accorded praise to the other. Before introducing them, he said to himself.

"The destiny of mankind lies in God's hand; to think otherwise is a delusion, and the spirit of 'Free Will' is only ignorance of the cause."

"Aaron, this is my friend, Alexander, as you know, recently of the West Indies. He studied with Mr. Barber at the Academy in preparation for joining me at college. Alex, this is my friend Aaron, a recent student of President Witherspoon and a scholar in his own right."

As they shook hands, Alex shot Aaron a rugged look. The latter, usually armed with a light heart, observed envy on Hamilton's brow. Alike in height, weight, age, and intellectual curiosity, they could have been friends under the right circumstances. Of the two, Alexander possessed a higher drive to charge forward, though without considering the consequences. He represented the real definition of audacious: fearless, brave, hardy, dauntless, venturous, daring, bold, brassy, bodacious, and brazen, as Jefferson would discover two decades later.

Having made the same request to advance from class to class with as much rapidity as his exertions enabled him, Alex entered King's College in late 1773 or early 1774. It was then a three-story structure with a cupola that faced a vast low-lying meadow with a vista of the Hudson River in the background.

Alex's mind bathed in the diffuse light of the sinking sun of his past. A whisper of his future, thick with conviction in his thoughts. Because most of the thirteen or so students, in their midteens, frightened his ego, he stated this birthdate as 1757, two or three years younger than his actual age. His mastering of the books lent him by Knox, Livingston, and Boudinot whetted his appetite for the thousands of pages in the college library. He devoured them as a hungry bobcat does its prey.

"Mr. Hamilton," said President Cooper of King's College, "I enjoy your rapid progress through your studies."

Alex's brow lifted. "Do you have any suggestions for me?"

I would be delighted if you attended the evening gatherings at my residence."

He could not remember being so excited, the College of New Jersey's rejection, a distant memory. He rushed to his room and read until his eyes fell shut. The next night, wit like thunder and lightning abounded when Samuel Seabury and Cooper debated the day's politics with Alex. The West Indian youth was quick to interject his opinion.

"The destiny of humanity lies in God's hand; to think otherwise is a delusion, and the spirit of 'Free Will' is ignorance of the cause."

INTERLUDE III
A WEDDING -
CALM BEFORE THE STORM

An incident unrecorded in the annals of history happened at the gala reception, sumptuous dinner, and brilliant ball following the wedding of William Livingston's daughter, the beautiful, gay, and intelligent Sarah, then seventeen years old, to the twenty-eight-year-old lawyer, John Jay. At Liberty Hall, the blessed event occurred on April 28, 1774, at the completed two-story Georgian-style house situated amongst a treasured 120 acres on Elizabethtown's outskirts.

"There two hearts beat in rhyme, each to each," said Alex to his college roommate Robert Troup, while proceeding to the wedding.

With a shake of the head, he continued, "When two people can be unhappy nowhere because they love each other too well, John and Sarah fit the bill. He calls her Sally, and she calls him Mr. Jay. They walk till the dawn of day, in the dark and mysterious night, through mists of rain, under the throbbing fires of a million stars; love unveiled, shimmering over a sea of eternity."

Troup wondered what it would be like to have love hovering over him rather than heaviness, a shroud of anxiety towards dangerous romance. Alex pointed as they turned a corner; Troup raised his eyebrows, "The gardens you helped Mr. Livingston cultivate?"

"Yes! Provided by your mirthful friend."

Alex showed him his hands.

"I am impressed, Alex; the trees stand firm with buds."

Troup pointed, "Look at all those flowers highlighting the foliage."

"Mr. Livingston marvelled at my enthusiasm when I dug the many holes."

He glanced at the orchard.

"He warned me the bloom of youth occurs only once."

"I bet you failed to tell him you wanted to impress Miss Livingston, the bride's sister."

"I knew I should not have let down my guard."

"Worry not, my dear friend; my lips will stay sealed."

"Tell me the truth," asked Alex, "What about this cold front?"

"Normal for spring but not cold for me. Um, maybe the low fifties. Invigorating. You lived a spoiled life in the West Indies."

Alex with, a vibration in his stomach, squinted at Troup and said nothing. Upon entering the front door, the warmth of the vast interior fireplaces that flanked the two one-story wings grabbed Alex. He paced ahead of his friend. An ox could fit in either one, thought Troup. On his way to the tables abounding with platters of exquisitely prepared wild and raised game, "that great fat fellow," Troup salivated.

His head turned to the left and right, eying an army of more irresistible dishes. He sampled oleo, pigeon, sirloin of beef roast, venison, turkey, snipe, duck, partridge, trout, beef roast, leg of mutton roasted, hashed calf's head, and venison. He shunned the asparagus, fried sole, ham and boiled chicken, boiled beef, beans, and roasted pears. He considered finding Alex for a second, but desiring an avalanche of flavour against his palette, he continued to weave amongst the banquets bounty.

He targeted gooseberry pies, currant, and green apricot tarts; fruity, bitter, nutty. Sweet tastes coated his tongue. He mingled and marvelled at the flat, key-blocked cornices that topped the glowing first-story windows when not eating. Finding himself sitting next to the young Catharine "Kitty" Livingston, he blushed when she wet her lips before sipping from her glass.

"Most excellent," she informed Alexander's companion. "Came from the cellar of Lord Sterling."

Hamilton, engaged in a conversation across the room, kept a careful eye on Kitty, whose low-neck silk gown drew men's eyes. He could not but think she cast a heavenly light as her sleek fingers brushed her long hair. Her soft face fixed on Troup's round face, who wished to bathe in her dreamy, nostalgic portrait.

Her beauty stirred both men's hearts. Troup fought the impulse to stare into her eyes. Hamilton's spirit cried as his eyes turned from Kitty. Her pout resembled drooping summer flowers, he thought.

Kitty inquired of Troup, "Has Alex grasped the essential characteristics of Whig ideology?"

Troup thinking, *Alex, always Alex, does she not see me?* His dream was of Kitty dying as he realized he would never reach her shore, even be nearby. He cleared his throat and announced in a professorial tone.

"And what ideology might that be, Miss Livingston?"

She gave him a crooked smile, condescending or not he wondered.

"According to Mr. Liv-ing-ston," she said her father's name slowly, paused and looked Troup straight in the face.

"Greater parliamentary influence, trimming the crown's power, and protecting civil liberties."

"Well, Alex certainly softened his Loyalist views and continues to make strides towards becoming Continental. But being so versed in the history of England and well acquainted with the principles of the English constitution, which he admires, his views are as fixed as the laws of gravity."

"Or as wrong as a broken clock," announced Kitty.

Troup paused for a second or two, thinking, at least, the clock remains correct twice a day. More than most people.

"Better late than never," he replied, "but let me paraphrase Shakespeare, not 'as far from help as limbo remains from bliss.'"

She chuckled.

Troup thought her lips as smooth and soft as silk. He desired to touch them. "You appear wittier than I figured, Robert." The compliment lifted the hefty Troup but not as much as her calling him by his first name. He felt the spring wind lifting the clouds. His momentary joy abated as she changed the subject to her family.

"Did you know Mr. Troup, my sisters, and I were schooled at home in penmanship, English grammar, the Bible, and classical literature?"

With the slightest of sarcasm hidden behind a pleasing smile, Troup let loose, "And I might add, to have grown into graceful and capable young women."

Before speaking, Kitty wondered if there existed anything hidden in his compliment.

"Yes, we have. And freed from the kitchen, we reached out to think politically. Sarah served at times as Papa's secretary."

Troup wished to walk with her under the evening stars. Her personality cheered the day, animated the sun, inspired divine delights.

"You and Alex," she said abruptly.

He strained to hear her hushed coy voice. "Occupy the same room I am informed."

Thinking the world belonged to him, Troup smiled and let out an easy laugh.

"Yes, and have slept in the same bed since he entered college four months ago."

He knew his words caused her to flush.

"And how pray tell, did you meet my dear Alex?"

In a matter of fact way, Troup informed her.

"First, at a lecture on anatomy presented by Dr. Samuel Clossy. A few days later, I became acquainted with him at a dinner party given by President Cooper. He wanted to introduce a new student. We fast became friends exactly three months ago. I, too, suffered the hardship of an orphan around the same time that Alex's mother died. He confided in me that he thought of his mom as holy and pure from sin. We admitted to each other that our hearts still felt as empty as a bird's nest in December."

He paused, then looked across the room to his roommate, surrounded by several women. Hamilton's eyes were azure as a wave, inviting the women to play brightly. The hearts of his audience darted like the stars on a clear night. Troup turned to Kitty, who thought his countenance as honest as a mirror.

"I must admit jealousy abounded in me when he informed me Mr. Cooper granted him the status as an exceptional student, who could take private tutorials and audit lectures. But his extraordinary displays of the richness of genius and energy of mind won me over. We soon formed a club with Edward Stevens, Samuel, and Henry Nicholas, and Nicholas Fish to sharpen our debating, writing, and speaking skills."

Kitty thought his eyes as blue as the summer sky. She demanded, "The star of this club?"

"Alex, I must admit."

By the tone of his words, she knew her question had embarrassed him. She gave him a coy smile.

"Well, Mr. Troup, we also have something in common though we do not convene in the same club or share the same bed."

He thought her smile stretched like a quarter moon.

"My first impression of Alex was that he was good-looking and gentlemanlike, with an endearing face, and soft, natural manners," said Troup.

"After Alex presented Papa with his letters of introduction, Papa took him by the arm and said, "Girls, may I introduce Alexander Hamilton of the West Indies.'"

"His natural, graceful, polished movements pulled at me. We also became instant friends. It did not hurt that he possessed a slim and elegant figure. That, coupled with his rosy cheeks and his full, well-carved mouth, captured my fancy."

"I find," informed Troup, "his chiselled jaw combative for someone who walks with a buoyant lightness."

"Well stated, Mr. Troup. And his flashing eyes darted here and there."

She hesitated, swiped her hand through her hair, and puckered her lips.

"He amuses me."

Troup breathed deeply then looked at her, trying to rid himself of a taste of jealousy towards Hamilton.

"Oh, yes, those deep azure eyes," waxed Kitty, "exude beauty without the slightest trace of hardness or severity. They beam with grand expressions of intelligence and discernment than any other

"When we take walks and talk," Kitty stopped and weighed her words, "his manners and movements display such a degree of refinement and grace that I have never witnessed in any other man."

"Now, Miss Livingston, how many men have you known in your short life?"

"Well, Robert, I never kiss and tell."

Before going off towards her spiffy father, who stood engaged in conversation with the youthful Aaron Burr, she asserted to Troup, "The world, that all it contains, remains ever moving, The stars within their spheres forever turned. Sir Fulke Greville Lord Brooke, 1580."

She winked, and off she went.

Hercules Mulligan, the tailor extraordinary, had made a hand-sewn suit of French silk, patterned in cerise and cream, lined with horsehair, and backed with silk for the bride's father. Mulligan's skill and reputation as a suit maker in Manhattan Island during the Revolution would bring British officers to his establishment. Mulligan would also provide George Washington with valuable information of the enemy's military movements through idle conversation with them.

Across the room, the tall, black-haired William Livingston stood in conversation with the smaller Aaron Burr. "Liberty, a precious Jewel," said Livingston, "gives an inexpressible charm to all our enjoyments." Burr nodded, admiring his attire.

Livingston, an intimate and correspondent of Aaron Burr, senior, delivered a funeral Eulogium on the Reverend Mr. Aaron Burr, late president of the college of New-Jersey in October of 1757.

"Never underestimate your father's love of country and the strongly religious tone of his character."

Burr recited to himself a refrain from the Eulogium.

Of comfort, no man speak.
Let's talk of graves and worms and epitaphs.
Make dust our paper and with rainy eyes.
Write sorrow on the bosom of the earth.

"Your father would have wanted you to know: be weary of the Vanity of Birth and Titles, the vanity of Dress, and the airy Diversions of the gay world."

Livingston understood Burr's silence and let him measure the information.

The older man then asked, "Have you chosen a path to follow?"

"I have my doubts about one."

Livingston noticed a slight smile.

"I am concluding that the cloth of religion stands replete with abstruse Erudition and seems rather calculated to make one a critic or pedagogue than a good man or a Christian."

"I have long since believed," Livingston added, "that absolute religious beliefs clash with sense and cannot bear the touchstone of reason."

The small-framed Burr nodded in agreement.

"May I suggest you consider the law."

Before Aaron could reply, he noticed the cute, coquettish, somewhat spoiled, and always ready for flirtatious banter, Kitty.

She kissed her father on the cheek

"Excuse me, Papa, Aaron, and I have some catching up to do."

She grabbed his arm and whisked him away.

At first, they strolled amongst the guests. Enraptured by his dark and humid eyes, she asked, "Do you recall our walks when you stayed with us?"

"Under the evening stars."

"Let us go now."

"I fear, my lady, the weather, too cold."

He noticed her eyes fluttering like the gorgeous wings of a butterfly and thought of moonbeams glowing, casting light over the shadows of life's eternal struggle.

"I wish Aaron, as children, we had strolled hand in hand in the summer sun by the waters of a brook that transported the fragility of life towards yonder sea."

"When did you become a poet?"

"Oh, Aaron, you know how to corner a girl's heart."

"I do recall feeling safe in your presence. Our innocence then mocked the sun's blaze.

"I remember holding you in my arms and telling you that your future will be brighter than sunlight on winter snow, not weak and dim as the wintry sun."

"Catharine." She thought he never called her Kitty, "Your wisdom, silver-tongued like Patrick Henry's orations."

"Wow," she said and blushed slightly.

He enjoyed her eyes dancing with joy to the musical beams of his flattery.

Taking her hand, he quoted:

I see through the windows of your soul
Your youthful face fair as the fall harvest
The sun sank to harvest

Faded like the dreams of youth
A full moon casting its light
Fair as first love.

He thought her mien was like thousands of twinkling stars in a moonless night and as light as a petal blowing in the wind.

From across the room, Alex espied Burr releasing Kitty's hand. He feared the rumblings of a threatening storm in his chest, his eyes, seething flames of fire, his heart hardening to a sharp, keen, cruel, penetrating, piercing spear. Murmuring to himself, "It should be me who bathes in her dreaming, wistful eyes."

Troup, walking towards Alex, stared at a face as pale as the winter sky. He sensed his friend's temperament, smouldering in the bowels of a deep, dark cavern, ready to intensify in fiery resentment. His intensity, a cloud, growing dark and deep in mysterious skies.

Troup observed Alex, watching Kitty and Aaron bantering back and forth, their faces flashing like the sun playing on the water. He thought his roommate's pupils looked like burnt holes in a blanket.

Alex recalled walking and laughing with Kitty through the cold, the snow, the perfumes of night – after a storm, enjoying the moonlight, feeling the day's smiles, free from the dark shadows of his past.

"My friend, what troubles you?"

Alex dare not tell him, but Troup knew that seeing Burr basking in the morn of Kitty's dreamy, wistful personality touched a nerve.

Alex's insecurity was ready to burst forth, a malignancy bred in the womb of envy that flourishes nowhere else, fomenting magna. Behind his dry face, now looking more like leather than living tissue, his thoughts were scintillating with vindictive intent that could have been seen by a vessel at sea or a man on the moon. Alex unable to restrain himself, strutted off, without a degree of refinement or grace.

Quickly, though, Troup noticed his roommate hid his wrath under an undisturbed serenity of majestic repose. As he approached his foe, the wheels of Alex's malice spun like a windmill. His ego burnt like a flame through cannon smoke. A bright but not warm conversation ensued, foreboding danger. From that point in time, whenever he could, Alexander would damage the reflection of Aaron's tranquillity. On social occasions, his sincerity overflowed as glasses filled above the brim but as false as sand stairs.

As his core continued to fester from the scab of ill will, his venom would extend into the outer reaches of space and beyond the eyes of time. A complex interaction of Hamilton's personality within the social and political environment would produce high drama in America till friends and pleasures were gone. By the time of his death, he would become an exhausted well – threatening and commanding ruin.

CHAPTER 21

The Making of a Legend

They frowned at each other from across the Atlantic.
One felt righteous; the other felt strong.

The Colonies rolled their eyes, not wanting to pay taxes under the pretext that Parliament refused them representation.

The king and his inner circle glanced over the Atlantic, believing taxation the centrepiece of sovereign power.

Frustrated, the leaders of the Revolution shook their heads.

"Damn it," they said and refused to sit silently and watch the king and Parliament walk over their lives.

Rejecting this flawed philosophy's shield, the Revolution's sons moved towards picking up the sheaf of rebellion.

William Livingston said it best: "We must endeavour to make the best of everything. Whoever draws his sword against his prince must fling away its scabbard. We have passed the Rubicon, and whoever attempts to recross it will be knocked on the head by the one or the other party on the opposite banks. We cannot recede, nor should I wish it if we could. Great Britain must infallibly perish, and that speedily by her own corruption, and I never loved her as much as to wish to keep her company in her ruin."

Huffing out of breath, Robert Troup ascended the stairs to their room. Alex, intended to write an essay on political and economic corruption in Shakespeare's *Hamlet* and *Richard III*, but Myles Cooper asked him to consider corruption of power. Cooper suggested the Bard's comedy, *Measure for Measure*. The leading character, "whose blood is very snow-broth," finds himself consumed by a desire for a young woman who came to him for help.

Dressed and ready to retire to the library for a day of Shakespeare, Nicholas Fish, followed by Troup, stormed into the room. He turned to their voices, the space of the room between them.

"Have you forgotten the meeting in the fields?"

"Oh," he paused. Yes, he thought, for a second, blushing. "I did forget."

Six eyes blinked in unison.

The West Indian boy, drawn to the political drama between his adopted country and England, went off with his friends, the day of July 6, 1774.

The "Meeting," presided over by Alexander McDougall, was to consider a resolution on the Boston Port Bill.

As Alex listened to the orators, he said to his companions, "I am struck by what remains unsaid far more than by all the speaker's rhetoric."

"Alex, approach the stage," pleaded his friends, "and elucidate the omissions you have detected."

He weighed their suggestion as a grocer does his produce, thinking of the store in St. Croix. He recalled Rachael and James Junior fidgeting with a scale given to him by Nicholas Cruger as he made his way through the crowd to the platform. Acknowledged by McDougall, who welcomed him to the stage, he stood, all 5 foot 6 inches, before the boisterous crowd.

He hesitated for several seconds, the crowd glaring at the stranger and, in appearance, a mere boy, small-framed, and audacious. He perused the audience's faces, thinking they reminded him of the ledgers in the accounting books he kept for his past employer.

A series of fast-moving clouds played with the breath of summers' sunlight. He noticed the light cast on and off shadows over an older man's pockmarked face that looked like cobblestone. Beside him stood a woman whose youthful surface shone like a full moon. In the back of them was a tall gentleman whose presence resembled a weathered corn-stalk. Troup and Fish raised their hands, squeezed into fists, to the sky.

The crowd murmured. "The Collegian! The Collegian!"

About to embark, the lively face of Troup, flaming like the sun, caught his attention. As he began to speak, from the edge of his vision a woman looked like his mother was the last thing he remembered before starting. His words coursed like the free-flowing Hudson River.

"Friends and countrymen. England, ancient and firm, stands erect in its principles to govern us from an ocean as far as good stands above evil. Their King charges us with attempting to injure British commerce and subvert their Constitution. In doing so with the wave of his fist, he prohibits the landing and discharging, loading or shipping of goods, wares, and merchandise until restitution paid to the king's treasury. Thus, he bans the Boston Port to all ships, no matter what business ships might have. Medical supplies or food for the needy left offshore. The Royal Navy patrols the mouth of Boston Harbour to enforce his intolerable authority. The fist of

His Majesty's power so firm that our Boston brothers cannot bring hay from Charlestown to give to their starving horses."

Delight glowed from McDougall's face. How could such reason and passion come from a college student? He had heard his name but now wanted to know this youth.

"King and Parliament have violated our constitutional rights, natural rights, and our colonial charters. His capricious whim smells like a field of cows. The barbarous leaders of Great Britain violate natural justice. We must unite against his ignominious, cruel, and unjust edicts. The times call us to attention. We should act as one in opposition to this violation of the liberties of all. United we shall stand, divided we will fall."

Simultaneously, Troup and Fish turned to each other, remembering just last week they and Alex translated the Greek storyteller, Aesop's, *The Four Oxen and the Lion*. Alex recited those very words, "United we shall stand, divided we will fall."

"Rise my friends and countryman in defence of American liberty against the Generals of despotism. They now draw the lines of tyranny around our bulwarks of freedom and nothing but unity, resolution, and perseverance can save ourselves and posterity from a fate worse than death – SLAVERY. Tyranny without a covering now stares you all in the face. We must ALL unite to guard our Rights, or we will ALL be slaves!"

Off in the distance, a dog howled. Cheers pulsed from the crowd as Troup and Fish raised their fists again to the sky.

"But make no mistake, the applause, loud and lasting," Hercules Mulligan later told William Livingston, "A procession formed around him; it seemed endless as he joined his friends."

Alex kept his emotion well concealed as if it was just another day.

The next morning, "Alex," said Troup, "have you heard you have a following? The students admire you."

He looked at him with surprise, then realized how far he had come since landing in America. Leaning back in his chair, the corners of his mouth turned up. Troup and Fish brought him scented cards from anonymous sources. He grinned, more entertained than proud.

"You must feel good that people admire you," said Troup.

Alex's heart idled for a moment, ready to sprint forward as the wind of rebellion roared. In December 1774, he anonymously answered the much-read pamphlet authored by "A Westchester Farmer." The latter put forth, "our malice would hurt only ourselves for the English merchants would find new lines of trade if they lost the American trade."

The Collegian countered, "The enemies of the rights of humanity deceive the people because they wish to see one part of their species enslaved by another. That they have an invincible aversion to common sense smells in many respects. They endeavour to persuade us that the absolute sovereignty of Parliament does not imply our absolute slavery."

"Alex," said Troup. "The Farmer produced a mocking rebuttal to your first essay.

"Here," he handed it to his roommate.

Alex scanned it. "What nerve!"

"Your response, my friend?"

"To write a defence."

He produced a pamphlet of eighty-four pages, published by James Rivington on February 28, 1775.

At the Merchants Coffee House at the southeast corner of Wall and Water Streets, Troup told Alex in-between mouthfuls of food. "I like your argument because it centres on natural rights and construction of English and colonial history.

Yes," said Alex, "The fundamental source of his errors, sophisms, and false reasoning comes from total ignorance of the natural rights of humanity. These sacred rights must not rummage among old parchments or musty records. Written, as with a sunbeam, in the whole volume of human nature by the hand of the Divinity itself and can never be erased or obscured by mortal power."

Troup informed many patriots who authored the anonymous pamphlets, at first variously attributed to John Jay or William Livingston. Hamilton's college president, Myles Cooper, thought it absurd to imagine that so young a man could have written them. The two pamphlets, 60,000 words, enhanced his growing reputation. Prominent men and the public took notice of his name.

Troup and Fish rushed into their room on the morning of April 24, 1775. "Have you heard of the battles of Lexington and Concord?

Astonished, Alex looked up, "No."

"Citizens are charging like a tidal wave towards City Hall," said Troup.

"As mad as a wet cat," added Fish.

Alex dropped his quill and looked down at his parchment.

"My essay on Joan of Arc and Jesus must wait."

He jumped up and joined his two friends as they marched to the rhythmic pounding of eight-thousand footsteps, thinking his wish for a war waited around the corner.

The next day a handbill blaming Myles Cooper and four other "obnoxious gentlemen" for the deaths in Massachusetts circulated in every corner of the once tranquil town.

"Fly for your lives or anticipate your doom by becoming your own executioners," signed, Three Millions.

Alex blinked as Troup slouched into a chair across from him in their room at King's College on the warm night of May 10.

Before they commenced with their studies, they detected Nicholas Fish's earsplitting voice as he burst through the door. "They want to hang President Cooper!"

"Who?" asked Alex.

"Men, many men, who spent the evening listening at a public-house to John Smith and Joshua Hett Smith, who were most vocal."

After swallowing a proper dose of Madeira, a mob set off about midnight. They intended to seize Dr. Cooper from his bed, shave his head, cut off his ears, slit his nose, strip him naked, and turn him adrift.

An amber of fear crept through Alex. He looked at Troup and shook his head, his eyes bulging.

"We must act immediately!"

They then heard a commotion outside the three-story building of King's College.

"Nicholas, warn Dr. Cooper and take him out the back."

"I squared my shoulders," Alex wrote to the Reverend Knox, "and grabbed my courage; leaping on the stairs in front of the Doctor's apartment."

As he wrote, he assured himself, like any patriot, that the gang needed to be controulled.

"A crowd of rabble crashed through the gate, intent on getting their hands on the head of the college. Hearing venom in their toxicant mouths (no love milking their thoughts), and smelling liquor on the contorted faces of the vulgar multitude."

"He detained the mob," Troup wrote to Kitty Livingston, "as long as he could to gain the Doctor more time for his escape.

"I observed," Alex continued to Knox, "the mob stood armed with clubs, pigs at the trough. I recognized many a face from 'the meeting in the fields,' though now, they possessed more poison than a family of rattlesnakes."

"He tried to appeal to their honour," continued Troup to Kitty, "until they broke down the gate and rushed forward."

Kitty's face went ashen, sensing a clink of fear and brush of anxiety for Alex.

Alex's shoulders hunched.

"He let out a long breath before telling Fish and myself, "Hate with a target makes a deadly force."'

Describing his departure from New York in May 1775, in a poem published in the Gentlemen's Magazine #46 (London, 1776), Myles Cooper attributed his narrow escape from a revolutionary mob's clutches to the timely intervention of "that divine boy."

As for Miles Cooper, who lived in London until 1785, he often thought of Alexander. He intended to tell a particular friend and acquaintance with whom he went to dine with about the audacious Alexander. The gentleman, not being at home, the Doctor sauntered to a tavern, ordered a dinner, and crashed to the floor dead while it was being prepared.

The Revolution shuffled down the wrong road for Hamilton, bypassing his sense of public order. A dull ache settled into his heart. Alex read with dismay that the press and the types of the Tory printer, James Rivington, were carted off by a band of Connecticut militiamen. They then kidnapped Samuel Seabury, the Westchester farmer, and held him for thirty days with some other loyalists.

"I am always more or less alarmed," he wrote John Jay, who was serving in the Continental Congress, "at everything done out of mere will and pleasure without any proper authority."

"Though a committed revolutionary," he wrote Reverend Knox, "I fight against the dangerous excesses of mob rule to authority and care not that I risked my stature among the Sons of Liberty."

During breakfast, Robert Troup smiled before shovelling more food into his mouth.

"You look smart, robust, self-aware, confident today,' said Alex.

"I am when in your presence." His roommate hesitated before continuing.

"Alex."

"Yes, Robert."

"I see that lawlessness eats at you from the inside."

"Society requires order. If not, we devolve into beasts of prey."

Troup laid his hand on Alex's arm, wanting to make a further connection. "You correspond with the leaders of the revolt, but you are not yet old enough to vote or hold office."

Alex shrugged his shoulders. "But my age will not stop us from drilling in the newly formed Corsican Company, under Captain Thomas Fleming, an excellent disciplinarian, who served as adjutant of a regular British regiment."

"Where will we meet?"

"In the mornings at Saint George's graveyard."

"Where does the name Corsican come from?"

"In memory of the guerrilla activity on the island of Corsica."

A week later, the battle of Breed's Hill, June 17, 1775, resulted in four hundred casualties for the Patriots and 1000 casualties for the British.

"The dead lay as thick as sheep in the fold," said Nicholas Fish.

THE MEN WHO CHOOSE LIBERTY

Without looking at Alexander, Troup said, "Your preparation for the coming war is a beacon for all patriots."

Stiff-lipped, Alexander turned from his friends and looked out the window, sensing his fate waiting on the battlefield.

On June 25, 1775, General Washington made his way up Broadway in his carriage, pulled by six white horses, to take command of the Patriot forces in Boston.

Alex turned to Troup and Fish. "Our artillery company, the Corsicans, must have Liberty, or Death emblazoned on our round leather caps and our Green jackets, and a size or so too small."

Troup grimaced at the thought of tight clothes.

"And they must sport red tin hearts denoting, God and our Right, and I want the name changed to "Hearts of Oak," demanded Alex.

He never read *Measure for Measure*. Events moved so quickly after the extraordinary "Meeting in the Fields" that Shakespeare, Myles Cooper, and King's College vanished like a river running into an unknown sea of change.

The cynic in him believed the coming Revolution a family quarrel. He prayed it would provide for him the vehicle to actively risk his life, though not his character, to exalt his station in life.

CHAPTER 22

Give Me Liberty . . .

"Four British regiments sent to Boston closed its Port in
response to the 'Tea Party,'" related the thirty-one-year-old
Jefferson to his wife.

Surprise on her face, her lips bowed gracefully. Martha shook her head,
stood, and smelled the scent of a vase of flowers as the winter sun,
slanted and dull, lit the room.

Pouring another glass of chardonnay, he studied her with a lover's
unwavering attention. He wanted to stroke her hair, and wrap his arm
around her, but Boston's news cooled his desire.

"A mistake," she said, "one they will not forget."

"The times require the citizenry muster to the dangers impending over America from the hostile invasion of a sister colony."

He went back to reading the newspaper, realizing the darkening sky and the coming booms of thunder would allow his entrance upon the political stage. As Martha dropped into his lap, he blinked.

"The candles burn too bright," she told him.

"Not for making notes," he replied.

"I have other plans," she informed him. She let her hair down; her fingers massaged his scalp. Smiling, he lifted her with his two hands and kissed each hazel eye. She said nothing until they reached the bedroom.

"You forget your quill and paper."

Asked in July of 1774, six months after the Boston Tea Party, to script instructions for Virginian delegates to the coming Continental Congress in Philadelphia on September 4, 1774, Thomas accepted the task

He reminded the King, "It is neither our wishes nor interests to separate from Great Britain but, our own territories shall be taxed or regulated by any power on earth but our own."

His 6700 worded, *A Summary View of the Rights of British America*, met applause in the House of Burgesses, and George Washington referred to it as Mr. Jefferson's Bill of Rights.

Jefferson's ambition awakened – warm and bright.

In the back of the Burgesses on an extended bench, Patrick Henry stretched out his legs.

"Thomas," said Patrick, "your phrase a free people claiming their rights as derived from the laws of nature and not as the gift of their chief magistrate, circulates through the colonies."

A deep pleasure pumped from his heart. He enjoyed his celebrity and wanted more.

"I think war stands before us, Patrick. You must call the Virginian militia to move into a posture of defence."

"You have come a long way from digging in the words of philosophy."

Thomas lifted his head and smiled at him, his eyes bright as he thought of his future. "I want us to be prepared."

On March 23, 1775, at St. John's Church in Richmond, Virginia, Washington slumped in his seat at the Virginia Convention.

He did not look his height of six foot two. His long limbs and broad shoulders fit snugly under his brown silk suit buttoned tightly on his chest.

Jefferson trudged over and sat.

"Well, hello, George," he said frowning.

"Any news?" Washington asked from a dense brow. His steady right hand swatted a fly away from his straight nose.

"We need ten more votes to pass the resolution delivering Virginian troops for the Revolutionary War."

Jefferson slumped beside Washington, thinking he wanted his books and the quiet. The day of committees, votes, talk, and more talk had worn him out. Plus, he had a headache. The constant bickering annoyed him, but he reminded himself that achieving freedom required fortitude, and his spirit picked up.

Both men looked up when they heard the chair recognize Mr. Patrick Henry, the delegate from the county of Hanover.

"MR. PRESIDENT: No man thinks more highly than I do of the patriotism, as well as abilities, of the very worthy gentlemen who have just addressed the House. But different men often see the same subject in different lights; and, therefore, I hope it will not be thought disrespectful to those gentlemen if, entertaining as I do, opinions of a character very opposite to theirs, I shall speak forth my sentiments freely, and without reserve. This is no time for ceremony."

Washington turned and whispered to Jefferson, "Henry must rebuke our political opponents among the gentry as lovers of ease and security, or our cause is lost in the wind."

The mention of Henry's name still sent ripples of pain through Jefferson's delicate ego. No matter how much he tried to ignore this feeling, he failed.

"MR. PRESIDENT: I have, but one lamp by which my feet are guided; and that is the lamp of experience. I know of no way of judging of the future but by the past. And judging by the past, I wish to know what there has been in the conduct of the British ministry for the last ten years, to justify those hopes with which gentlemen have been pleased to solace themselves, and the House?"

Colonel Edward Carrington, standing outside the Henrico church and listening through an open window, exclaimed, "Right here, I wish to be buried." This desire his widow later satisfied.

"MR. PRESIDENT: They tell us, sir, that we are weak; unable to cope with so formidable an adversary. But when shall we be stronger? Will it be the next week or the next year? Will it be when we are totally disarmed, and when a British guard shall be stationed in every house? Shall we gather strength by irresolution and inaction? Shall we acquire the means of effectual resistance, by lying supinely on our backs, and hugging the delusive phantom of hope, until our enemies shall have bound us hand and foot?"

Several members of the convention shook with excitement from Henry's rhetorical dynamite. One who just turned forty-two thought, *what a birthday present!*

Jefferson experienced searing pain in his right temple and jammed his knee into the chair's back in front of him.

"MR. PRESIDENT: There is no retreat but in submission and slavery! Our chains are forged! Their clanking may be heard on the plains of Boston! The war is inevitable, and let it come! I repeat it, sir, let it come."

The Burgesses members watched as Henry assumed the position of a condemned galley slave, loaded with fetters, awaiting his doom. His form was bowed; his wrists crossed; his manacles were almost visible as he stood as an embodiment of helplessness and agony. After a solemn pause, he raised his eyes and chained hands towards heaven, and prayed, in words and tones that thrilled every heart, "Forbid it Almighty God!"

He then turned towards the timid loyalists of the house. They were quaking with terror at the idea of the consequences of participating in proceedings that would be visited with the penalties of treason by the British crown.

Slowly, he bent his form nearer to earth, saying, "I know not what course others may take," and he accompanied the words with his hands still crossed, while he seemed to be weighted down with additional chains.

"It is in vain, sir, to extenuate the matter. Gentlemen may cry, 'Peace, Peace,' but there is no peace. The war is begun! The next gale that sweeps from the North will bring to our ears the clash of resounding arms! Our brethren are already in the field! Why stand we here idle?"

Henry stopped speaking and bent his body.

Washington thought he appeared transformed into an oppressed, heartbroken, and hopeless felon. After remaining in this posture of humiliation long enough to impress the imagination with the condition of the colony under the iron heel of military despotism, he arose proudly. He exclaimed, "but as for me . . ."

The words hissed through his clenched teeth, while his body was thrown back, and every muscle and tendon was strained against the fetters that bound him. With his countenance distorted by agony and rage, he looked for a moment like Lacoön in a death struggle with coiling serpents; then, the loud, clear, triumphant notes, "GIVE ME LIBERTY!" electrified the assembly.

Jefferson adjusted his position in the chair, wondering where Henry found his thoughts. How could a man who rejected reading books find such words?

"MR. PRESIDENT: "What is it that gentlemen wish? What would they have? Is life so dear, or peace so sweet, as to be purchased at the price of chains and slavery? Forbid it, Almighty God."

A hush roared in the Burgesses.

For many listening, it was not a question but a stern demand, which would submit to no refusal or delay.

"The sound of his voice, as he spoke these memorable words," an observer wrote, "was like that of a Spartan paean on the Field of Plataea, and, as each syllable of the word 'Liberty' echoed through the building, his fetters shivered; his arms were hurled apart, and the links of his chains were scattered to the winds. When he spoke the word 'liberty' with an emphasis never given it before, his hands were open, and his arms elevated and extended; his countenance was radiant; he stood erect and defiant; while the sound of his voice and the sublimity of his attitude made him appear a magnificent incarnation of Freedom, and express all that can be acquired or enjoyed by nations and individuals invincible and free.

"MR. PRESIDENT: "I know not what course others may take; but as for me, GIVE ME LIBERTY!"

After a momentary pause, only long enough to permit the echo of the word "liberty" to cease, he let his left hand fall powerless to his side and clenched his right hand firmly as if holding a dagger with the point aimed at his breast.

He stood like a Roman senator defying Caesar while the unconquerable spirit of Cato of Utica flashed from every feature, and he closed the grand appeal with the solemn words, "OR GIVE ME DEATH!"

Standing silent for several heartbeats, Jefferson realized Henry's words sounded with the awful cadence of a hero's dirge. Fearless of death, and victorious in death, he suited the action to the word by a blow on the left breast with the right hand, which seemed to drive the dagger into the Patriot's heart.

Thomas Marshall told his son that evening, John, the speech was "one of the boldest, vehement, and animated pieces of eloquence that had ever been delivered."

The next morning Washington told his wife, Martha, "Henry made dry sentences dynamic, mixing adverbs and adjectives and nouns. His mesmeric words carried the resolution, one of the grand revolutionary declarations of history."

Patrick's creation blasted through the hard grey skies; untouched and un-trampled, his words flowed over the colonies' terrain, painting over it.

A few weeks later, the raw-boned, sturdy as bedrock Henry stopped Jefferson at the Burgesses' entryway, "Have you heard Mr. Jefferson that on Wednesday, April 19, the Battles of Lexington and Concord resulted in bloodshed."

"Yes, the birth of civil war drops upon us."

"The British royal marines removed fifteen-half barrels of gunpowder," informed Henry, "from the public magazine at Williamsburg, Virginia to the HMS *Magdalen*."

"Lord Dunmore," replied Jefferson, "promises freedom to the slaves and Williamsburg to ashes should there be further injury or insult to the royal prerogative."

Back at Monticello, work-related headaches dominated Jefferson's days, but Philadelphia's landscape gripped his imagination.

"My malady," he told Martha, "will not serve as an excuse for me to not attend the Second Continental Congress in Philadelphia this coming summer."

"Who will you replace?"

"Washington, who now commands the reins of the Army of the Revolution."

"My dearest husband, with a mouth for history, I see that your palate tastes the rebellion."

A grin flashed on his face. Flushed with enthusiasm, he jumped up, grabbed a quill, and wrote in his journal.

Martha knew Monticello would be quiet without his footsteps echoing around her. She felt abandoned. Stupid, she told herself, and she pretended to smile.

Armed with his notebook, Jefferson organized his thoughts as his carriage crossed Market Street in Philadelphia in the late afternoon.

The sun seemed more robust than usual, and he observed, its light bold and bright as he heard about the battle of Breed's Hill (June 17) in Charlestown, Massachusetts.

"Over one several hundred men killed and hundreds more wounded."

He absorbed the news and swallowed the fact that the tide of history rushed towards him.

The civil government was suspended in Massachusetts. Boston was now occupied by General Gage, he learned.

Benjamin Randolph, a Quaker cabinetmaker, who lived on Chestnut, a narrow cobblestoned street, housed Jefferson. His lodgings were close to

Philadelphia's population centre, now more a financial and cultural centre than he remembered when there in 1766 for vaccination against smallpox.

He heard the risings and fallings of vendors hawking their wares and carriages passing on the street through his window. He dreamed of Martha's hands, rubbing his temples and massaging away his headache. He wished to have his fingers comb through her hair and kiss her lowered lashes.

When writing to Abagail about Jefferson, John Adams commented, "Misery takes the upper hand when it comes to separation."

The following morning, possibilities and angles raced through Thomas's mind as he recorded his views on how to approach the coming crisis. There would be no time for cupcakes and lemonade he realized as he rushed off on June 21, bearing his credentials from the Virginia Convention to the Second Continental Congress. He recognized the decked, gable-roofed Pennsylvania State House, completed in 1748 with balustrades between the chimneys and surmounted by a centrally located cupola. Approaching his fate, he struggled to set aside any insecurity.

He lumbered towards the first floor. The two chambers, about 40 feet square, separated by a spacious centre hall about 20 feet wide, were elbow to elbow with men.

"For a State House," he wrote Martha, "it lacks elegant furnishings. The chairs, tables, curtains, screens, and did not appear appropriate. The open fireplaces dormant but the heat in the room from its occupants' emotions, strong."

Congress appointed a committee of five on June 23, "To draw up a declaration to give popularity to the cause." The committee members were John Rutledge of South Carolina, William Livingston of New Jersey, Benjamin Franklin of Pennsylvania, John Jay of New York, and Thomas Johnson of Maryland. On the following day, June 24, the committee reported the draft of the *Declaration of the Causes and Necessity of Taking Up Arms*, said to have been written by John Rutledge.

On the 26th, and, after more debate, the declaration returned to the committee, and John Dickinson and Thomas Jefferson added to it. The latter learned that the youngest member of the convention, John Jay was slightly younger by twenty months. The fact disappointed the Virginian.

"Mr. Jefferson, as the committee asked us to join their deliberation," said Dickinson, "would you be my guest for breakfast at my country estate, Fair-Hill, on the outskirts of Philadelphia?"

The Virginian's heart skipped a beat. *To work on a committee with the Penman of the Revolution, he thought.* The man who wrote *Letters from a Farmer in Pennsylvania*, he recalled the words, "Although a constitution is perpetual, the power of the government is not unlimited."

"Yes, tomorrow morning is fine," replied Jefferson.

A short, stocky man approached Jefferson. He fumbled a bit. "Mr. Jefferson, I presume?"

"Mr. Adams, I believe."

They hit it off as both men itched for independence.

Later that evening, by his desk at his room on Chestnut Street, Thomas reviewed the Rutledge declaration. Pride and regret moved through him. Not up to the task, he realized. He wandered over to the open window; the air smelled of lilies and roses and rang with voices and horse trots. For the next hour, Jefferson split himself between Rutledge's declaration and writing his own.

Between grievances and action, liberty and tyranny, either way, he mused, the memories of the last year will never fade. His paragraphs, big and small, he knew were part of him. He could refine them, finesse them, submit them. He eased back in his chair, circled his beliefs as they dressed his mind. All there, he thought, as his quill finished sentences on the parchment. The wonder, the joy, without the smallest tug of sorrow. His cup of satisfaction was overflowing.

"You ought to put more on your plate, Thomas," said Dickinson, "the morning meal – the most important."

Jefferson stared down at the scrambled eggs and sausage heaped in front of him. He added two spoons of sugar to the tea and downed it.

His head buzzed as his host walked to the window, looking out at the sunlight piercing his estate's gardens and lawns. He stood for several moments before coming back to the table with Jefferson plopped down, who in his heart longed for Martha's arms and the serenity of Monticello.

The Virginian sighed and lifted his chin and then took two big mouthfuls of his breakfast. The Pennsylvanian lit a cigarette. Jefferson pulled back, his eyes narrowing against the smoke. Dickinson's face grabbed his attention.

"Rutledge's version, too stilted! My style better suits the occasion," said Jefferson

"I must say, Thomas, I would have preferred that King George III considered our earlier petitions."

"Not an easy time," informed Jefferson, "holding revolutionary views."

"I worry," added Dickinson. "How do we treat the honest loyalist?"

"Unfortunately, the tree of liberty must be refreshed with the blood of patriots and tyrants; it is its natural manure."

"The cause of freedom requires dignity and should not be sullied by turbulence and tumult."

Jefferson thought him a conservative sort of rebel.

"I fear tavern meetings and nocturnal societies that rule the community," stated Dickinson.

"A little rebellion now and then is like storms in the physical world."

"We have moved beyond the point where reconciliation seems probable. It saddens me," stated Dickinson.

"Franklin said it best," replied Jefferson, "Rebellion to tyrants is obedience to God."

"Those who believe riots and tumults are the only way to solve the problem," asserted Dickinson, "are much mistaken."

"Can I get that in writing?" asked Thomas.

Dickinson laughed then said, "May I quote Aristotle. 'Patience is so like fortitude that she seems either her sister or her daughter.'"

Thomas narrowed his eyes at him and began to arrange his thoughts. "I have as much as any patriot."

They crossed over from the dining room and started to the garden. With a cigarette in hand, Dickinson addressed his younger colleague.

"The past humiliation of France and England's complete success in the Seven Years War marked the birth of the revolt of the colonies. It allowed England to decree that certain goods exported from the colonies to European countries pass through British ports. They required that most products of those countries and their possessions imported into the colonies sail by way of Britain, to collect customs."

Jefferson thought the British authorities wished to dominate the market for transactions through monopoly, never realizing their self-defeating actions. Both men were unaware that the revolt of the colonies, a reaction of the prevailing system against itself, and the coming conflict would turn all of Europe upside down in commerce and politics.

"Have you read Turgot?" asked Dickinson.

The French economist and statesman, thought Jefferson, who recognized the folly of British policy. He noticed how bright Dickinson's eyes were, how the light caught the edges of his pupils. He wondered why they looked at the problem differently and, with a quick smirk, said to himself, *the older man remains mired in his ways.*

"Turgot feels we are sure to win our independence," put forth Jefferson. "If the English should conquer the seacoast, it could only be by devastating it. We could then retreat to the interior and harass the English on the coast; or, we will bend while force remains on us, only to spring up again at the first opportunity."

"His pertinent premise, I believe," stated Dickinson, "right reasoning requires the colonies not to break off trade with England but to remove any all possible obstacles to trade with her."

"It flies in the face of common sense."

"But common sense remains not that common."

After an apologetic glance, Dickinson continued. "It is the only wise course, for when the conflict begins, we are poorly prepared for military preparations; either with passive resistance or through an energetic war based on the adequate organization of the army and finance. We have little powder or lead, few guns, little cloth or leather, or means of making them, and are in general almost destitute of supplies for an army. As they were cheaper and better in England than anywhere else, that is the place to purchase them."

Jefferson and the revolution leaders focused on the commercial profit the English merchants would gain, missing the opportunity to get from England the cheapest and best supplies with which to fight England.

"The enterprise and the apparatus of fighting the British," concluded Dickinson, "absurd!"

This was something that Hamilton noticed and never forgot, but he failed to see the reasonable cause. Back at Chestnut Street, his night self-criticized his morning self on a sketch not done well. Always more to do, Jefferson mused.

He drafted his "crème de la crème" for the committee but decided to give the draft one more swirl before submitting it. Thinking his draft right and hoping the members of the committee agreed, Jefferson still despaired. It must be superb, he thought.

Wanting more time to bathe, dress, go over his words, check and recheck his grammar, he wished to hold back the clock's hands. By eight in the morning, he started, winding through the streets to Congress's entrance foyer with its soaring ceiling room where the committee met. Dickinson and his elves already there, he noted. He acknowledged Dickinson's hello as he rushed to assemble by John and Ben, whose smiles were quick, spontaneous. Soft on Franklin, even a little sly, and delighted on Adams.

"As I habitually disagreed with the Philadelphian," Jefferson wrote to Martha, *on principle, my interest in the Declaration piqued. I prepared a draught of the Declrn committed to us. I submitted this fair copy to Dickinson in private before reporting to the committee. He objected – too harsh –needs softening. As he held the distinction of elder statesman, I felt if he and I could agree, it would seem natural to suppose that the committee would the more readily accept our compromise draft. After a private consultation with him, I left him my draft. He made several corrections and three significant suggestions in his handwriting.*

Upon meeting with him again in private, he informed me the corrections were principally in phraseology or altered to suit his sense of rhythm and style.

His three suggestions:

First: to take notice of Lord Chatham's plan of conciliation and to pay tribute to his great abilities;

Second: to show appreciation of the great men in Parliament and the cities and towns in England that acknowledged the justice of the American cause

Third: to comment on Lord North's proposal but I disregarded it altogether.

"The Rutledge and Jefferson drafts," William Livingston wrote to William Alexander (Lord Stirling) on July 4, 1775, "revealed the faults common to our Southern gentlemen. Much fault-finding and declamation, with little sense or dignity. They seem to think a reiteration of tyranny, despotism, bloody, &c, all that is needed to unite us at home and convince the bribed voters of the North, of the justice of our cause."

"When I reported the draft to the committee," continued Jefferson to his wife,

> *Mr. Dickinson looked both surprised and annoyed. Out of regard for my sensitivity, he took my draft. He altered, he said, only half a dozen minor phrases and put his suggestions in the form of queries.*
>
> *Mr. Dickinson and Mr. Livingston still retained the hope of reconciliation with the mother country and unwilling their objectives thwarted by offensive statements.*
>
> *Dickinson seems so honest a man & so able a one that he garners indulgence even by those who do not feel his scruples.*
>
> *The committee desired him to retouch it and requested him to take my paper and put it into a form, he could approve, which he did in the form now approved & reported to Congress, who accepted it July 6.*
>
> *His statement, entirely new, preserved only the last 4. paragraphs & half of my second draft.*

Thomas rubbed a dimple under his chin, thinking, *I should never have given him my draft.* He shook his head as he leaned back in the chair as he pictured Martha combing her auburn hair.

He stepped out and closed the drama with Dickinson.

"The truth of the matter," Livingston said to Hamilton. "Dickinson certainly embodied a few of Jefferson's phrases and ideas, but not more so in those than in the other parts of the Declaration. It seems obvious at a glance that Dickinson produced an amplification and revision of the outline and structure of Jefferson's draft. Throughout my friend's text in the beginning, in the middle, and at the end are long passages copied almost verbatim from Jefferson. It appears apparent, too, that, far from softening Jefferson's words, Dickinson strengthened them!"

Be assured that Dickinson contributed the bold and quotable words, 'Our cause is just. Our union is perfect. Our internal resources are great, and, if necessary, foreign assistance is attainable' that appear at the close of the Declaration and not those of Mr. Jefferson."

Jefferson pronounced, "Dickinson retouched my former draft."

Towards the end of his years, he said, "Dickinson wrote an entire new statement, retaining only the last four and a half of the paragraphs of my draft."

"Nothing in the two drafts revolved around polarities of radicalism and conservatism, timidity, and boldness, weakness or strength. What upset Jefferson," Livingston said to Hamilton, "Dickinson altered his style and method of presentation!"

Hamilton sighed, "The Virginian's pride refused to accept a revision." He smiled and managed both a smug and sympathetic look. "That the text of the *Declaration* as adopted by Congress, the result of collaboration on the part of the two men, struck a nerve,"

William Livingston shrugged. "Jefferson's ego bruises easily." He stopped to weigh his thoughts before informing Hamilton. "Both men expressed hope for a restoration of harmony. Both declared the aim of resisting violence and not of intending something else. But whereas Jefferson employed a circumlocution to express this idea, Dickinson wrote bluntly!"

Alex mimicked the expression of Livingston. He filed the information in a compartment of his mind and nodded in response, thinking Jefferson an odd sort of fellow he had no desire to know.

CHAPTER 23

The Son of a Butler, Boiling Water, and the Other George

Horatio Gates sailed for North America in August of 1772, in the 14-gun HMS *Kingfisher*'s maiden voyage, commanded by Thomas Jordan, a friend of the family who arranged the paperwork for the passage. Elizabeth Horatio, a small, rosy-cheeked woman, snug with her devotion, watched a dolphin nudge another. Then, a dolphin game of play began as they swarmed at high speeds taking turns chasing each other.

As their flippers glistened in the sun, she recalled the conversation that led the couple to re-settle in British America. "Advancement in the British Army requires money or influence," said Horatio, standing by the draughty window, his jaw tightened. She knew the son of a butler possessed little of either. "I have spent considerable time trying to secure through influential patrons a prestigious position under the government but to no avail." A hiss in his voice warned Elizabeth about his feelings. "I am disgusted with the politics of England.

"It is time to leave. Retire, my dear husband, at the rank of major and let us emigrate to America."

"Can we live on my retirement of half-pay?" Horatio's eyes blazed like a furnace.

"Yes, and lest you forget, Colonel Washington offered his assistance."

Through a window of his past, Gates saw few advancements as a professional soldier, and his many failures to rise in rank irked him, the crunch and rattle for glory as a commanding general raging within him. "Let me mull it over."

George Washington, born in 1732, and the eldest child of the second marriage of the thirty-seven-year-old Augustine Washington and the twenty-three-year-old Mary Johnson Ball, the Northern Neck's belle, and the Rose of Epping Forest, spent his early years in the port town of Fredericksburg, Virginia. He played by the courthouse and stone prison and watched ships with tobacco, grain, and iron sail to London.

Beyond the sleepy sea, he watched the sun peak brightly, ready to start a new day. His goals remained silent with a shadow of sadness as he wondered where the sails of fate would take him. In a homespun dress and a straw bonnet, Mary Washington, after her husband died in the spring of 1743, screamed at her son, "Git over here! You must do like I say! No diving from rocks, ever again, I have seen it!"

George chuckled and rolled his eyes, not enjoying her loud voice slipping through his thoughts. With her pipe in hand (she loved her Virginia tobacco), she informed him, "You will pay if I ketch you. You need to help me on the land. No polished society here." His father had left George one of his farms and land and lots in Fredericksburg. The orphan bonded with his oldest half-brother, Lawrence, who inherited the Little Hunting Creek estate that he renamed Mount Vernon after Admiral Vernon. Lawrence had served with Vernon in the War of Jenkins› Ear, a battle with Spain in the Caribbean. Three months after his father›s death, Lawrence married Ann, the daughter of the richest man in Virginia, William Fairfax. At Mount Vernon, George became acquainted with Fairfax, who took a liking to him. He invited the eleven-year-old boy to his estate at Belvoir. «George,» said Fairfax, «I consider you a devoted friend.»

"I trust you, Sir."

"And I appreciate that." George smiled, having no doubt he made a valuable companion.

"You do not hide your weaknesses or pretend to have strengths; I admire that in a man."

George knew that his fate rested in the hands of the older man. "You are good at math. Would you like to learn to survey?" As sure as 2 and 2 equal 4," said George as he giggled. He informed his younger brother, Jack, "Spend more time with the family at Belvoir; it is in their power to help us on many occasions. I am under many obligations, especially to the old gentleman."

In 1748, the sixteen-year-old George surveyed lands for the Fairfax family across the Blue Ridge Mountains and into the Shenandoah Valley's depths to create leaseholds for sale. He noted his month-long exploits in a diary, *A Journal of my Journey over the Mountains.*

"George," said Fairfax, "I enjoyed your description of the lands and your trek over the mountain." His benefactor's words sang gently within George and woke him up to do more with his life. "I documented it for you." Fairfax scratched his chin, studying George, sensing the quiet, gentle young man behind his humility. While surveying more lands in the Shenandoah

Valley in the spring of 1750 for the Fairfax family, he bought fifteen hundred acres for himself. A year later, he bought more, and years later, he bought even more.

Before his brother's death at Mount Vernon in July of 1752, George had lobbied Lt. Governor Dinwiddie to consider him for the adjutant general of one of the newly created militia districts. Through William Fairfax and his brother's connections, Dinwiddie appointed George to the position with Major's rank, and the six-foot-two-inch twenty-year-old exchanged his sextant for a rifle. Lawrence's widow, Anne Fairfax, upon remarrying, moved from Mount Vernon. Upon her death in 1761, George inherited the estate.

Major Gates did mull it over; upon her father's death, the couple sold his estate and left England. But, Elizabeth knew the military life still beckoned her husband. Exhausted from trying to gain a military command, the petulant and despairing Gates left England in 1772, more than ever wanting change. With George Washington's help, he purchased a 659-acre plantation on the Potomac River near Shepherdstown in Berkeley County, Virginia. Elizabeth Gates called their new home Traveller's Rest.

Made a lieutenant colonel in the militia, Horatio Gates also served as a local justice. The short, stocky man studied the colonies' dissent towards the mother country, hoping to seize military command.

Major Gates understood that the Colonial leaders needed his military expertise. He resided close to Charles Lee's residence, Hopewell, a 2,752-acre estate with a log and limestone farmhouse. Lee, an English veteran, possessed the honour of being adopted by the Mohocks, aka Mohawks, into their tribe under the name of Ounewaterika or Boiling Water, *one whose spirits are never asleep.* In 1756, Lee married the daughter of the Seneca Chief White Thunder. His marriage to the chief's daughter entitled him to a seat and the privilege of smoking a pipe in the Indian councils. His mind tried to focus on the space in the air between them. He decided he preferred the bottle to the pipe. The chief's daughter bore him fraternal twins that he abandoned along with their mother when he returned to the 44th Regiment.

Major Gates, a frequent guest at Mount Vernon, lingered in the central hall, observing maps on the walls and hearing the slim, tall Charles Lee blow his trumpet. No matter how hard Lee blew, Gates admired him. The Major knew men said, "Lee stood vain to the verge of insanity, with an acid of the tongue, exhibited a mean spirit and envious of all."

"Burgoyne owed his success in Portugal to the fact that he listened to me!" Said Lee.

"I played a vital part in his victory at the Battle of Vila Velha on October 5, 1762. Because of his politics, the ministry praised him and passed me over for command."

Before entering Washington's study to discuss Lexington and Concord's recent battles, Gates remembered how much he owed Lee. He pulled him from the battlefield during Braddock's tragic misstep at Monongahela.

"He did save my life," he mumbled to himself.

"Are we not masters of our house?" asked Washington.

"Not as long as we remain colonies subject to British tyranny," replied Lee, whose expensive tailored uniform smelled of dog.

No wonder his dogs, eleven in total, prowled around Mount Vernon, lunged and nipped at anyone who approached and sat under the table during dinner.

"King George III is a mongrel between pig and puppy, begotten by a wild boar on a bitch wolf." Washington's cheeks flushed bright pink.

"The dispute between the mother country and the colonies," continued Lee as he petted his dog, Spado, "represents the ongoing universal struggle for human freedom. We must resist with arms or suffer enslavement."

"England requires the thirteen colonies," said Gates, "to supply the raw materials of sugar, tobacco, dyewoods, rice, naval stores, beaver, and other furs, indigo, and wood products. In return, the colonies buy the expensive finished goods of British factories."

"If a revolution is needed to set us on the road to becoming great," Washington interjected, "let us stand shoulder to shoulder with the planters, the New England merchants, the shippers, and the Sons of Liberty."

"The King is a fool and his ministers rogues and villains," said Lee.

He recently praised America as "the last asylum of liberty" (predating Paine's 1776 Common Sense) in an essay "To the Citizens of Philadelphia" under the pseudonym Anglus Americanus.

"I hear," said Gates, "many military men have no desire to return home to England when their tours of duty here have ended. They see in the colonies, everything is new, business booms, towns, and cities are lively places, people are well dressed, and one sees few beggars on the streets."

"The real issue that separates the colonies and mother country is not economic but constitutional," said Lee.

"Are we subject to Parliament?" asked Washington. "Or only to our colonial assemblies?"

"Simply put," said Lee, "it is this! Do those whores in Parliament have the legal authority to rule us?"

"We must demolish those badges of slavery that suffocate the natural spirit of freedom."

"The day of decision is here," stated Gates, "either we are an independent commonwealth within the British Empire subject to the king only or pawns of Parliament."

"While in NY, Penn, Mass., and Virginia, I ascertained there is not a man who is not determined to sacrifice his property, his life, family, and children, in the cause of Boston."

"Gentlemen," said Washington in a voice thick with conviction, "we need someone who holds the public's confidence and can counter-punch General Gage."

He stopped and stared at Gates and Lee. He noticed they offered little eye contact, thinking the British too reserved.

"I must retire and give this some thought," said Lee, "but before I do, we must demolish those badges of slavery associated with tyranny."

For the first time, Washington seemed to relax. Major Gates glanced at him and noted his calm, steady, blue-grey eyes. With a deliberate, deferential, and engaging manner, Colonel Washington smiled.

Gates observed his sandy brown hair obscured under his fashionable powdered mane tied in the back. The skin on his face was pockmarked. He suffered from an attack of smallpox when he was 18 that made him immune to the disease. When it later ravaged the Continental Army, he did not suffer. The Major felt superior to the aristocratic Virginian, and pain and anger marched in step with his thoughts.

"Colonel, I will always be at your assistance," announced Gates. Washington gave him a slow, pleasing sideways glance. Gates slept soundly that night and dreamed of commanding an army, longing for fame.

As victory and adoration stood within reach, he heard a knock on his door and a voice urging him to the parlour.

CHAPTER 24

Free of the Cloth

Burr, standing on the vast expanse of the lawn at Nassau Hall, enjoying the fall sun's warmth, decided to confront the religious leanings pressing against him. He turned, giving the Hall a long look, and went off to the home of Reverend Joseph Bellamy – a friend and disciple of his grandfather – who had established a school of divinity.

"It is natural for your creative capacity," said the Reverend, "to question the natural order, the given."

"So, this is all right to do." He fell silent for a moment, counting the pox marks on Bellamy's face. "But this leads me," continued Burr, "to question the character of religious directives and the ultimate itself, religion."

"This," asserted the man of the cloth, "is not acceptable."

"But, I struggle with this quandary."

"One must believe." He took Burr's hand but felt its coolness.

"You must follow your father and maternal grandfather's calling to take heaven by voice."

Burr, thinking if he ceased to question religion, he would be free to challenge everything else. He decided to doubt everything. Having nothing against God, he objected to its followers, who lacked toleration.

"Reverend, a religious calling finds no meter in me. Others must conduct the music of theology. The road to Heaven is open to all alike."

Burr watched him nod, hold his tongue, and then shift his attention – totally to another student. Stripped of the cloak of religion, Burr started a journey. In love with the moment, hoping for adventure, he jolted forward.

After returning from Sarah Livingston and John Jay's wedding, Aaron informed his uncle that he decided on the law as a career. No whoops and shouts, but from his angle, he observed Aunt Rhoda's face light up. By May 1774, the eighteen-year-old lived in Tapping and Sally Reeve's sycamore-shaded home, studying jurisprudence with his brother-law

On a Sunday visit to his cousin, Thaddeus Burr, at Fairfield, he met the 28-year-old Dorothy (Dolley) Quincy, John Hancock's finance, and Hancock's aunt, Lydia. Dolly's eyes widened. Her lips pursed, she studied Aaron. He cleared his throat, then stepped back when she touched his arm.

Thaddeus wrote to Tapping Reeve, "Burr came to us on Sunday evening, spent the Sabbath with us. Mrs. Hancock is vastly pleased with him. And, as to Miss Quincy, if Mr. H. was out-of-the-way, I don't know, but she would court him. Burr went off to Greenfield last night."

Aunt Lydia feared that he or any man should gain her affections and defeat the purpose of connecting her with her nephew. She guarded her against the approach of any invader upon Mr. John Hancock's rights. Miss Quincy bemoaned that her chaperone seldom allowed her a moment alone with the young, handsome man. Always polite, the charming young Aaron paid attention to the older woman and her aunt. He enjoyed the time, listening to their voices carry in the warm air, the barking of his uncle's dogs, and lilac's scent.

Dorothy Dudley, a friend of Miss Quincy, wrote to a friend in Philadelphia,

> *Aunt Lydia is well acquainted with Mr. Timothy Edwards, a son of Rev. Jonathan Edwards. I stopped at his house. Mr. Edwards has a nephew living with him, whom he has adopted and treats in all respects as his son. Aaron Burr is his name. He is a young man of fascinating manners and many accomplishments.*
>
> *He is much charmed with Miss Quincy, I have heard, and she, in turn, is not insensible to his attractions, but Madame Hancock keeps a jealous eye on them both and would not allow any advances on the part of the young man towards the prize reserved for her nephew.*
>
> *When the knot is tied that makes them one; she is free to breathe.*

The rumour monger could not correctly identify the house owner, confusing Timothy Edwards for Thaddeus Burr. And here Aaron Burr met his first serious episode of gossip and conjecture that would plague him throughout his life.

'The pert, petulant, pretty Dolly craved attention." Aaron informed his sister. "She lacked any heartfelt fluttering in her breast for me though pleased by my consideration."

Aaron turned, expecting to see a law student, and watched Tapping walk towards him. Sally smiled and poured him and Tapping a glass of lemonade from a half-filled pitcher.

"From what I hear, Aaron," said Sally, "her education is shallow and her intellect not much better."

Aaron arched an eyebrow, "Never too late to learn."

Reeve chimed in, "Welcome home. I trust things went well," as they clanked their glasses.

Sally patted his face. "My brother, the gallant. Attentive to a woman's feelings."

Aaron laughed and kissed her hand. Armed with his family and close friends' constant Whig talk, the words of sedition became a familiar echo in Burr's life corridors. His uncle's commencement address in 1767, "On Liberty," was always flowing through his mind.

With notebook in hand, he continued to read military history and studied ancient battles.

Henry "Light Horse Harry" Lee had inspired in Aaron an appreciation of the strategy and tactics of Hannibal, Greek general Epaminondas of Thebes, and Aristides of Athens.

Lee drew sketches of Hannibal's evasive tactics that allowed his forces to defeat the superior Roman legion leaders. To sharpen their understanding of such evasive tactics, the two students took turns using imaginary troops, and the other maneuvered a counter-strategy.

They admired Epaminondas's methods of deploying cavalry on his flanks in battle, They realized this changed warfare, which was not lost on them when they engaged in the war with England. From Aristides, they learned to use cavalry in unorthodox ways to support the front lines. Harry Lee wrote a treatise on the calvary that President Witherspoon praised before an assembly of all the students.

"If only Washington studied these generals," Burr later told Sally, "or listened to those that did. The Americans would have won the war earlier on their initiative, not on the British generals' lack of enterprise."

"Some act with wisdom and some otherwise," he murmured. When in the future he passed a monument to Washington or heard his name, he stiffened.

When the news of Concord and Lexington reached him in April 1775, his destiny invited him to the adventures of war and youth's dreams. He drew the breath of the forthcoming revolution, and the fire of war pierced his thoughts. Reading ancient heroes, he became influenced by their courage, loyalty, generosity, self-sacrifice, and magnanimity; he looked forward to his future. He took to heart John Dryden's words, "All things are subject to decay, and when fate summons, monarchs must obey."

Hearing of Bunker Hill's Battle, June 17, 1775, though most of the action took place on nearby Breed's Hill, Aaron rushed to enjoin Matty, Mathias Ogden. Matty was then wooing Hannah Dayton in Elizabethtown.

As Aaron rushed towards the Dayton house, a bolt of lightning pierced the grey sky. He looked up, knowing destiny waited. Approaching the door, Aaron made his presence known to the family inside the house. Hannah jumped out of her chair and rushed towards her Aaron as he witnessed a pained look on Matty's eyes. Hannah winked at Aaron.

"We must join the patriotic cause of liberty."

Later in the day walking, with Aaron and Matty, Hannah told Aaron, "He is yours. Make sure you both come back."

"Of course," said Aaron, "The stars will it."

"Wonderful," Hannah said. She turned to Matty, "Keep a journal so when you come home . . ." Matty kissed his sweetheart good-bye.

They went off to Cambridge with letters of recommendation to Joseph Reed of Philadelphia, an aide to Washington, from a member of the Continental Congress, Elias Boudinot.

For a moment, a piercing hush besieged them. The pain of leaving his sweetheart, Hannah Dayton, marched through him with a terrible intensity.

"Matty, a world of new possibilities await us beyond our ordinary experiences and limitations."

Matty bit his lip, and his eyes widened, "I hope I have the talent, ability, and potential."

"Inspiration will awaken us to the impossible."

"I wish I possessed your confidence."

Aaron winked at him, "God told me so." He then laughed heartily.

Approaching the blue hills of Cambridge, Massachusetts, on August 1, they carried an additional letter. Dolly whispered in her finance's ear the name of the President of the Continental Congress, John Hancock, whose growing influence the British authorities had misgauged.

In 1768, his sloop, the Liberty, was impounded by British customs officials for violation of the revenue laws after arriving from England. John Hancock, who made his fortune smuggling Dutch tea into Boston, did not want his bottom line disturbed. The Tea Act undercut the price of his Dutch tea. Riots ensued as infuriated Bostonians needed the supplies on board.

When formally charged with smuggling, his attorney, John Adams, Sam's cousin, succeeded in getting all charges dropped. Besides smuggling tea, Hancock's contraband portfolio consisted of paper, glass, French molasses. The joke in Boston was that "Sam Adams writes the letters to newspapers, and John Hancock pays the postage."

Hancock's profits were still well in the black while Sam Adams' sharpened pen waited for fresh ink.

CHAPTER 25

General Road Builder

oratio Gates swaggered into the parlour, seeing Colonel Washington for a moment with his chin nearing his chest and a frown that made a difference in his appearance. Beside the Colonel sat Henry Lee, who cradled a cup of hot coffee in his hands, his head over it and inhaling the rising steam as his dog, Spado, rested his head on Lee's scuffed right boot. Washington thrust a newspaper to Major Gates, who took out his granny spectacles and blew out a small breath; his shoulders rose slightly.

Friday, April 21, 1775. BLOODY NEWS. PORTSMOUTH, April 20, 1775. Early this morning, we were alarmed, with an Exprefs from Newbury-Port, with the following letter, to the Chairman of the Committee of Correspondence in this Town.

Sir, Newbury-Port, April 19, 1775.

This town has been in a continual Alarm since Mid-day, with Reports of the TROOPS having marched out of Boston to make some Attack in the Country – The Reports in general concur, in part, in having been at Lexington – And it is very generally said they have been at Concord.

Gates lifted the ornate porcelain pitcher of coffee and poured it into his mug; his mind was churning as he adjusted to the news. The three men looked at each other without speaking. Their minds were standing at full alert, hearing the bullets beyond the open window.

For the second time in two days, they attained a closeness, thoughts brushing, eyes locked for a moment. They knew now a war inevitable as the sun rising.

"My friend Edmund Burke asked me to write him about the cause of the French and Indian War and your military experience, Colonel. I will take some notes?" said Lee.

Washington sat elegantly in his chair, his face gripped with anticipation. His mind was on the future, not the past.

"As a matter of fact," said Gates, "did it not gestate when an influential family along with a group of prominent Englishmen and Virginians formed the Ohio Company in 1748? Their goal was to subdivide 200,000 acres in the upper Ohio River Valley that they believed offered immense economic and financial potential."

"Yes," said Washington, who knew quite well the influential family to be Lord Fairfax and Governor Dinwiddie.

"According to my godfather, Horace Walpole," said Major Gates, "the Company planned settlements and using hand tools and horses opened an 80-mile wagon road to the Monongahela River." He hesitated.

"The French, though," added Lee, "considered this area a vital link between New France (Canada) and Louisiana."

"They took the offensive," said Washington, "and marched southward and westward, from Fort Niagara on Lake Ontario, expelling English traders and claiming the Ohio River Valley for France in 1753."

"This did not bode well," said Major Gates, "for selling land grants to investors and settlers." George neglected to tell the men that Governor Dinwiddie and his deceased brother Lawrence were significant shareholders in the Ohio Company.

"Is this when you began your military career, Col. Washington?" Lee snarled, avoiding eye contact as he scratched Spado's belly. Washington inspected the skinny man, thinking, *Did he always have a belligerent hangover?*

"Governor Dinwiddie of Virginia ordered me to carry a summons to the French troops occupying two new forts near the Forks of the Ohio in Western Pennsylvania to remove from British territory."

The truth roared at Major Gates, who knew from Horace Walpole that George benefitted from his friendship with Colonel Fairfax. Governor Dinwiddie needed the support of Fairfax, who was president of the Virginia Council, and he suggested to the Governor that the 22-year-old Washington man the diplomatic mission to the Forks.

GW's Incredible Adventure

Proudly, George recalled the soft sounds of peregrine falcons to heavy rain to black vultures to insects, the size of a woman's fist, and feeding on Eastern elk, leaving the carcass for the red wolf after his small party left on October 31, 1753.

He followed a familiar traders' path the distance of nearly 250 miles through an ancient woods that consisted of gigantic trees, several feet around, very tall and close enough together that their branches formed a canopy over the forest floor. It blocked sunlight to the ground and prevented low bushes from growing. Thus, the grounds were open, dark with deep shadows, even at midday and movement unhindered.

Lee looked down his nose at Washington, who seemed a mile away; his temple twitching. Upon arriving at the Forks," said Washington, "I meet Tanaghrisson, the half King, a Mingo chief, who asked me the purpose of my party. Were we the vanguard of invaders who would steal their land or allies who will drive away the French?"

Lee thought any child could give the correct answer.

"Leaving the Forks, we visited the French forts, asking 'by whose authority and instructions you have lately marched from Canada, with an armed force, and invaded the king of Great Britain's territories? It becomes my duty to require your peaceable departure.'"

"What did the damn frog-eaters have to say?" asked Major Gates, who grinned annoyingly, jealousy feigning trust and emotion.

"I imagine," said Lee, a vigour appearing in his empty eyes, "they politely told you to go to hell."

"As to the Summons you send me to retire, I do not consider myself obliged to obey," was their response, replied Washington.

He studied Lee for several seconds before speaking. "I returned to Williamsburg in January 1754 and reported the French commanders' refusal to vacate the forts."

Lee, gnawing on a fingernail, said, "Shit!" as he pulled a slither of it away from his mouth.

Washington shook his head at him.

He continued, "On my journey to Fort LeBouef, I had passed through the area of The Point, where the Allegheny and Monongahela Rivers meet to form the Ohio River (present-day Pittsburg). I recognized its strategic importance and upon my return to Williamsburg informed Governor Dinwiddie of the need to immediately dispatch a force to establish a fortification at the forks of the Ohio."

"Yes, Colonel. I know the geography," said Lee, who glared at Washington.

George neglected to tell him that death had hovered over him during his marches to the Forks. His friend, Christopher Gist, pulled him from a swift, icy river. Fired upon by a French sentry, bullets put a hole in his hat, and he spent a freezing night on an island.

After my return, Governor Dinwiddie asked me to write an account of my adventure in the Ohio Country," said Washington.

"Published on both sides of the Atlantic," said Lee.

"The Virginia General Assembly praised my undertaking and rewarded me 50 pounds, and the Governor kept me on the payroll."

Gates looked up with a pang of hunger never filled, thinking George rides the horse of luck.

"After your return, if I recall correctly, Governor Dinwiddie sent William Trent and a small force of Virginia militiamen."

"They departed," said Washington, "on February 17, 1754, to find a place well suited for a fort at the headwaters of the Ohio."

"You are correct," said Lee in a liquor-soaked utterance. "They named the fort Prince George, but in early April, French soldiers descended to dislodge the English with an overwhelming force of 1,100 troops and Indians"

"As a point of order," said Washington, "Governor Dinwiddie sent the Virginia soldiers to build the fort at the forks of the Ohio before he learned from me of the French refusal to abandon the Ohio Valley."

Lee chimed in; his bloodshot eyes narrowed. "During this period you received a promotion by the governor to Lieutenant Colonel of the Virginia Regiment and was told to organize and command a sufficient force to move as soon as possible to reinforce Captain Trent."

Washington's eyes sparkled, and his face seemed reassured.

"This occurred after the death of Colonel Joshua Fry, who died from a horse fall."

George then complained his salary was too low, but his benefactor told him it would increase. Both Gates and Lee knew the hand of William Fairfax directed Washington's commission.

GW's First Military Adventure

"The following spring of '54, I returned to the frontier, leading two regiments to protect fellow Virginians who were erecting a warehouse for the Ohio Company at the forks of the Ohio. To do this, my frontiersmen constructed a road that could support heavy supply wagons and artillery carriage from Winchester."

"What was the distance?"

"80 miles from Alexandria to Redstone Creek, (present-day Brownsville, Pennsylvania), on the Monongahela River."

Staring sightlessly at Washington, Lee remembered being offered shares in Virginia's Ohio Company when he arrived in 1754. He recalled the happy faces of the fellow officers he socialized with who had bought land grants.

"I learned from the Indian chief, 'Half King,' on May 27," said Washington, "that the French expelled Captain Trent and his small group of Ohio Company men constructing Fort Prince George at the fork."

Lee's eyes flickered past Washington to the beady-eyed Gates.

"Upon further questioning," continued Washington, "I learned of a French force about five miles away."

Lee seemed to stare through Washington. His arms folded across his chest, realizing they had covered this topic before. He yawned.

"Without me asking," said George, "the Half King or Tanacharison, then informed me he hated all French because they threatened to boil and eat his father."

Gates gagged ever slightly and tried to force a smile.

Lee, wondering if they intended to use any salt, said, "The heathen bastard probably deserved it."

Washington lifted his eyebrows as he glanced at Lee.

"A few days later my friend Christopher Gist, who farmed less than 20 miles to the North, appeared. He informed me that a French force of 35 men passed through his land the day before, heading towards the Great Meadows."

Major Gates gritted his teeth, and his shoulders rose considerably. Seated straight in his chair, Washington crossed his right leg over the left and patted his fingers together. Memories galloping through his mind; he said, "I decided to march all night in the pouring rain through the pitch-black mountain forest to the Half King's camp. We arrived in the pre-dawn darkness."

Lee, wondering what the subtext was, poured some liquor from his cask into his black coffee mug. With about forty soldiers and Mingos, we moved out to ascertain the French intentions." Gates relaxed with attentiveness in the eyes. Lee, with a cold gaze fixed on the anxious Virginian, studied him with unwavering attention.

"At 7 AM from a rocky glen, we observed the lax French party drinking coffee and eating warm bread. Surprised, at seeing our men, a shot occurred," said George, "and all hell broke loose."

Gates' mouth twitched, thinking in a battle, best to surprise than be surprised.

"My men fired at the French from the rocks and high ground from two sides killing the enemy."

"You wrote," said Major Gates, "of this incident to your younger brother, John."

"Yes."

George recalled his letter, "I, fortunately, escaped without a wound, tho' the right Wing where I stood was exposed to & received all the Enemy's fire and was the part where one man was killed & the rest wounded. I can with truth assure you, I heard Bulletts whistle and believe me there was something charming in the sound."

Major Gates thought maybe a calming sound but not charming.

"The letter ended up published in the London Magazine," said Lee, "and read by George II."

"Horace Walpole informed me that your description of the affair circulated in England, and George II noticed it," said Gates.

The Major withheld that Horace Walpole told him of the king's comment regarding bullets' charming sound. "He would not say so if he had been used to hear many."

Lee thought George the luckiest man alive or a liar.

"In fifteen minutes, my soldiers killed ten while we suffered only one fatality."

This volley of fire in America's backwoods marked the prelude to a world war lasting from 1756 until 1763. Every major power in four continents fought – North America, Europe, Africa, and Asia.

"My father, Major General John Lee, told me, 'Fire fast and move even faster in battle.'"

With a crooked smile and tightness in his eyes, he knew George won a battle that did not deserve a celebration of significant military achievement.

Amused by Lee, Washington said, "Some of the enemy tried to flee down along a narrow path, where they encountered the tomahawks of Tanacharison's braves."

Gates imagined their heads hurting, their bodies hurting, everything hurting too much.

"Twenty-one men captured, some of them wounded."

"One of them, Ensign Jumonville?" asked Lee, who had heard of an incident."

"Yes," frowned Washington, who blinked a few times before saying, "As I was interrogating Ensign Jumonville, Tanacharison, the Half-King, rushed up with a tomahawk and split his skull. His braves then started killing and scalping the wounded before I put a stop to it."

Gates, in his mind, hearing harsh half-stifled yells.

"I refused them their 'trophies,' the scalps of the injured, and Tanacharison scowled in disgust."

Lee said, "a scalp to an Indian means more than a pocketful of silver coins to a white man."

George held back from telling Lee, "You are a smart man's man."

Neither Gates nor Lee mentioned that Washington bore responsibility for the atrocity.

They knew that George knew it. It lurked deep in George's soul, like a splinter festering. He could not forget it, the blood oozing from the officer's head.

"The French, learning of Jumonville's death," said Lee, "sent a force led by Ensign Jumonville's brother, Captain Louis Coulon de Villiers and their savages, thirsting for revenge."

A glassy-eyed George said, "Yes, 800 French and Indians marched towards my 300 Virginians."

Lee yawned.

"I forwarded a request to Williamsburg in hopes of receiving additional troops."

"Why waste the parchment?" asked Lee. Washington ignored him.

"Like the damn reinforcements might get there in time," murmured Lee in a hushed tone.

Washington turned to him, amused with his eccentric behaviour and coarse language.

"For your information, Charles, 100 regulars arrived under Scottish Captain MacKay, a brave and worthy officer."Lee poured himself another drink, which he cradled in both hands.

"About this time, the half-King left the Great Meadows with 80 Mingos," said George.

"He told you, Colonel, correct me if I erred that you would be caught at the little thing upon the meadows and proposed you leave."

Sweat poured from Washington's brow; his eyes turned inward as he nodded in the affirmative.

"How did you know that?"

Lee chuckled. "Family connections."

"My mission compromised and my options limited," said George, "I realized attacking The Forks without reinforcements and artillery out of the question. If I went back to Virginia, the French were free to make incursions in the entire area and beyond. I decided to retreat to the Great Meadows and prepare for a French attack."

The Great Meadows, was an open grassland between Chestnut Ridge to the West and Laurel Hill, an eastern ridge of the Allegheny Mountains in southwestern Pennsylvania, extended 55 miles southwest to northeast.

"Immediately at the end of May, the 30th, I believe, I began construction of a stockade, calling it Fort Necessity."

Lee observed Washington's rigid position and dire face as the Colonel continued, "I waited during the month of June for the French and Indians to arrive at the Great Meadows, praying for reinforcements."

Smugly, Gates wondered why any intelligent commander would not attempt to ambush the advancing enemy force.

"During a drenching rain at noon on July 3, 1754, the French attacked."

George neglected to tell the two men that he refused to abandon his Stores-Baggage-&ca as his horses had not returned with provisions because he knew his reputation would suffer.

Both men studied Washington with a lover's unwavering attention.

"Struggling against them and the elements, I realized our half-built stockade offered little protection. The trenches filled with water, our ammunition low and our powder wet, we continued this unequal fight with an enemy sheltered behind trees, ourselves without shelter, and the enemy fired from all sides incessantly from the woods, until eight o'clock at night."

The battle ended when the French officer, not wanting to cause war the English, offered Lt. Washington terms of surrender. George lost 1/3 of his force

"Ah," Gates said with his chin raised. He looked down at George. "The surrender document in French that you signed acknowledging your culpability for assassinating Ensign de Villiers at Jumonville Glen."

The memory remained, and George wanted to crawl outside himself.

"I accepted the terms as translated to me and felt it paramount to the safety of my soldiers, Major."

Gates, smug in knowing that this embarrassing debacle caused Washington to resign his militia commission and return to private life.

"Well, Colonel, the press heralded you a hero in Williamsburg," said Lee, knowing William Fairfax had put out the word.

"Getting the men back alive is always a good thing," said Gates.

With a gleam in his eyes, Washington said, "After this incident I received a promotion as the ranking officer in the Virginia Regiment."

Lee winked at Washington with a half-grin in place, like a casual handshake. Washington sighed and softened, wanting to slip this past event of his life from his thoughts, ease it down through his mind and toss it to the wind. In the thick soup of their plans, the three men longed to command an army. The faint sound of a battle in a distant field called to them. Lee poured himself another brandy and gulped it down and poured another. The conversation drifted to when the three men met during General Edward Braddock's expedition to the Point, known as the Forks of the Ohio.

The Battle of the Monongahela or A Catastrophe in the Wilderness

Braddock, a sixty-year-old lifetime soldier, with no combat experience or knowledge of the geography, politics, or people of the North American colonies had listened silently to the Duke of Cumberland, Prince William Augustus, the third and youngest son of George II.

Learning he would command a British force against the French at a fort they were constructing at the Forks of the Ohio, (Fort Duquesne) Braddock thought, finally.

"I need someone I can trust, General," said the Duke.

Braddock smiled and puffed out his chest. "I am your man, Duke."

"The Ohio Company built its headquarters store at Wills Creek in late 1753, and in 1754, they built a stockade on a ridge above the Creek."

"I heard about this," said Braddock as he removed his glasses to wipe the lenses."

"We, England, need the French out of this territory. I have friends who have invested in the Ohio Company, and if you succeed, it would be a good investment for you."

The Duke stopped and winked at Braddock, who cast a sceptical look but knew the Duke to be a man of his word.

"The royal governors will provide you with funds and supplies."

"I look forward to serving my country's interests and attacking the French at the Point."

The General arrived in Alexandria, Virginia, in February of 1755. He soon learned some hard facts: instead of the 15 miles of mountains he had to cross, 125 miles stood as the actual figure, 50 of which were steep ridges between his men and the French post at the Forks of the Ohio. And the royal governors failed to provide him with adequate provisions, carriages, horses, and so forth.

His mind still hazy from the month-long voyage, he learned at the King Street Tavern of George Washington's efforts and that he had blazed a trail to the Point.

"I congratulate you on your safe arrival," said George, grinning.

Braddock looked up at the tall and muscular Washington. "I need your advice. My mission is to drive the French from the Forks of the Ohio."

"You will need scouts. I know the region. The ways of the Indians. The wilderness."

Braddock gazed at Washington, as the voices in the crowded tavern surrounded their conversation.

"I would want a commission, General, suitable."

The General cut him off. "I cannot give you a commission with a rank above Captain."

George's face contorted. He bit his tongue.

"Possibly, I can offer you service as a volunteer aide-de-camp."

George hid his ambition and went on to sell himself as best he could. William Fairfax did the rest. Wanting to increase his knowledge of military art and further his fortune, George paid his way on the expedition. As a member of the General's officer corps, George met Lieutenant Colonel Thomas Gage, a future opponent in war, Lieutenant Charles Lee, and Major Horatio Gates.

On a trip to Philadelphia from Alexandria, Braddock met with Benjamin Franklin, who sold supplies to the British for the expedition. The American tried to warn him about Native American warriors' fighting prowess, but the General insisted his troops stood prepared, ready for anything.

Back from Philadelphia with his supplies, Braddock moved his 2,100 soldiers. They consisted of two regular regiments, the 44th, and 48th, by Colonels Sir Peter Halkett and Thomas Dunbar, respectively, and American colonial militia units to Wills Creek in Maryland.

He renamed the stockade Fort Cumberland.

While inspecting his force at the Fort, the General informed his Indian chiefs, "An army has but one supreme leader and I insist there must be rules to war. No scalping! That is not the way of civilized men." The chiefs considered his order to be akin to sending a squaw on a mission to hunt the white buffalo.

He went on to say, "Pull back your barbarous acts and show respect to your defeated enemy."

They studied him like a vampire waiting to take a bite.

His clipped voice filled with a rage, demanding, "Your military capabilities and tactics must bend to my will." As the wind roared, most of the Indians walked away; their dark eyes cast a vicious, severe disdain.

General Braddock's army left Fort Cumberland on June 6, 1755, to remove the French from the Forks of the Ohio. On June 10, the violent pains and fevers of dysentery seized Washington. For nine days, he rested at Bear Camp then rode in a wagon with the army's rear division.

Thick woods and steep ridges slowed the march to 5 or 6 miles a day, and by June 18, the General worried that French reinforcements would arrive before he reached Fort Duquesne. Braddock asked his aides for suggestions. He liked Washington's idea to split the army, the best troops, horses, wagons, and a limited number of artillery pieces to push ahead of the supply train.

With his legs crossed in Washington's Mount Vernon library, Lee blurted out as he flipped a scrap of a muffin to Spado. "The egotistical son of a bitch Braddock, split his force."

"Looking back, Charles, not a good idea," said a blushed Washington. "I tried to dissuade my superior officer, Colonel Sir Peter Halkett, of this flying column strategy, said Major Gates.

Three hundred ax-wielding grenadiers and various American militia units cut down trees, and they blasted the stumps to create the 12-foot-wide road for the 1,300 men, followed by the general's personal guards and Braddock in red uniform with gold trim. Behind the flying column were heavy artillery, and supply wagons, flanked by the British regulars.

Towards the end of the one-mile-long procession a supply column of 800 followed, with most of the baggage commanded by Colonel Thomas Dunbar.

At the very end were slaves, free blacks, herdsman, ladies of low morals, camp followers, a flock of civilians, spouses of soldiers, servants, and a strong detachment of troops to guard against attack brought up the rear. The army still only covered five or six miles a day following Washington's earlier path towards Fort Necessity's ruins.

On July 6, a small French and Indians party attacked the British, first in the rear and later along the right flank. Several, including one woman, were killed and scalped before a weakened Washington and British troops drove off the attackers. During this skirmish, the English soldiers panicked and shot one of their Indian scouts, the son of Monacatootha, an Oneida sachem and leader of the small group of Indians with Braddock.

On the evening of July 8, a weakened Washington arrived at camp as the army prepared for battle near the Monongahela River. To avoid ambush in the rugged area, Braddock crossed and recrossed the river without encountering the enemy.

"I shudder when I remember the goddamn current on my body," said Lee.

"Yes, added Gates, "as we waded through knee-deep water on that cold summer day where Turtle Creek enters the Monongahela."

"I remember the smug son of a bitch announcing, "Nothing now stands between Fort Duquesne and us."

"Both damn sides jumped out of their pants when they discovered one another," said Gates in a deliberate, unhurried voice.

Washington recalled the enemy rushing forward to meet the British, who had assembled near their second river crossing at Turtle Bay.

"That blockhead, incompetent Braddock blundered when he failed to occupy a grassy hill to our right, allowing the enemy to flank our central column."

The British fought European style with massed ranks firing in a volley. Their red uniforms made easy targets for the Indians, who hid in the woodlands. Fighting from behind trees and bushes, they changed their places as soon as they fired. Creeping or laying on the ground while they reloaded their weapons, which they did very quickly, the enemy continued their assault.

"The asshole Gage's failure to stop his men from retreating," said Lee, "and colliding with the advancing body of troops contributed to the resultant panic."

"I still hear in my dreams," said Gates, "the French and Indians shooting and their howling war hoops."

"Believe me," said Lee, "they did not exceed three hundred men; while ours consisted of well-armed troops, chiefly regular soldiers."

Washington chose not to inform his guest that he knew Braddock's soldiers encountered 250 French soldiers and 600–700 of their Indian allies on July 9, 1755.

Instinctively, the American militia on that afternoon tried to seek cover, but the enraged Braddock, with sword's flat drove them back into formation. The thick woods, filling with smoke, and the panicked British soldiers firing blindly, killed or wounded many American militiamen, recalled Washington.

"The quick and efficient response of the French and Indians," said Gates in a detached and clinical voice, "despite the early loss of their commander – led many of our men to believe they had walked into an ambush."

Gates's memory spread like a wave as he remembered the bullet that tore through his body. Twenty years had passed, but the tide of that pain still washed over him.

"The men, Major Gates, struck with such a panic, behaved with more cowardice than it is possible to conceive," stated Lee in a hollow voice. "The officers behaved gallantly, to encourage their men, for which they suffered considerably, there being near sixty killed and wounded; a large proportion of the force."

"To their credit," replied Washington, "the Virginia troops showed a good deal of bravery, and suffered dearly; for I believe, out of three companies there, scarcely thirty men lived. Captain Peyrouny and all his officers down to a corporal killed. Captain Polson received nearly as hard a fate, for only one of his men lived."

Gates, who liked to talk, but not listen, said, "The cowardly behaviour of those they call regulars exposed all others, who continued to do their duty, to almost certain death."

"In spite of all the efforts of the gallant officers, the vermin ran, as sheep pursued by dogs, said Lee. "It was impossible to rally them."

Washington closed his eyes and saw General Braddock lying, dying, and Sir Peter Halket and other brave officers dead on the field. George then recalled Braddock imploring him to come closer, and he heard the General ask him to take his scarf, blood-soaked, as a token of appreciation. The memory made George swallow the pain again and absorb the tragedy. It never went away.

For four hours, frightened, leaderless soldiers attempted to remove the enemy from the high ground as withering fire poured in from all sides. Nothing worked, and the army broke and ran, Lee helping the wounded Gates towards safety. At Jumonville, the fleeing survivors bumped into Colonel Dunbar, who promptly burned or buried his artillery and supplies and joined the retreat to Fort Cumberland.

A mile from the site of Fort Necessity on July 14, Braddock died. Washington ordered his body buried in the middle of the road and told the troops to march over it to prevent the Indians from discovering his corpse and desecrating it. At Fort Cumberland, George wrote a letter to his mother and Governor Dinwiddie describing the battle that the Governor dispatched to England.

Regular soldiers, who were struck with such a panick, that they behavd with more cowardice than it is possible to conceive. The Officers behav'd Gallantly in order to encourage their Men, for which they sufferd greatly; there being near 60 killd and wounded; a large proportion out of the number we had! The Virginia Troops shewd a good deal of Bravery, & were near all killd. I believe out of 3 Companys that were there, there is scarce 30 Men left alive. I luckily escaped without a wound.

The British press complimented the courage of the Virginians and disparaged the British regular's conduct. The General's defeat left American settlements in Pennsylvania and Virginia vulnerable to French and Indian raids. By surviving and leading the soldiers back to Virginia, his "safe Return" allowed for "an uncommon Joy" among all "true Lovers of Heroick virtue" according to William Fairfax. Washington's reputation as a military man bloomed.

"How fortunate," mused Gates as he shifted on the chair in Washington's library "that you escaped without a wound."

"I can still hear," said Washington, "bullets piercing through my coat, and my horses falling to the ground."

"Lucky for you, George, the hulking beasts did not flatten you into a pancake," said Lee.

Washington shook his head from shoulder to shoulder as he remembered the screams and agony of Captains Orme and Morris, two of the aides-de-camp, who suffered wounds early in the engagement. The anguish he then experienced returned. Lee and Gates noticed the sweat on his face.

"Being the only person left to distribute the General's orders, I did what I could," said Washington. "Still not half recovered from a violent illness that confined me to my wagon for above ten days."

Lee did not remember Washington in his adverse condition, helping organize a general retreat and a successful rear guard action.

Of commissioned officers, the prime targets, the British suffered greatly: out of 86 officers, 26 were killed and 37 wounded.

Of the 50 or so women that accompanied the British column as maids and cooks, only 4 survived. The French and Canadians reported 8 killed and 4 wounded; their Indian allies lost 15 killed and 12 wounded.

In total – 456 killed, 422 wounded, along with the unscathed, stumbled back to Virginia under the command of Washington.

For his self-proclaimed actions during the battle, George became known as the "Hero of the Monongahela." He returned to Virginia with what remained of the Virginia militia.

"What did he do in his sickened condition during the battle?" Lee mumbled to Spado in a low growl.

After the death of Joshua Fry, his connections granted him official recognition as Commander-in-Chief of the Virginia regiment.

Fry collaborated with Peter Jefferson, Thomas's father, on an influential map of Virginia in 1752.

At twenty-three years of age, the "veteran" officer strutted some in the June of 1755. For the next three years, George served as colonel of the Virginia Regiment, but it never reached its manpower goals.

In 1756, he travelled up the Atlantic coast to Boston, meeting Governor William Shirley of Massachusetts, who he asked to grant military status to him and his troops but without success. The next year, 1757, George visited Philadelphia to ask John Campbell, Lord Loudoun, to allow him to play a major role in a campaign against Fort Duquesne, again without success.

In 1758, when General John Forbes led a second British expedition to remove the French from the Forks of the Ohio, Col. George Washington, commander of the Virginia Regiment, served under him. George fought with Forbes over the route to Fort Duquesne, wanting to travel by Braddock's Road from Virginia. Forbes chose to go thru Pennsylvania by way of Laurel Hill, a 90-mile route without rivers to cross. He forsook Fort Cumberland, a 160-mile trek that lacked forage, had narrow passes and many river crossings.

During the expedition, Washington's military experience consisted of being a decoy for the French, who thought his presence on Braddock's Road meant the British were coming from that direction. By way of Pennsylvania, the mere surprise presence of the British forced the French to blow up Fort Duquesne and sail away to Canada.

Refused a commission in the British Army, Washington resigned from the provincial militia. In January of 1759, he married the dainty, five-foot – tall, rich widow, Martha Custis, who knew how to read and write. George took up the life of a Virginia plantation owner at Mount Vernon, aided by Martha's 300 hundred slaves and nearly 18,000 acres of land worth at least 40,000 pounds.

The building of the two roads to Pittsburg allowed travelling to western Pennsylvania or west to the Forks of the Ohio. The difficult and dangerous route opened to thousands of Americans new economic opportunities. It granted Washington's friend Lord Fairfax and the Ohio Company profits, not as great as would have occurred if General Forbes had taken Braddock's Road. Gates grimaced, realizing that twenty years had streaked by, and he mulled over a thought while Washington stood outside his hand-carved library door speaking to a messenger. He asked Lee, "Will there be war with England?"

Lee cracked his knuckles, menacingly, and said, "Absolutely."

With one side of his head raised, Major Gates asked, "Is George up to the task?"

With one-half of his upper lip tightened, Lee answered, "With the right help."

Their eyes danced in a shared understanding.

With a slight smile, Lee said, "Command will land on his shoulders."

Major Gates peered sightlessly at Lee, thinking their time had arrived.

Repeating himself he whispered to Lee, "Is Colonel Washington up to commanding a rebel army?"

Lee searched his memory between sips of brandy, "He delivered a message to the French from Virginia Governor Dinwiddie to vacate their position at the Point."

Major Gates said in a voice detached and clinical, "He fulfilled an errand."

Lee nodded; his thoughts turned inward.

Major Gates's face hardened in concentration. "Upon his return, the governor ordered him to go back to the Point with reinforcements for Col, Gist. "

He attacked a French party and soon found himself besieged by a greater French force that demanded his surrender and let him return to Virginia."

Lee crossed his arms and lifted his chin as he spoke. The Major noticed the tightness around his eyes as he shook his head and spoke, "He served under Braddock during the General's failed expedition and his failed health."

Gates arched his eyebrows, "He knew the way back to Virginia."

He then shot a glance over the top of his granny glasses. Lee absorbed the fact and swallowed the truth; George was one lucky son of a bitch. His only experience during the Seven Years War was an expedition to the Forks of the Ohio commanded by General John Forbes," mused Gates. "As a damn decoy!" Said Lee.

"Not very impressive," replied Gates.

Lee formed a tight fist with his right hand and pounded on the square table.

"No actual warfare as the Frogs ran from Fort Duquesne," said Gates.

"Well, Major, not exactly. Let us not forget the friendly fire incident. After hearing shots, he rushed out to help Lt. Colonel George Mercer's 500 soldiers of the Second Virginia Regiment. They were looking for the enemy during General Forbes march to Fort Duquesne.

"The two parties met in the dark and opened fire on each other."

"One officer and several privates killed and many wounded, I heard," said Major Gates.

"The reality, Major, hundreds of men were killed and wounded."

With alertness in their minds, the two men's eyes opened wide in surprise and recognition. They realized his four trips to the Forks of the Ohio and afterward assisting Virginia counties in reorganizing and training their militias summed up Washington's military experience. They were not impressed.

"Yes, greater than that of any other son-of-a-bitch American, and he lives in the largest and most important of the colonies."

"No one," said Gates, can deny he possesses' an impressive appearance, stands quiet, and shows confidence in manner."

Lee clenched his fists, trying to controul his temper. "His self-serving work in the military committees of Congress influences his compatriots, but God knows, he lacks experience and knowledge in handling large groups of men."

"But never discount his experience as a political leader in Virginia, and his plantation at Mount Vernon stands him in good stead."

Their jealousy smelled like bad liquor on the breath.

Gates scratched his chin. "More a road and fort builder than a military officer."

"Soon to be, General Road Builder," said a smirking Lee.

"I can only hope that the slow-witted George would read a book on military strategy and then listen to me," said Lee." He hesitated, locking his eyes in a mutual understanding with Gates.

"He has a greater chance of winning the lottery."

Horatio laughed, running his fingers through his thinning hair and seeing how Washington personified the quick-witted American farmer soldier's myth over a British officer.

"I know one thing," said Lee, "I want in. Screw the king and his sycophant advisors and the power-hungry Parliament."

Washington returned, exhibiting more teeth than usual. He studied the men with a level gaze, then excused himself. "Public business calls."

The two men thought for a moment of embracing their host but unable to face their emotions; they just stood. Washington observed their slow grimace, oblivious to the roguish charm that they failed to see through. With a nostalgic yearning, they wanted the command waiting for George. Through their host's mediation, Gates received the appointment of Adjutant General with the rank of Brigadier in the Continental Army. Gates bolted to the camp at Cambridge, Massachusetts, seeing his light shining. Lee lobbied to become Commander-in-Chief of the Continental Army but, in time, settled for second in command.

CHAPTER 26

Comings and Goings

Before leaving his home at Scotchtown for the Second Continental Congress, Patrick Henry's daughter Patsy ran towards him with tears in her eyes.

"Mother is dead."

His eyes swelled with tears as he thought of the twenty-one-year marriage to his beloved Sarah, who gave him three sons and daughters. Sorrow gathered around him as storm clouds around a mountain. For days on end, the man of many words fell silent.

In early May, Patrick departed for Philadelphia, accompanied by an armed escort to prevent his arrest. He thought of Sarah and promised to make her proud.

The Second Continental Congress participants made their way through Philadelphia's crowded streets to Smith's New Tavern. Before entering, Patrick Henry knew that a date with history waited for him. His heart raced as he looked up at the two-story building in the shape of a cross. Although Patrick preferred the countryside's isolation, he admired the decorative gables and pediments on all four sides.

"Let us ferment rebellion under the true banner of liberty of conscience," he said.

"How should Congress proceed?" asked John Adams.

"It would be a great Injustice if a little island should have the same weight in the councils of America, as a great one," said Henry.

Samuel Adams, his round face glistened in a halo of sweat, said, "Some of the delegates feign patriotism."

"Quacks in politics who would intimidate the populace," added Richard Henry Lee.

"What we need," said John Adams, "a man who speaks with a town meeting's passion and language."

The men's heads turned to Patrick.

Waiting for the delegates to the Congress to come to order, Samuel Adams made an impatient sound. Finally, the gavel sounded, and the debate began on the floor of Congress.

"How dare this Congress, like some foreign imperial power," sneered a delegate from New York, "sit in judgment on the decrees of a British legislature."

Tension increased; Henry slouched in his chair, blowing on his coffee, watching the delegates with heightened curiosity.

"I wonder," said another delegate. "whether some degree of respect be not always due from inferiors to superiors & especially from children to parents?"

The blue-eyed Patrick felt the chamber's anxiety and thought of all the times he sat under a tree, living with wild things, thinking about the future, and what waited for him.

"No Englishmen, no Scots, no Britons, only a set of wretches dare to complain," said another delegate.

On March 23, 1775, Patrick gazed at his fellow members, their brows furrowed and looking like tired children. He rose, wondering were a majority of delegates ready for freedom?

"Many men's eyes," he paused, "float in the clouds and fail to see freedom's benefits. The subtleties of despotism wear many vestments, and some of them can be glamorous and attractive."

Jefferson recalled Henry covered some of this territory before in the House of Burgesses.

"Something exists sweeter than life and something larger than peace, and if I may be bold enough to interpolate, something safer than security. The liberty of every individual as a citizen of a free country and as a child of nature must be honoured."

Watching the representatives from the corners of his vision, Jefferson witnessed that Henry's words were achieving their desired effect; the earth was no longer flat.

"It is no longer a question of Parliament's right to tax but of its right to govern. There is no longer any room for hope under this system. If we wish to want freedom, we must fight! – I repeat it, sir, we must fight! An appeal to arms and the God of Hosts is all that is left us."

The delegates from New York twisted in their seats, staring at Henry, considering his words treasonous.

"Is life so dear and peace so sweet," continued Patrick, "that we accept the price of chains?"

A few of the delegates from Pennsylvania glowed like ghosts on Halloween night.

"Guard with jealous attention the public liberty. Suspect everyone who approaches that jewel."

Jefferson observed a sign of pleasure on Henry's face, remembering Patrick failing in so many ways, but knew a new Henry exhaled.

"The King acts as a Tyrant, a fool, a puppet, & a tool to the ministry." He paused. Several seconds passed – some sense of anger raged inside within a hot dose of patriotism.

Some voices from the back of the Assembly yelled, "Give us liberty or give us death!"

Henry stood for a moment, frozen, wondering about the future. Finally, he said in an entirely different voice.

"Separation and armed resistance, now. It is not possible to couple empire with liberty. Without individual freedom, we have nothing!"

* * * * *

In early September of 1775, the king knelt at the royal chapel at St. James' Palace, built by Henry VIII on the site of a former leper hospital.

"The rebellious war becomes more general and turns for the purpose of establishing an independent empire. What shall I do, father?"

Shifting his weight from his left knee to the right, he wheeled awkwardly but corrected his balance. He smiled a superior kind of smile.

"I need not dwell upon the fatal effects of the success of such a plan. The object, too important, the spirit of the British nation, too high, the resources with which you hath blessed us too numerous, to give up so many colonies that we planted with great industry, nursed with great tenderness, encouraged with many commercial advantages, and protected and defended at much expense of blood and treasure."

A thought, like a shadow from a bird of prey, drifted across his mind. He laughed softly.

He knew that the plague of politics had touched him, leaving him vulnerable.

"It now becomes the part of wisdom, and (in its effects) of clemency, to put a speedy end to these disorders by the most decisive exertions."

He sighed and widened his eyes, hoping for divine inspiration. He then heard, "Increase your naval establishment, and significantly augment your land forces, but in such a manner as may be the least burdensome to your kingdoms."

* * * * *

James Wilkinson shrugged, then smiled, but as a mask.

At the Potomack and Monocracy rivers' confluence, the warm air of the summer solstice pressed upon a group of men and women.

"Hot," murmured the waiting patients, their shadows growing in length, their hands swatting at mosquitoes under the gleeful yolk of late afternoon.

Inside the log cabin, a young doctor stood, concocting a potion of rhubarb, hemp, mota, and chicory for a patient with a severe headache.

He learned to bleed and purge impurities from the body, and his grandmother boasted, "He has inherited a gracefulness of address and ease of manners."

At the age of nineteen, James Wilkinson returned from medical school in Philadelphia to Maryland and sat down in the practice of medicine in March/April of 1775.

After the Battle of Lexington and Concord, his days of watching geese skimming upon the river's waves, a summer thunderstorm whipping the virgin forest, a herd of elk trampling the ground was replaced by a passion for arms that haunted his every thought.

He rode sixty miles round trip to attend drills of a rifle company. In July of 1775, not three months since setting up his medical practice, the news of Bunker Hill and Washington's command of the army reached his ears.

Like many of his generation, he pounced on a career of arms.

"At my expense," he told his mother. "I must skedaddle to the voice of the rebellion."

Late summer 1775, James arrived at Cambridge as a volunteer and joined a rifle company commanded by Colonel William Thompson of Pennsylvania. He learned the company lacked artillery supplies and possessed only enough cartridges for twenty-four rounds a man.

He commented to a fellow volunteer, "On entering the camp near Boston, the familiarity that prevailed among the soldiers and officers of all ranks, from the colonel to the private struck me as odd. I observed, but little distinction, and I could not refrain from remarking to the young gentlemen with whom I made acquaintance, that the military discipline of their troops similar to the civil subordination of the community in which I lived."

Struck by the unexpected, he surveyed the camp.

At night by candlelight, he grabbed his quill and wrote home. "The Continental Army, of which General Washington took the command at Cambridge, July 3d, 1776, rated at 14,500 military. Without a shade of uniformity in its organization, pay, dress, arms, or exercise; destitute of subordination and discipline, and fluctuating from day to day at the caprice of the men, inclined them to absent themselves or to rejoin their colours."

He paused for a moment.

"The British Army under General Gage in Boston consists of twenty regiments of the line, estimated at less than 10,000 men."

* * * * *

On his hands and knees at his boarding house, Jefferson was looking for Martha's letter that the wind blew off his writing table. He yearned to touch her silky skin, smell her tumbled hair, admire her soft curves, feel her moist lips, and missed the pianoforte, the harpsichord, the dancing, Monticello. He picked it up, and as most of the work he focused on done, before sealing the letter, he added the note, "The Continental Congress in Philadelphia readying for the coming conflict."

He rose. He could see it. Independence still rough, the house, half done, with walls and stairs, yet to come. Rounding a corner, he went through the Pennsylvania State House's back door and heard men in the cloakroom. He spotted Elias Boudinot and Samuel Chase talking. The majority of the Assembly waiting to meet, he assumed.

"Not much longer now," John Adams boasted to a group of men. "Washington's army resides in Cambridge, ready to thrash the Redcoats."

Jefferson strolled over and said fast and loudly, "Liberty is pure Virtue, and if the British cannot learn this simple truth, the hell with them."

Adams nodded, and in a moment, expounded, "Our revolt was effected before the war commenced. It was in the hearts and minds of the people."

Jefferson's beliefs brushed over his, a pleasing feeling that stirred the juices of his ambition.

"This radical change in the principles, opinions, sentiments, and affections of the people," continued Adams, "is the real American Revolution. A revolution without a prior reformation would collapse or become a totalitarian tyranny."

Jefferson responded in a voice crackling and raw, "My sentiments exactly."

The Aftermath
of the Fourth Son

J ames Hamilton, the senior, drifted from one of the Virgin Islands to another.

With a light-hearted banter about the unfairness of life, he ignored the foibles of his past.

He stared at the reality of experience in the face.

Pain with no relief. More pain without the thought of comfort. Whiskey with the kick of a mule, warming his belly and dulling his senses.

He missed the boys, but as he wrote to his brother, "I still have dreams I must act on."

He liked to recall his golden attribute between the whiskey, his looks but cursed that it caused nothing but trouble.

Yes, women flocked to him, he remembered. He carried no regrets of leaving more than one with a full belly before departing for the West Indies to pursue his dreams as a merchant and escape his responsibilities as a father.

Handsome, charming, and undemanding, he recalled stepping off the ship in Nevis, a community cash-poor; he soon learned.

Not a sound business decision, he realized.

He soon resettled at St. Kitts and worked at Basseterre's port, the island's capital.

His romantic dreams of success and riches faded like the beauty of a wilting flower.

At 9 AM or 5 PM, he attracted women like bees to honey, always informing them, "My family owns a coat of arms that dates back to the fourteenth century and owns a castle called the Grange in Scotland near Glasgow."

During a night of boozing in St. Lucia, James, while trying to adjust his position on the barstool, fell to the floor. As he staggered up, an image of a laughing Rachael Lavien flashed before him.

A searing hurt from a dull knife curled through his heart. Agony flowed through his blood.

"For fifteen years, did I not do the best I could?" he cried out.

The wind of time, never still, continued to capture his looks, and hard drink hampered his ability to make a living.

His nose and complexion reddened by liquor; women now turned from him as if he contacted the plague. And he limped from the harshness of life

However, rumour clanked like a church bell that he fathered several children while intermingling with slaves and that two of his sons in 1791 sparked the Night of Fire revolt on St. Dominque.

Fifty thousand slaves rose with hooks; machetes and torches put fire to over 1,000 sugar and coffee plantations.

Flames extended as far as the Bahamas.

The slave revolt in the French colony led to the founding of the state of Haiti in 1804.

He kept retreating until reaching the southern end of the Caribbean, stirring the powder of hope into another glass of hard liquor until he sat for a moment, organizing his thoughts on how to proceed.

As an act of last resort in March of 1774, he entered a program for impoverished British subjects on Bequia's tiny secluded island, south of St. Vincent.

It was a lawless refuge for indigenous Caribbean natives and runaway slaves, who cared not that he bragged his Scottish nobility.

They sneered at him because he dressed like an Englishman, of sorts. Even he realized that he wore out too many suits and sped by too many avenues of opportunity.

He contracted for twenty-five acres of timberland along the shore of Southeast Bay, not suitable or allowed to do business in sugar production as if he could tell the difference between fertile soil and beach sand.

Required to sign a statement acknowledging that the ground "existed" for poor settlers' unsettled him.

His mind thumped, sharp and dark. His joy was reduced to a black-and-white rainbow of failure and broken hope.

There would be no woman to pave his path, he realized.

His humility turned darker than the black of a moonless night.

In exchange for living on the seven square mile island, for at least a year, the property would be transferred to him, gratis.

In 1776, he and a man named Simple shared seventy acres, a step up from 25.

The British bureaucracy recorded them as the only poor residents.

He swore over his ifs, as "if," did not stand stiffly in a poor man's pocket."

When he thought about Alex, his eyes opened wide in guilt; though the fourth son possessed a picture in his mind of himself and Alex: the latter's head tilted and a smile streaming between his ears.

Near the end of his life, when desperately in need of money, he wrote his son, then well-known.

Regretfully, Alex passed on the request.

The days of the son of a Scottish laird growing up in a fog-bound castle always burned in his memory under the scorching West Indies sun.

His life was left behind as his ship sailed out.

Blind to the green aura of the hills that skirted the volcanic cone, he never walked on the sandy beaches nor noticed the jagged cliffs.

His saturated wit, or what remained, allowed him to settle on St. Vincent in 1793, where the claw of death hooked him six years, later on, June 3.

A moment before expiring, James the senior dreamed he was a predatory tiger swaggering through life, ready to pounce when the mood struck.